Seen and Unseen

Studies on Performing Arts & Literature of the Islamicate World

VOLUME 5

The titles published in this series are listed at *brill.com/spal*

Seen and Unseen

Visual Cultures of Imperialism

Edited by

Sanaz Fotouhi
Esmaeil Zeiny

BRILL

LEIDEN | BOSTON

Cover illustration: Hoda Afshar, *Westoxicated #5*, from the series *Under Western Eyes*, 2013 Archival Pigment Print. 104 × 90 cm / edition of 5.

The Library of Congress Cataloging-in-Publication Data is available online at http://catalog.loc.gov

Typeface for the Latin, Greek, and Cyrillic scripts: "Brill". See and download: brill.com/brill-typeface.

ISSN 2214-6563
ISBN 978-90-04-35700-6 (hardback)
ISBN 978-90-04-35701-3 (e-book)

Printed by Printforce, the Netherlands

Contents

PART 3
Interrogating Visual Representations

Acknowledgments

What eventually became this book would not have been possible if not for serendipity and the support of Dr. Noraini Md. Yusof and the staff at the Institute of Malaysian and International Studies (IKMAS), National University of Malaysia (UKM). They made it possible for Sanaz to travel to Malaysia, as a visiting scholar at UKM, where she met Esmaeil and the idea for this book emerged. We thank the staff at UKM for making this happen.

List of Figures

Notes on Contributors

Syed Farid Alatas

is Professor of Sociology at the National University of Singapore. He also headed the Department of Malay Studies at NUS from 2007 till 2013. He lectured at the University of Malaya in the Department of Southeast Asian Studies prior to joining NUS. In the early 1990s, he was a Research Associate at the Women and Human Resource Studies Unit, Universiti Sains Malaysia. Professor Alatas has authored numerous books and articles, including Ibn Khaldun (Oxford University Press, 2013); Applying Ibn Khaldun: The Recovery of a Lost Tradition in Sociology (Routledge, 2014), and "The State of Feminist Theory in Malaysia" in Maznah Mohamad & Wong Soak Koon, eds., Feminism: Malaysian Reflections and Experience (special issue of Kajian Malaysia: Journal of Malaysian Studies), 12, 1–2 (1994), pp. 25–46. His areas of interest are the sociology of Islam, social theory, religion and reform, intra- and inter-religious dialogue, and the study of Orientalism.

Christiane Gruber

is Associate Professor of Islamic Art in the History of Art Department at the University of Michigan, Ann Arbor. Her primary field of research is Islamic book arts, paintings of the Prophet Muhammad, and Islamic ascension texts and images, about which she has written two books and edited a volume of articles. She also pursues research in Islamic book arts and codicology, having authored the online catalogue of Islamic calligraphies in the Library of Congress as well as edited the volume of articles, The Islamic Manuscript Tradition. Her third field of specialization is modern Islamic visual and material culture, about which she has written several articles. She also has co-edited two volumes on Islamic and cross-cultural visual cultures. She is currently finishing her next book, entitled The Praiseworthy One: The Prophet Muhammad in Islamic Texts and Images.

Jared Ahmad

is a lecturer in International Relations at the University Manchester. He holds an M.A. in Literary and Cultural Theory (2009) and a PhD in Politics from the University of Manchester (2015), and his research interests are situated between the fields of Cultural Studies and Political Communication. In particular, Jared's research focuses on the changing nature of contemporary media discourses and visual and verbal representations of "Islamic" terrorism throughout the "war on terror" period (2001–present). His work has been published in the journals Critical Studies on Terrorism, Media, War and Conflict, Global Media and Communication, and the Journal of International Relations Research. He is currently working on a book entitled The BBC, the War on Terror and the Discursive Construction of "Al-Qaeda" that will be published in 2018 by Palgrave-Macmillan as part of their "New Security Challenges" book series.

Layla Hendow
is currently doing an AHRC funding PhD at the University of Hull on the topic of Recycling and Waste in late 20th Century American Literature. She completed her BA in 2013 at Lancaster University and her MA in 2014 at University of Warwick. She is a creative and academic writer and specializes in 20th Century American and British Literature, postmodernism and poststructuralism, and themes of pollution, waste management and the body.

Raihanah M. M.
is an associate professor of literary studies at the Faculty of Social Sciences and Humanities, National University of Malaysia (UKM). Her PhD was on Constructs of Multicultural Identity in Malaysian Fiction. Since then, she has received numerous national and university research grants in the areas of Muslim diaspora, Minority Fiction and Popular Culture. She has published extensively in these areas. She recently received a university grant to study the themes of socio-cultural imperfection in popular media.

D. Bruno Starrs
holds Masters Degrees from Bond University and the University of Melbourne and a PhD from the Queensland University of Technology in Australia. He is a published novelist, playwright and short story author, winning the Open Category of the Dungala-Kaiela Writing Awards in 2015 and 2016. Starrs has been widely published in academia, is a former Research Fellow at the National Film and Sound Archive in Canberra and until recently worked as Senior Lecturer in Cinema at the Universiti Teknologi Brunei.

Esmaeil Zeiny
is a Research Fellow at the Institute of Malaysian and International Studies (IKMAS), National University of Malaysia (UKM) and Honorary Research Fellow at the Department of Creative Arts and English, La Trobe University, Australia. He received his PhD in Postcolonial literature in English from the

National University of Malaysia. His research interests lie at the intersection of political theory, cultural studies and literary studies. His work addresses questions about identity, representation, colonialism and postcolonialism.

Hoda Afshar

born in Tehran, Iran, is now based in Melbourne where she practices as a Visual artist. She completed a Bachelor degree in Fine Art—Photography in Tehran and began her career as a documentary photographer in 2005. She is currently a PhD candidate in the department of Art at Curtin University, and a lecturer at Photography Studies College in Melbourne. In 2006, World Press Photo selected Hoda (as one of the top ten young documentary photographers in Iran) to attend their Educational training program. She has been exhibiting locally since 2007 and also internationally in major photography festivals such as Pingyao international festival of photography in China (2012) and PhotoVisa festival of photography in Russia (2013). Hoda has also been shortlisted for prestigious photography awards such as the Josephine Ulrick and Win Schubert Photography Prize and the Moran Contemporary Photographic Prizes. In 2015, she was selected as the winner of National Photographic Portrait Prize. Through her practice, Hoda reflects on issues related to power relations, displacement and post-identity politics. Her artwork attempts to open lines of communication in a world both homogenized by global economy and unsettled by mass migration. She tests diaspora, exoticism and cosmopolitanism for artistic and uncanny image-making possibilities.

Sanaz Fotouhi

holds a PhD from the University of New South Wales and a BA and MPhil from the University of Hong Kong. Her area of interest lies in diaspora and migrant writing in English. Her first book *The Literature of the Iranian Diaspora: Meaning and Identity since the Islamic Revolution* (IB Tauris, 2015) is the one the first of its kind that examines the body of diasporic Iranian writing in English. Sanaz is also a creative writer and a filmmaker.

Introduction. Visual Cultures of Islam: The Seen, Unseen and the in Between

Sanaz Fotouhi and Esmaeil Zeiny

In our modern world, we are continuously bombarded with visual images as a means of communication. The large variety of constructed visual cues that we see everyday, including everything from still images such as antique oil paintings to modern abstract art, photographs, posters, to moving visual feats of physical impossibilities on our televisions and computers received by way of advertisement, movies, YouTube clips, and news images, all contribute to the way we decipher the world around us; they, all collectively, inform and create what we call a visual culture. Just like the way various cultures are formed through social etiquettes, political desires, our histories and religious beliefs, and even the geographical location in which we live, visual cultures, too, are informed by repeated visual cues that we encounter in our everyday life. These visual cultures—which stem in our social cultures—not only shape how certain images should be read and understood but they also influence and affect our opinions, beliefs and values in powerful ways. Namely, they also influence our social cultures and attitudes. So, in effect, especially in today's world where the visual image in its various forms has become the most powerful tool of communication, it is difficult to separate the two. Our social cultures and visual cultures are continuously and seamlessly feeding off each other in extraordinary ways to help us make sense of our changing world. Unless we tune into this connection, it is easy to miss the influence of visual cultures in the way we understand and see our world. That is because visual cultures, like and as part of other aspects of our social cultures, are deeply embedded in our collective psyche, influenced by our national and personal histories, reinforced by politicians and businessmen, and our biases, to the degree that unless we stop and think about how we have been directed to read those images around us and their meanings, it is easy to miss this connection and be blindly guided by the very images we see in front of us.

As much as providing us with clues on how to navigate this complex world around us, visual cultures can also lead to the construction of certain repeated images, biases, stereotypes, and definite ways that we can position ourselves in the world against the Other. While infinite opinions are being visually reflected and formed—and studied—on the representations of every aspect of our human lives and others,' for example, anything from how we see queer and transgender people, the human body image, various wars, poverty and wealth, etc., this collection brings into focus a diverse study on the visual cultures surrounding the representation of Islam and Muslim people. The understanding of certain ways Islam and Muslim cultures are visually represented and the way they are approached by the authors in this book—not only by non-Muslims in the West, but also by Muslims themselves—however, requires some contextualization as this book sits on the cusp of where visual cultures feed into debates surrounding the historical, social and cultural representation of Islam in the West. Neither the visual representation and analysis of Islam and Muslim identities nor the concept of visual culture, however, is a new phenomenon that we claim to establish in this collection. On the contrary, this book is rooted and inspired by already existing theories and analyses of visual cultures as well as the visual representations of Islam. For us to situate this collection fully, however, we need first a fuller grasp of the definition of visual cultures that we engage with, as well as the history and situation of visual representation of Islam and Muslim people within a Western context.

Although it has only been recently, since the visual image has become our most powerful tool of communication, that there appears to be an interest in visual culture, the human engagement with the images we see and construct has deep roots in history. Ever since the Age of Enlightenment, knowledge and information began to be systematically and regularly retrieved from observation and display; from then onwards through the eras of industrialization and colonialization to the current globalized world, visual culture has continued to form the way we think and interpret the world (Kromm & Bakewell, 2009). While the undercurrent of visual analysis in a social context has played a significant part in our human history's perception, the term, visual culture—in the way we understand it today—to refer to the system of study of images in a social setting, is only a 20th century phenomenon, dating back only to scholars and writers such as John Berger, Laura Mulvey, and Maurice Merleau-Ponty in the 1970s. The first book-length study of this topic dates only to Pal Miklos's 1976 Hungarian book Vizuális Kultúra—*Visual Culture*.

In the modern interpretation of it, as a term, visual culture refers to visual aspects of culture and Visual Culture as a discipline. Visual culture and the importance that is placed on it, emphasizes the crucial significance and the potential power of images in our cultural life. Social sciences, in the past, were always assumed to be 'disciplines of words' which left very little space for images. It was thought to be the miniature scale of the logocentric world. The "social sciences had either depreciated or relegated the use of images to simply a secondary documentation or supplementary illustrations to written text" (Zeiny, 2017, p. 76). However, over the last two-and-a-half decades, the interest in the visual aspect of social life has risen significantly to the extent that Visual Culture as a discipline has emerged to figure out the significance of the roles of images, still or moving, in our culture, to "realize how pictures and their viewers make meaning, and to consider what it intends to negotiate a great number of images in our daily lives" (Zeiny, 2017, p. 76).

Visual Culture, as a spin-off of Cultural Studies, is interested in studying how a visual culture is produced, enacted and consumed. Visual Culture which contains many forms of still and moving images ranging from fine art to film and television advertisement to YouTube clips etc., has now become an inter-disciplinary field of study abandoning the conventional and traditional practices of art historical inquiry to include theories and perspectives from fields such as sociology, anthropology, cultural theory, literature, gender studies, film and media studies. What is vitally important to Visual Culture Studies is marking boundary crossing between these fields. For example, it is important to realize "how and why art images take advantage of commercial imagery or what it means when images, still or moving, improve or deteriorate the status of a group of people in a society" (Zeiny, 2017, p. 77). With the recent spate of images and the relevant technologies, 'visual culture' is the everyday life rather than just a part of it (Lister & Wells, 2000). This phenomenon of visuality of culture has become considerably significant that it requires its own discipline of study regarding all kinds of visual information, the meaning that images produce, pleasure and consumption, containing the study of all visual technologies from "oil painting to the internet" (Mirzoeff, 1998, p. 3). It is now obvious that Visual Culture is not just the study of images but rather the centrality of vision in our everyday life and the production of meaning which is a major backbone of 'visual culture.'

Of essence in understanding visual culture is the close relationship between 'representation, meaning and culture.' But what is the connection between these three components that makes it so essential in this study? Culture, as a highly complex phenomenon, is a broad concept with a variety of different definitions which keeps changing over time. On the conventional level, culture was assumed to be a whole body of outstanding and noble ideas represented through the fine arts such as the classic works of literature, painting, music and philosophy. This sort of notion described culture as the "best that has been thought and said" (Arnold, 1932, p. 6) in a society and categorized the culture into the 'high culture' for the elite and the sophisticated; and 'low culture' also called 'mass culture' or 'popular culture' for the widely distributed forms of popular fictions, television programs, and comic books for the general population (Zeiny, 2017). However, the recent definitions of the term have it that culture, by and large, is considered as learned and communal values, beliefs, perspectives and customs. In terms of Anthropology, culture is considered 'a whole way of life' accommodating a vast range of activities within a society. Apart from this all-encompassing anthropological perspective, Irving (1984, p. 138) believes culture is "the shared and learned information people use to generate meaning and order within a social system." Following this view, culture is not inherited, but learned; it is not instinctive but origins from one's social milieus.

Drawing upon Stuart Hall's definition of culture, we argue that culture is the shared practices of a community, society or a group through which meaning is produced from the textual, aural and visual world of representations. Culture is not just a fixed set of components such as paintings or television programs but it is also a set of practices which assist individuals and groups make sense of those things (Hall, 1997). It is, indeed, the manufacture and transference of meanings between individuals in a group or a society. Thus, it is safe to contend that there is a diversity of meanings and interpretations about any particular given topic or object in any culture. People may share the same culture but there other different individual interpretations of a certain topic, object or image. It is precisely this diversity and plurality of meanings and interpretations that scholars of Cultural Studies are studying. The Cultural Studies scholars focus upon the "patterns and practices of culture, their links to social groups and the power connections between those groups as they are made and mediated by forms of culture" (Zeiny, 2017, p. 77). In the vein of this view, culture is the everyday symbolic and expressive practices that happen as we live. It is highly impossible to take out the cultures of everyday life from practices of representation, visual or otherwise. What has emerged to be termed as the 'cultural turn' has now been replaced by the 'visual turn' where images and representations saturate our world.

Representation has seized an important place in the study of visual culture as it connects meaning and language to culture. Representation is the process by which meaning is created and exchanged between members of a culture through the use of language, signs and images which stand for or represent things (Hall, 1997). Languages are the medium through which feelings, ideas, and thoughts are represented in a culture. More than ever, our language is ultimately becoming more visual. Representation through language, in this case a visual language, as Hall (1997) further argues, is therefore crucially important to the process through which meaning is constructed in a culture. In the vein of this view, meaning is a matter of intervention or creation which is created and constructed by people. Hall (1997, p. 3) says: "it is the participants in a culture who give meaning to people, objects, and events ... it is by our use of things, and what we say, think and feel about them—how we represent them—that we give them a meaning." Therefore, it is now clear that meaning is the result of social convention, produced and constructed through representational processes. Visual representations, in today's globalized world, have become the predominant "representational system" (Hall, 1997, p. 1). That is how they can be considered as an increasingly powerful medium for the production of meaning.

In this context, the term "visual culture" places great importance on the visuality of our world, and describes a philosophical and epistemological posture that endorses visuality as fundamentally important to the constitution of the world. This growing centrality of the visuality in our life, argues Martin Jay (1994, p. 3), is "ocularcentrism" or "scopophilia" where the practice of looking help people understand the world and their surroundings (Cartwright and Sturken, 2001). The world which was once so logocentric has now been progressing towards a shift where images and visuality have saturated our surroundings. While the shift from lexicality to visuality popularizes the status of visuals and enhances engagement with them, it engenders a fear about their potential capability to shape and change attitudes. After all, visual pronouncements are almost always cultural products loaded with values, ideologies and taken-for-granted beliefs of the cultures which produce them, and the ones which consume them. As critical theorist Douglas Crimp elucidates, "an image [still or moving] isn't simple negative or positive but rather is the product of social relations ..." (Takemoto, 2003, p. 85). Despite it all, whether we like it or not, visuality is the way in which particular ways of seeing the world are conceived and it has a dramatic influence in "how we see, how we are able, allowed, or made to see" (Foster, 1988, ix, in Ros, 2007).

Derived and informed by socio-political and historical changes, this conceiving of a particular practice of looking and seeing is influenced by the "information that exist both prior to and separate from the [visual] text itself" (Howells & Negreiro, 2012, p. 17). Therefore, understanding the influence of the visual pronouncements requires special consideration of the relation between particular images and the audiences' underlying notions, beliefs, narratives, and ideologies. Given the fact that images have the ability to quickly influence viewers both cognitively and emotionally, these visual representations would gradually form a desired method of reading and viewing. Once reproduced repeatedly, these visual representations construct a fixed set of meaning for certain issues, perspectives, cultures, and groups of people. Oftentimes when these visual codes are constructed towards making sense of a different culture, or other people who are unlike us, they can lead to a process of Othering or a kind of hierarchy. Informed by political, social, and historical thoughts and belief systems, they can lead to pigeonholing the represented in specific ways. Especially if these representations occur in a loaded setting, for example, where a historical, political and social binary is already embedded in the culture such as East vs. West, these representations more often than not feed off and into that unbalance and hierarchy.

While giving the viewers the power of subjectivity and judgments, these visual pronouncements, especially if they are continuously misrepresenting or selectively representing, could lead to the objectification, silences and oppression of those represented. This defines what we may refer to as visual imperialism; it is the ubiquitous form of representation that manufactures our perceptions, determines our desires, and regulates our choices in a way that one mode of representation and the reading of a group or another culture become dominant. This type of representation also often leads to a kind of gap between representation and the reality of the lives and cultures of those who are represented. As Susan Sontag explains, images are potent entities that profoundly intervene with one's perception of 'reality.' She states: "Notions of image and reality are complementary. When the notion of reality changes, so does that of the image, and vice versa." (1982, p. 354). To put it in another way, "images can become perceived reality, and reality may turn out to be nothing but projected image ..." (Gruber & Haughbolle, 2013, p. xiii).

In the way we are conditioned to read images, misrepresentation and selective representation are part of the process of 'Othering' which is the backbone of visual imperialism.' Visual imperialism is "the colonization of the world mind through the use of selective imagery that acts as a representation of a dominant ideology." (Kuehnast, 1992, p. 184). Ideology plays an important role in visual imperialism. An ideology reflected in an image, which informs the audiences what and how to see and think, conjures up the pedagogical functioning of visual culture. Even when visual culture is consumed to be entertained, it functions pedagogically. This spectacle pedagogy of visual culture, to borrow the term from Garoian and Gaudelius (2004), is the risky and continual form of propaganda at the disposal of cultural imperialism. It is in this context that visual imperialism leaves no space for a possible plurality of interpretations. Bereft of such plurality, visual imperialism reproduces ideologically informed images that are often easy to read as one-dimensional by the uninformed viewer. An example that best illustrates such short of plurality is the often Western cliché representation of Islam and Muslims, which sums up Islam and those who practice it to very few reductive images. What resists and challenges this dominant reductive vision is a plurality of vision which enhances the feasibility of multifaceted perspectives, discourses and understanding.

This is where this volume comes together. It intends to open up a space for dialogue, to highlight and examine the dominant and sometimes not-so-dominant visual cultures that have informed the way Islam is represented at both local and global levels through the inclusion of multiple realities, media, perspectives, discourses and interpretations.

The idea for this book was also conceived at the cross-section of multiple realities of what it means to be Muslim when we, Esmaeil Zeniy and Sanaz Fotouhi, met in Kuala Lumpur where Sanaz was invited to present a paper as part of the Institute of Malaysian and International Studies (IKMAS) seminar series in National University of Malaysia (UKM). The presentation brought to gether an interesting mix of people who identified themselves, in one way or another, as Muslim, each of whom was unique in their approach and understanding of what it entailed. Here was Sanaz, a Muslim born Iranian woman, a selective practitioner, who has been living in Australia for the last decade or so, alongside Esmaeil an Iranian Muslim man who had been in Malaysia for the last seven years. We were in dialogue with the Malaysian staff at UKM's School of Language Studies & Linguistics, the majority of whom are feisty Muslim women, some of whom observe the *hijab*, and some who do not. In dialogue, we realized that inherently we shared a common thread, our association with Islamic thought and culture. Yet, in this similarity, we were also very inherently different. While the similarities and differences were utterly clear to us, for which we respected each other, we were also aware that the diversities and complexities of Muslim identities are usually unseen to those who are unfamiliar with it.

We also recognized that each of us has grappled with the representation and misrepresentation of Islam and Muslim people both in our own personal lives and scholarly work. Sanaz, who has worked extensively on Iranian writing in diaspora, has always grappled with the representations of Iranian Muslim women in texts and to some extent visually. She has examined aspects of this in her book *The Literature of the Iranian Diaspora*. Esmaeil has also always been dealing and concerned with this sort of (mis)representation in the course of his study on the post-9/11 Western representation of Islam and Muslim women, and diasporic Muslim women's life narratives.

What both of us realized in our studies of this topic is that the visual representation and analysis of modern day Muslims people and Islam, especially in the West still has its roots deep in a history that informs Westerns and Eastern understandings of each other. One can argue how the Middle East, Islam and Muslim people are portrayed today on our glitzy computer screens and through various visual platforms in the West dates back to the way Western painters recorded and depicted certain regions and areas of the East in a way that served the purposes of the larger missions of Western Empires. If we trace this back, during the colonization era, it became "a major preoccupation of nineteenth-century painting, an East which was, in turn, 'Imagined, Experienced, [and] Remembered'" (MacKenzie, 1995, p. 44). As an obsession for the West, representing the Orient has its roots in the first Westerners' journey to the Orient in search of exotica and excitement whose travel accounts encouraged many male artists to travel there for painting. The creation of these paintings led to the emergence of the Orient as a source that provides the West the deepest and most recurring images of the Other. These visual representations of the Orient, over the centuries, have continued to bolster the stereotypes of the 'Other' and celebrate the differences to sustain the power of the dominant culture. These differences that are constructed imaginatively as the real ones are being contracted are the result of what Benedict Anderson (1983) calls "imagined communities." "Imagined communities" are formed through the invented links out of which emerges exclusive group identities The creation of Western identity delineates who is part of the community and who is on the other side. Baily Jones (2007, p. 8) argues that it is precisely "this creation of imaginary difference that separates one group from another."

Of the groups of people who have been left outside the Western communities and who have been historically and constantly subjected to Orientalist stereotypical depiction are Muslims, especially Muslim women whose body has long been a site of contention. The visual and pictorial representations of these women, over the centuries, have been created to reinforce differences and has denied the representation of their personal and individual experiences. Thus people in the West have been presented with the cliché portrayals of Muslim women as veiled and powerless victims of patriarchal societies in primitive lands, tribal, and frozen in a hazy past. Created often by male members of the society, and most times with a larger political agenda, this depiction continues to date, becoming darker after the events of 9/11, and even more misconstrued with the emergence of ISIS and other extremist Islamic groups. What we see in post-9/11 visual contexts is thus a continuation of a colonial strategy and rule in depicting the 'Other' but in a new form that serves the purposes of our current era. The 9/11 events and President Bush's 'Axis of Evil' speech gave birth to the explosion of visual discourses about Muslim women's oppression in Islamic societies. It now seems an established rule in the West to represent the East in need of Western liberation. The rule is the same in every medium including painting, photography, news, film, literature and music. What gives power to this stereotype is a persistent repetition that associates Muslims and East with the 'veil,' 'Orient,' and 'Arab.' These are all words with different layers of textual and visual history, referring to real places and real times but the meaning of which have been weighed down with certain negative and historically rooted associations that grossly stereotypes and pigeonholes those who are represented—and even sometimes those who are representing them.

We all know that "Islam is not homogenous; it is a diverse set of practices that vary from culture to culture" (Akbarzadeh & Smith, 2005, p. 4). Yet, for various complex social, political and historical reasons, the diversity of Islamic cultures, thoughts and practices of the global Muslim population in the West has been glossed over. For the majority, in our highly image dependent world today, these reductive perceptions are constructed visually. And most times, what is seen, or what is at least projected, is enough to construct an image around which many can claim a certain degree of understanding, even if that representation is misinformed, simplistic or far from the truth. But for the complex and critical mind, it is what is unseen, what is under the veil of representation that can offer a multifaceted and truer understanding of Islam and Muslim identities.

At the other end of the spectrum, Muslim countries within themselves are prone to this type of visual exploitation. Muslim local home-grown ideologies and perceptions yield to imperialist representations as well. A prominent example is the use of visual culture by the radical terrorist organizations of Al-Qaeda and ISIS. In the context of 'war on terror,' the visual culture of conflict began to appear and images became weapons. Al-Qaeda has begun its 'Electronic Jihad' by producing images that invited jihadists to a fight against America and its allies. In constructing these 'call outs,' they were careful to employ and produce images that feed off and increase anti-American/British sentiments. When images from Abu-Gharib prison became public in April 2004, they were instantaneously appropriated and re-circulated in a wider culture. This redistribution was in the visual forms of murals, posters, ads, comics and websites (Anden-Papadopoulos, 2007). The most iconic image of this abuse scandal is the picture of the hooded prisoner standing on a box. His wide open arms stand for Christ on the cross which conjures up devotional images that depict revered and tormented figures that remain decent in spite of their humiliation (Mitchell, 2004). The hooded man was regenerated as murals and posters in Baghdad and along with the images of Lynndie England holding a detainee on a leash, it made it to the murals in other Muslim countries such as Iran (Apel, 2005). The transformation of these private shots into public visibility was to augment the anti-American/British sentiments. Having exploited the Abu-Gharib pictures, Al-Qaeda recruited more mujahidin to launch its operations. Abu-Gharib images drove jihadists to new lengths and Al-Qaeda started filming its hostage taking and beheading episodes to communicate its power of violence to target populations. This is nothing new. Just as much as the West has used certain images of Islam and Muslims to highlight certain differences, Muslim states have also historically been using visual representations to instill their cultural ideologies.

The problem with these types of visual representations is their extreme power and potency to lure people into holding beliefs that compromise or complement the state's or a specific group's ideology. They possess the power to persuade others to share certain views and values. That is why we refer to this kind of control as visual imperialism. The most important facet of ideologically constructed images, or visual imperialism, is that "they appear to be natural or given, rather than part of a system of belief that a culture produces in order to function in a particular way" (Sturken & Cartwright, 2001, pp. 21–2). The persuasion of people to hold the same perspectives as that of the state, which results from the dominant ideology, could be linked with Roland Barthes's concept of myth (1977). In Barthes's concept of myth, there are two levels of meaning of images. These two levels are denotative and connotative meanings. The denotative meaning is based on its literal and descriptive meaning whereas the connotative meaning hinges on the cultural and historical context of the image. Connotative meanings also rely on personal and social knowledge of those circumstances; thus, connotations could be different personally and culturally. At this level of connotation, Barthes uses the term 'myth' to refer to cultural beliefs and values. 'Myth' for Barthes is "the hidden set of rules and conventions through which meanings, which are in reality specific to certain groups, are made to seem universal and given for a whole society" (Sturken & Cartwright, 2001, 19). Therefore, myth makes the connotative meaning of a particular image seem denotative, literal and natural. Akin to Barthes's notion of myth, the ideologies of the West towards representations of Islam and Muslims are usually connotations parading as denotations in the context of visual imperialism. Thus, visual imperialism of Islam in this context refers to the collection of visual images, defined in the broad sense, that perpetrate and perpetuate the myths about an Islamic race, geography and culture. These images which have been used to substantiate imperialist rhetoric to extend their colonial projects gave birth to a dominant reading of certain races and issues.

This is the context in which this collection is set. Deriving from this broad definition of 'visual imperialism,' essays in this collection thus tease out, explore and analyze how various mediums within the Western and Muslim visual culture have constructed a limited perspective or understanding of a certain issue and groups of people. Anchored in this belief, this collection, *The Seen and Unseen* seeks to question these dominant readings, to agitate the singular and fixed meanings and to proffer in the audience the feeling that ideologies can work through seemingly simple artefacts and sympathetic images. This edited volume takes the position to demystify the visual representations of Muslims, to interrogate the naturalness of the given reality and to highlight the carefully orchestrated construction of any given reflection of reality on Islam and Muslims. Instead of simply reiterating the meaning of stereotypical representation, the task of this volume is to detect and interrogate the apparent taken-for-granted assumptions made of the images of Islam and Muslims. *The Seen and Unseen* deals with this fixed and stereotypical way of looking at Islam and Muslims, and explores alternative and challenging visual representations which have set out to reconstruct and dismantle these already existing belief systems.

While in dialogue with, and adding to the already existing scholarship, this volume approaches this topic from a vantage point of diverse multiple perspectives and through an analysis of multiple visual resources. The unique attribute of this volume is the diversity of voices and global representations that it offers. Covering issues from Indonesia to Brunei, Iran, Egypt, France, and England and even on cyberspace, by international scholars, this volume provides examinations of different ways that visual cultures have formed the way representations of Islam and Muslim people are understood, misunderstood, misrepresented, or even embraced visually. The scholars in this volume draw on historical images in paintings, books and their covers, photography and modern art, news representations, and images on cyberspace to demonstrate their arguments. What adds to the uniqueness of this collection is its representation of the diversity and sometimes contradictory—yet reality of—visual perspectives that construct and adhere meaning to the way Islam and Muslim people are seen in a Western context.

The three parts in this volume each explore a vastly different approach to visual representations of Islam from around the world. Essays in part 1, Imaging Histories, explore and expand some of the historic approaches to the visual depiction of Islamic worlds, not only in their historical context but by tracing their impact into the modern world today. In his essay "The Arrest of Diponegoro: Visual Orientalism and its Alternative," Syed Farid Alatas, for example, analyzes the function of Orientalist representation of the historical event 'The Arrest of Diponegoro,' the Indonesian anti-colonial hero, painted by the Dutch painter, Nicolaas Pieneman and compares it with the Indonesian painter, Radin Saleh's version of the same event painted in 1857 which suggests a 'counter-orientalist view.' Whereas the study of visual orientalism is a well-developed field in the context of Middle East, it has never been a well-trodden path in the context of the Malay world of Indonesia and Malaysia. Utilizing Ibn Khaldun's the Science of Human Society as a normative method, Alatas makes a case for art as poetics as a valid method and demonstrates how art as poetics can complement the sociological study of ideologies such as Orientalism. In "Images of the Prophet Muhammad: Brief Thoughts on Some European-Islamic Encounters," Christiane Gruber, a multilingual Swiss-American-Turkish scholar traces some of the historical myths surrounding visual representations of Prophet Mohammad in different Islamic thoughts, and engages with the way those historic ideologies have affected the way the modern world responds to the visual representation of the Prophet and the various consequences of it.

Part 2, Unseen Reality, includes essays exploring the impact of visual representations of what it means to be a Muslim in the West in the socio-political context of our modern. They explore a vast range of representations from the male Islamic fantastic terrorists, to the way Muslim women celebrate their own culture of veiling, and a visual association between Muslim women, patriarchy and oil. Jared Ahmed, in his "Nightmarish visions? Shifting visual representations of 'Islamic' terrorism throughout the 'war on terror,'" takes us into a specific local understanding of the concept of terrorism and its specific visual association with Islam in the West. By drawing on examples from the UK news images, he investigates the various ways in which the phenomenon of 'Islamic' terrorism has been made visible within the mainstream western news media. In "Oil and Women: Invisibility as Power in Nawal El-Saadawi's *Love in the Kingdom of Oil*," Layla Hendow, makes the connection between two seemingly unrelated and unseen issues of women and oil as pieces of commodity in El-Saadawi's highly visually depicted novel in the Islamic world, offering us a new way of reading the book, and seeing the connection with oil and power at large. In "'World Hijab Day': Positioning the Hijabi in Cyberspace," Raihanah M. M., takes us onto the platform of social media and examines the representation of *Hijab* as a form of empowerment by Muslim women from around the world. She examines the relatively unheard of World Hijab Day through analysis of the celebrated day's Facebook page. Engaging with the photos and comments, it brings to light a new perspective of the *hijab* as a symbol of pride for the women, and a celebration of its solidarity on the social media platform.

Part 3, Interrogating Visual Representations, brings together essays that examine the self-representations of those from Islamic countries through a variety of visual mediums, through photography, cinema, and book covers. Papers in this section bring to our attention the conflict and conundrum of visual representation. They remind us that no matter how certain authors or artists try to represent a certain idea or even themselves outside of the stereotypical modes of representations, there is still a chance that they will be read within the established framework. This part examines the way artists and writers are using the already known image of Islam as a way to challenge it, reframe it, and offer alternative readings. In "Contemporary Bruneian cinema in the context of Sharia Law," Bruno Starrs an Australian film lecturer in Brunei, explores Bruneian cinema, as an unseen representation of the Islamic experience. Situating the film in the seemingly strict Islamic context of Brunei, Starrs brings to the fore how *Yasmine*, a government-funded film from a female director about a martial arts-obsessed schoolgirl who happily defies her father, rarely wears a veil, enthusiastically chases boys and drives a racy, eye-catching car, challenges stereotypes and offers alternative perspectives on Islamic female empowerment within Brunei's society. Esmaeil Zeiny's "Visual Discourses of (Un)veiling: Revisiting Women of Allah" reviews Shirin Neshat's much-written-about Women of Allah (1993–97) series of photography to highlight its immediacy and relevancy in today's world. This relevancy origins from the rife anxiety and uneasiness towards Muslims and Muslim women in the West where hate crimes and Islamophobia are on the rise. While emphasizing the series potentiality in shattering the centuries-old stereotypes and questioning Iran's confining rules upon women, he accentuates its dialogical and pedagogical function. Moreover, he brings to surface images of veiled women in murals, posters and paintings of the 1980s and 90s Iran which bear uncanny resemblance with Neshat's Women of Allah. Exploring the series' relationship with these images, Zeiny contends that Shirin Neshat's series is dramatically influenced by these images and calls them the 'Iranian Women of Allah.' He further suggests that both of these works merit comparison because they are both dialogical and pedagogical in function. On a similar theme, as a unique attribute to this volume, in her "Visibility and veiling: Iranian art on the global scene," award-winning Australian-Iranian photographer and academic Hoda Afshar draws on her own experiences and work to demonstrate the challenges and trepidation of being a 'Muslim' identified visual artist in the West. Zeroing in on the 'interpretation and reception' of some of the works of well-known Iranian artists in the West, Afshar criticizes the exorbitant visibility of the veiling in their works and reveals how these works in the global art scene can serve ideological interest. Finally, Sanaz Fotouhi's "Changing the Cover Page," concludes the collection, as it explores the shifting nature of book covers by Iranian writers in diaspora. She examines the unseen relationship between Iranian book covers in the West and their transient nature in relation to social media and social interests emerging from Iran and how social media has opened up a new kind of interest in the visuals that represent Iran for the Western world. Here she directs us towards a world where we are seeing the beginnings of a new kind of movement of visual representation, beyond the hackneyed images of half-veiled women which have, over the last several decades, come to represent Islamic cultures.

Moving across geographical borders and political boundaries, and going beyond the margins of disciplinary practices, this volume questions principal presumptions that have long held sway in debates on Orientalist representations of the Middle East and Muslim people, and visual cultures. In particularly distinctive ways, each of the diverse essays in this book provokes a reassessment of political reinterpretation of visual cultures of the way Islam and Muslim people are produced and reproduced in a Western context. The diversity of these essays, formed at the intersection of the different opinions and experiences of the scholars researching them, provides a lively and unique perspective in the way visual representations of Islam is understood and addressed across a range of platforms and a wide geographic space, with the hope that the collection will offer alternative and fresh perspectives for analysis and understanding of already existing visual cultures that define the Western relationship with the Islamic world.

References

Akbarzadeh, S. and Smith, B. (2005). *The Representation of Islam and Muslims in the Media: (The Age and Herald Sun Newspapers)*. Melbourne: Monash University.

Anden-Papadopoulos, K. (2007). The Abu Gharib torture photographs: News frames, visual culture, and the power of images. *Journalism*, 9(1), 5–30.

Anderson, B. (1983). *Imagined Communities*. New York: Verso.

Apel, D. (2005). Torture culture: Lynching photographs and the images of Abu Gharib. *Artform* (Summer).

Arnold, M. (1932). *Culture and Anarchy: Landmarks in the History of Education*. Cambridge University Press.

Bailey, J. R. (2007). (Re) Envisioning Self and Other: Subverting Visual Orientalism Throughout the Creation of Postcolonial Pedagogy. Dissertation, The University of North Carolina at Greensboro.

Barthes, R. (1977). *Image Music Text*. Translated by Stephen Heath. New York: Hill and Wang.

Foster, Hal. (1988). *Vision and Visuality*. Seattle, WA: Bay Press.

Garoian, C. R. & Gaudelius, Y. M. (2004). The Spectacle of Visual Culture. *Studies in Art Education*, 45 (4), 298–312.

Gruber, C. & Haugbolle, S. (2013). *Visual Culture in the Modern Middle East: Rhetoric of the Image*. Indiana University Press.

Hall, S. (1997). The Spectacle of the other. In Stuart Hall (Ed.), *Representation: Cultural Representations and Signifying Practices*. London; Sage Publication Ltd.

Howells, R & Negreiros, J. (2012). *Visual Culture*. Polity.

Irving, K. J. (1984). Cross-cultural Awareness and the English-as-a-Second-Language Classroom. *Theory Into Practice, 23*, 138–143.

Jay, M. (1994). *Downcast Eyes: The Denigration of Vision in Twentieth Century French Thought.* Berkeley: University of California Press.

Kromm, J. & Bakewell, S. B. (2009). *A History of Visual Culture: Western Civilization from the 18th to the 21st Century.* Berge Publishers.

Kuehnast, K. (1992). Visual Imperialism and the Export of Prejudice. An Exploration of Ethnographic Film. In Crawford, P. & Turton, D. (Eds.), *Film As Ethnography.* (pp. 183–196). Manchester: Manchester University Press, Granada Center for Visual Anthropology.

Lister, M. & Wells, L. (2001). Seeing Beyond Belief: Cultural Studies as an Approach to Analyzing the Visual. In T. van Leeuwen & C. Jewitt (Eds.), *Handbook of Visual Analysis.* (pp. 61–91). London: Sage.

MacKenzie, J. M. (1995). *Orientalism: History, Theory and the Arts.* Manchester: Manchester University Press.

Miklos, Pal. (1976). Vizualis kultura: Elmeleti es kritikai tanulmanyok a kepzomuveszetek korebol. (Elvek es utak), (Hungarain Edition). Magveto.

Mirzoeff, N. (1998). What is Visual Culture? In N. Mirzoeff (Ed.), *The Visual Culture Reader* (pp. 3–13). London: Routledge.

Mitchell, W. J. T. (2004, June 27). Echoes of A Christian Symbol. *Chicago Tribune,* Retrieved from http://articles.chicagotribune.com/2004-06-27/news/0406270291_1_torture-humiliation-image.

Sontag, S. (1982). *A Susan Sontag Reader.* New York: Farrar, Straus, Giroux.

Sturken, M. & Cartwright, L. (2001). *Practices of looking: An introduction to visual culture.* Oxford University Press.

Takemoto, T. (2003). The Melancholia of AIDS: Interview with Douglas Crimp. *Art Journal, 62*(4), 80–91.

Zeiny, E. (2017). From Visual Culture to Visual Imperialism: The Oriental Harem and the New Scheherazades. *3L: The Southeast Asian Journal of English Language Studies, 23*(2), 75–86.

PART 1

Imaging Histories

∵

CHAPTER 1

The Arrest of Diponegoro: Visual Orientalism and Its Alternative

Syed Farid Alatas

Orientalism and Its Visual Dimension

Orientalism refers to an orientation in which non-European peoples, the people of the so-called Orient, are imagined in a stereotypical and distorted manner. Orientalism began during the period of the European Enlightenment and further developed as European relations with the Muslim world took the form of direct or vicarious colonialism.

Orientalism was to be found among scholars, statesmen and lay people in Europe since the eighteenth and nineteenth century. Among scholars, poets and artists, Orientalism found expression in philosophies of history, social theories, novels, poems and visual arts. What they all had in common was the basic distinction between the Orient and Occident, between East and West. The characteristics of the Orient are that it was weak and defeated, while Europe was powerful and articulate. The Orient was irrational while the West rational (Said, 1979, p. 57). In the case of Islam, it was seen to be fake or fraudulent as opposed to the Christianity that it originated from (Said, 1979, p. 59).

During the colonial period, Orientalist distortions and stereotypes functioned to justify colonial rule. This function continues into the post-colonial period. On this Said said:

> So far as the United States seems to be concerned, it is only a slight overstatement to say that Moslems and Arabs are essentially seen as either oil suppliers or potential terrorists. Very little of the detail, the human density, the passion of Arab–Moslem life has entered the awareness of even those people whose profession it is to report the Arab world. What we have, instead, is a series of crude, essentialized caricatures of the Islamic world, presented in such a way as to make that world vulnerable to military aggression.
>
> SAID, 1980

Orientalism is what Said called an imaginative geography that divided the world into two equal parts. The larger and "different" part was called the Orient (Said, 1980).

Orientalism was expressed in various modes including the visual arts. Europe of the nineteenth century produced a great many paintings depicting the Arab East and West as well as the Ottoman lands and Iran. Arabs and other Muslims were depicted as not only exotic but also erotic. Nudity was a frequent theme as were the harem and odalisques. Well-known Orientalist painters include Anne-Louis Girodet (1767–1824); Antoine-Jean Gros (1771–1835); Jean-Auguste-Dominique Ingres (1780–1867); Eugene Delacroix (1798–1863); John Frederick Lewis (1804–76) and William Holman Hunt (1827–1910) (Lemaire, 2001; Stevens, 1984).

Visual Orientalism, therefore, refers to the use of selective imagery that acts as a representation of an Orientalist thought-style. There are numerous examples of Orientalist painting, for example, from nineteenth century Europe. In fact, much of the attention to Orientalist paintings is directed to the Middle East and North Africa. Although there are several works on visual Orientalism and many scholarly debates on the topic, it is not the purpose of this chapter to enter into these debates. Among the interesting issues raised in revisionist perspectives in the existing literature is the idea that Orientalist art is not merely a reflection of the political economy of Western domination but was produced in the context of cross-cultural interaction, between the colonizer and the colonized (Beaulieu & Roberts, 2002). This is also argued in Eaton's work on visual culture in the context of interaction between British realist art and Mughal 'vernacular' art, their mutual influence, and the emergence of styles and forms that enabled Indian painters to critique colonial politics and aesthetics (Eaton, 2013).

This chapter, on the other hand, brings attention to another part of the so-called Orient, Indonesia during colonial rule. Rather than deal with general issues concerning visual Orientalism, it discusses a specific case of Orientalist paintings from the Dutch East Indies of the nineteenth century. The artist was the Dutch painter, Nicolaas Pienaman (1809–1860). Through Pieneman's depiction of the arrest of the Indonesian anti-colonial hero, Pangeran Diponegoro (1785–1855), it is possible to discuss some features of Orientalism. Pieneman's painting of Diponegoro's arrest is an example of how a visual representation of an historical event reflects the dominant orientation of the time, that is, colonial ideology. What is also interesting is to compare Pienaman's depiction with that of the Indonesian painter, Raden Saleh (1811–1880). His interpretation of the same event, which I suggest, presents a counter-Orientalist view. The study of visual Orientalism is a well-developed field in the context of various regions of the world, but not so in the context of the Malay world of Indonesia and Malaysia.

The next section provides a brief discussion of the methods of the human sciences in order to make a case for poetics as a valid method. This is followed by a discussion on art as poetics. I then turn to the paintings of Pienaman and Raden Saleh to discuss aspects of their respective orientations. I conclude with some remarks about a science of human society that is methodologically pluralistic.

The Methods of the Science of Human Society

The modern human sciences are lacking in methodological pluralism. Premodern traditions are more pluralistic. An example of this pluralism can be seen through the eyes of the fourteenth century Muslim theoretical historian, 'Abdul Rahman Ibn Khaldun (1332–1406).

Ibn Khaldun discovered a new science that he called the science of human society (*'ilm al-ijtima' al-insani*). He did so as a result of his dissatisfaction with the existing science of history. He was critical of the dominant method used by the historians of his time that they inherited from earlier generations of scholars. Ibn Khaldun argued that the method they used did not allow them to distinguish truth from error on the grounds of the possibility (*imkan*) or absurdity (*istihalah*) of reported events.

> We must distinguish the conditions that attach themselves to the essence of civilization as required by its very nature; the things that are accidental (to civilization) and cannot be counted on; and the things that cannot possibly attach themselves to it. If we do that, we shall have a normative method for distinguishing right from wrong and truth from falsehood in historical information by means of a logical demonstration that admits of no doubts. Then whenever we hear about certain conditions occurring in civilization, we shall know what to accept and what to declare spurious. We shall have a sound yardstick with the help of which historians may find the path of truth and correctness where their reports are concerned.
>
> IBN KHALDUN, 2005, I, P. 56 [1967, I, P. 77][1]

---

1 Citations in square brackets refer to Rosenthal's English translation of Ibn Khaldun's theoretical work, *The Muqaddimah*, in which he founded the new science.

Of paramount concern to traditional historians was the reliability of the trans-
mitters of information and the reliability of the sources. They tended to be
less concerned with the inherent possibility or absurdity of events as they are
reported. For Ibn Khaldun, on the other hand, the possibility and absurdity of
reports can be ascertained from logical demonstration from what is known
about the essence of society. Ibn Khaldun, like his fellow Muslim heirs to the
classical Greek tradition regarded the method of demonstration (*burhan*) to
be the most reliable in terms of yielding certain knowledge. Ibn Khaldun's new
science of human society was conceived as a body of generalizations that were
demonstrable from certain premises or *muqaddimat*,[2] which include the following: (i) human society is a necessity (Ibn Khaldun, 2005, I, p. 67 [1967, I,
p. 89]); and (ii) The physical environment influences humans socially, psycho-
logically and physically (Ibn Khaldun, 2005, I, pp. 71, 132, 138, 140 [1967, pp. I,
94, 167, 174, 177]).

According to the tradition that Ibn Khaldun operated out of, method, conveyed by the term *mantiq*, referred to the convention that made it possible to
distinguish right from wrong (Mahdi, 1957, p. 160). This convention includes
the formulation of definitions (*hudud*) through recognition of the essence
(*mahiyat*) of phenomena, and arguments that lead to judgment or apperception (Ibn Khaldun, 2005, III, p. 91 [1967, III, p. 137]). Knowledge is attained
when either conception (*tasawwur*), that is, the perception of the essence of
things, or apperception (*tasdiq*), that is, the judgement establishing the corre-
spondence between the concept and the phenomenon in question, is attained.
Conception in turn involves knowledge of the five universals, that is, genus
(*jins*), difference (*fasl*), species (*nu'*), property (*khasah*) and general accident
('*ard al-'am*) (Ibn Khaldun, 2005, III, p. 94 [1967, III, p. 102]). Ibn Khaldun
noted that every phenomenon has both its own essence and accidental conditions or properties. It is necessary to know both the essence of events and their
accidental conditions in order to be able to distinguish truth from falsehood.
This approach constitutes a critical approach to historical information (Ibn
Khaldun, 2005, I, p. 53 [1967, I, pp. 72–73]).

While this is the general convention, it was recognized that deductive reasoning or demonstration was not the only method of reasoning that led to
valid truth claims. The Muslims followed Aristotle in recognizing other kinds of

---

2   The *muqaddimat* are assertions whose demonstration do not fall within the scope of the new
    science of human society but taken as self-evident. See Mahdi (1957, p. 172).

analogical reasoning apart from demonstration.[3] These include (Ibn Khaldun, 2005, III, pp. 93–94 [1967, III, pp. 140–141]):

1. Dialectics (*jadal*). This form of analogical reasoning does not produce certain knowledge because its premises are not necessarily held to be certain. Rather dialectics refers to a form of disputation that aims to arrive at the truth by exposing false beliefs;
2. Rhetoric (*khitabah*). This refers to analogical reasoning that uses forms of speech that are directed to influencing or persuading rather than instructing people.
3. Poetics (*shi'ir*). This employs a form of reasoning that instructs via the use of parables (*tamthil*) and similes (*tashbih*). Knowledge is achieved through the stirring of the imagination rather than through demonstration or persuasion.

The purpose of this brief discussion on methods is to suggest that there is a need for a more pluralistic approach in the human sciences. In modern social sciences education there is a sharp distinction made between the so-called scientific method and those of literature and the arts. The development of a strict dichotomy between art and science meant that truth and beauty were entirely separate domains. There emerged a methodological dualism (Brown, 1978, p. 15), that is, "two orders ... separate but unequal" (Gouldner, 1962, p. 210, cited in Brown, 1977, pp. 26–27). In the methodological dualistic world of social science, the analyst had to either emulate physics or art (Brown, 1978, p. 16). The former engaged in science that was higher up in the hierarchy of knowledge for it was science, not art, that represented reality. For social scientists, being true to science means that the subjective state, feelings, interpretations and imagination of the scientist must be excluded from any account of social reality. Such an attitude takes us away from the idea that knowledge can also be attained through the stirring of feelings and imagination, and that poetics is as valid a method of reasoning or argumentation as demonstration or the scientific method. These methods did not divide communities of scholars in terms of epistemological approaches. In the world of Ibn Khaldun, not only demonstration but also poetics and other methods were all recognized as valid methods of arrival at knowledge.

---

3 So called because the logical method argues from analogy in which the common properties of a set of objects are established and universal propositions are examined by making connections between those common properties. See Cohen & Nagel (1934, pp. 286–287).

The Arrest of Diponegoro: Art as Poetics

Art, including paintings and other visual arts, instructs via the stirring of imagination rather than demonstration or persuasion. Art is as poetic as the literary arts. A painting is both form and content. As form it is an artefact that consists of, for example, paint and canvas. It also has content in so far as it depicts or represents something. The content takes the viewer "away from the present moment into the realm of our imagination and experience" (Sidell, 2012, October 16). How do we receive a painting? As we allow the painting to unfold, we gradually become aware of the feeling that it produces. The painting does more than just express the artist's feelings or views (Sidell, 2012, August 30). This aspect, of course, is not to be denied. But, the artist also painted a moment that unfolds in the viewer a particular feeling and experience that we must be aware of (Sidell, 2012, November, 19). Looking at art as poetics gives us a way to reflect on themes that are generally the subject of history, anthropology, sociology and literature by both our imagining ourselves experiencing the space and time of the painting as well as understanding how it expresses the beliefs, sentiments and values of the artist. This can be seen from our reception of the paintings of Pieneman and Radin Saleh.

Raden Saleh Sjarif Boestaman was born in 1811 in Semarang, Java into a Hadhrami Arab family, the bin Yahya. As a young man, he received instruction in art in Bogor from the Belgian artist A. J. Payen. Saleh was later able to obtain support from the Dutch government to go to Holland to study art.

In 1857, Radin Saleh completed his painting depicting the arrest of the Indonesian hero, Pangeran Diponegoro, the Javanese prince who rebelled against Dutch colonial rule.[4] After leading an unsuccessful revolt against the Dutch during the five-year Java War (1825–1830), Diponegoro was captured and sent into exile. The painting was completed in Java. Prior to that, Saleh was in Europe where he spent twenty-five years studying and training as an artist. His time in Holland was supported financially by the Dutch government. His presentation of the painting of the arrest of Diponegoro to the Dutch king, William III, was ostensibly to thank the Dutch government for its support (Carey, 1982, p. 1). The first ten years of his life in Europe were spent in Holland while the next fifteen saw him gain experience and tutelage in Germany, France, Belgium, England and Italy (Kraus, 2005, p. 264).[5] While in Holland, Saleh would have come across the painting of the Nicolaas Pieneman,

---

4   On Diponegoro see Carey (2007, 2014a). For Indonesian translations of both these works see Carey (2012, 2014b). On Raden Saleh's painting see Carey (1982).

5   On the life of Raden Saleh, see Soekanto (1951) and Marasutan (1973).

entitled *De onderwerping van Diepo Negoro aan luitenant-generaal baron De Kock* (The Subjugation of Diponegoro to Lieutenant-General De Kock) (See Figure 1.1). Both his and Pieneman's painting depict the same scene of the arrest of Diponegoro just outside the entrance to the Residency House at Magelang on 28 March 1830.

The general scene, common to both paintings is of De Kock gesturing to Diponegoro to enter a carriage that was to start him on his journy into exile, while Dutch officers and Diponegoro's followers look on (Carey, 1982, pp. 1 2). But, there are important differences between the two. According to Carey, the Pieneman painting is "stiff and formal" (Carey, 1982, p. 2). The day is bright. Kraus notes that there is no sign of resistance and everyone, Dutch and Javanese alike, seem relaxed. Diponegoro and his followers look submissive. Diponegoro is placed on a step lower than De Kock, while De Kock is pointing him out of his own country (Kraus, 2005, pp. 282, 285). The Pienaman painting certainly depicts the event from the point of view of the colonizer. The colonized are potrayed as weak and defeated while the Europeans as authoritative but at the same time benevolent.

In a letter to his German friend, Duke Ernst II of Saxe-Coburg and Gotha, Saleh referred to his painting by the title *Ein historisches Tableau, die Gefangennahme des javanischen Häuptlings Diepo Negoro* (A Historic Tableau of the Arrest of the Javanese Headman Diepo Negoro) (Figure 1.2) (Kraus, 2005, p. 281). Rather than being a subjugated person, Diponegoro is treated in Saleh's painting as a victim (Kraus, 2005, p. 286). The tones of the painting are dark and muted. Far from looking relaxed, Diponegoro has a provocative and challenging look. Diponegoro is also placed at the same level as De Kock. Furthermore, De Kock is placed on the left of Diponegoro, that is, the feminine side in the Javanese spatial order, as Kraus perceptively noted (Kraus, 2005, p. 285). Diponegoro is not being pointed out of his country but looks like he is being invited into the carriage by a helpless looking De Kock. The Saleh painting depicts the event of the arrest of Diponegoro from the point of view of the colonized. The Javanese hero is potrayed as dynamic and defiant. Also very interesting is that Saleh himself is featured in the painting, firstly head bowing respectfully before Diponegoro and, secondly as one of his followers (Carey, 1982, pp. 5, 25). He is figuratively caught alongside Diponegoro. It is as if Saleh is identifying himself with the anti-colonial struggle of Diponegoro (Maharani, 2013, November 30).

A very interesting feature of the painting is that the heads of some of the Dutch officers are not in proportion to their body size. This is not an error as the same problem is not seen with the Javanese in the painting. Kraus' interpretation is significant—"the 'error' is not an error but a message: the heads of the Dutch officers are the heads of *raksasas*, or monsters" (Kraus, 2005, p. 285). Many had failed to consider the possibility of this interpretation. This failure is reflective of a larger methodological problem. It is the failure to consider underlying meanings.

The oversized heads is only apparently an error. It veils, to those who do not see, the inner meaning and intention of Radin Saleh which was to potray the Dutch in a critical light. If in the interpretation of Saleh's painting, the move from the outward form to the inner meaning is not made it can then be suggested, as Carey did, that Saleh's presentation of the painting to the Dutch king indicates that he "had few motives for national pride in his original choice of subject-matter" (Carey, 1982, p. 3). Carey approvingly quotes Bachtiar who referred to the presentation as a very unnationalistic gesture, but very much in accord with the relationship of a grateful artist and his aristocrat patron, the relationship of a courtier and his king" (Bachtiar, 1978, p. 48). Along similar lines, Wright suggests the possibility that Raden Saleh's painting was commissioned by the Dutch to show the outcome of the Java War in a way that it could function to warn potential rebels (Wright, 2001, p. 58; cited in Kraus, 2005, p. 288). In other words, Wright did not see any anti-colonial element in Saleh's painting.

Kraus' contribution to the understanding of Saleh's painting is important because it raises the methodological issue of interpretation. For Kraus, Saleh's painting has two levels of meaning: there is the "upfront meaning for the Dutch viewer and a second clandestine meaning for a Javanese public" (Kraus, 2005, p. 285). The Dutch tended to see De Kock as a polite and fatherly figure, while the Javanese saw him as a female *raksasa* with a monstrous head. Unable to comprehend the clandestine meaning, the Dutch explained the oversized heads in terms of Saleh's incompetence (Kraus, 2005, p. 285).

In this sense, Saleh can be seen to have drawn from Islamic tradition. Kraus' two levels of meaning can be restated in terms of the appearance-reality dichotomy which corresponds in Islamic tradition to the *zahir-batin* dichotomy. Reality as well as the words we use to describe it have their outer forms and inner meanings. The terms *zahir* and *batin* are Qur'anic, which refer to both the outer and inner dimensions of God's bounties and of sin.[6] Also, the Qur'an consists of verses that have both outer forms (*zahir*) and inner meanings (*batin*). But, it is not only the *ayat* of the Qur'an but also the *ayat* or text of the world that have the outer forms and inner meanings. The general principle is

---

6 *Luqmān* (31): 20. "He has bestowed upon you His favors inwardly and outwardly."; *Al-An'ām* (6): 120. "Forsake the outwardness of sin and its inwardness."

that text and reality, natural or social, is to be understood by moving from the outer forms to the inner meanings.

The *zahir-batin* distinction has a number of types:

- The *zahir* and *batin* of texts refer to the exoteric and the esoteric respectively, and the movement from literal to figurative or metaphorical meanings.
- In the study of society the *zahir-batin* distinction refers to the facts on the one hand and to the laws and motive forces underlying social and historical change on the other. This is the Khaldunian sense of the *zahir* and *batin* (Ibn Khaldun, 2005, I, p. 5 [1967, I, p. 6]).
- concerning the study of human conduct, the *zahir* refers to overt action and behavior, while the *batin* refers to the intentions underlying such acts.
- The *zahir* also refers to the overt practices of a religious community, while the *batin* refers to their 'hidden' practices.
- The *zahir* refers to the outer form of rituals and other practices, while the *batin* refers to the inner experience that accompanies these practices.

The *zahir* and *batin* also correspond to the distinction made by Said Nursi between *mana-yı ismi* and *mana-yı harfi*, that is, the aspect of things that look to themselves, and the aspect that looks to God. Replying to a student, Re'fet, Nursi said:

> When you look in the mirror, if you look at it for the glass, you will intentionally see the glass; in it, Re'fet will strike the eye secondly, indirectly. Whereas if your purpose is to look at the mirror in order to see your blessed face, you will intentionally see lovable Re'fet. You will exclaim: "*So blessed be God, the Best of Creators!*" The glass of the mirror will strike your eye secondly and indirectly.

In the first instance, the glass of the mirror is 'the meaning which looks to the thing itself,' while Re'fet is its 'significative meaning.' In the second instance, the glass of the mirror is 'the significative meaning,' that is, it is not looked at for itself, but for another meaning; that is, the reflection. The mirror, on the other hand, verifies the definition of its 'significative meaning,' which is "it points to the meaning of another" (Nursi, 1995, pp. 155–6).

H. J. de Graaf remarked that he did not find the painting very beautiful and that the heads were a little too big (de Graaf, 1978, p. 15; cited in Kraus, 2005, p. 285). Graaf is like the one who looks at the glass of the mirror and, therefore, sees only the glass. He misses what is reflected in the mirror, that is, the possible hidden intention underlying the overt action and behavior. In the case of Saleh's painting, the overt or the *zahir* is the oversized heads of the Dutch officers. The *batin* is the clandestine meaning that Kraus attributes to Saleh, the reference to De Kock as a female *raksasa*. If we do not go beyond appearnces and inquire into Saleh's intention or clandestine meaning, the Arrest of Diponegoro would be read as a depiction by a grateful colonized subject. On the other hand, if the inner meaning is grasped, Saleh's painting is seen as expressing as anti-colonial stance.

Others who noted the anti-colonial stance of Saleh's painting are Alwi Shahab who remarked that "this was a revolutionary and ant-colonial work of art" (Shahab, 2002, December 22). C. Louis Leipoldt, the well-known Afrikaans writer,[7] takes a critical position against Pienemann and interprets Raden Saleh's painting as depicting Diponegoro's indignation and anger as the result of his arrest by the Dutch (Leipoldt, 1932; cited in de Jong, 2003).

Kraus' main objective is to explain the impact of the West on Saleh and his modernity. That there is such an influence is widely recognized and not contested. Ricklef notes that Saleh, along with some others, are examples of Indonesians adopting wholly European styles in the visual arts (Ricklefs, 2008, p. 153). While this is not to be denied, there is more to be said about Saleh's painting if we are to be more nuanced in referring to European influence. For example, Kraus was also able to recognize the element of opposition that can be gathered from Saleh's painting. Indeed, what we see is the Javanese skillfuly learning the art of the oppressor, performing Orientalist art in form which is yet counter-Orientalist in content.

Raden Saleh's paintings in general have been referred to as illustrating the case of Orientalism inverted (James, 2012, June 13). This was indeed true when Saleh through mastering European techniques, painted the Dutch countryside. But, when Saleh painted, for example, Asian hunt scenes, it would be more appropriate to refer to this as a matter of auto-Orientalism. Auto-Orientalism refers to the adoption of Orientalist views of the Orient by the Oriental herself. It remains squarely in the tradition of Western scholarship or art on the Orient. The difference is that the knowing subjects are so-called Orientals themselves. This is the meaning of auto-Orientalism as discussed by Lie (Lie, 1996, p. 5). On the other hand, Saleh's painting of the arrest of Diponegoro can be referred to as a case of auto-Orientalism in form but not necessarily content. In content, Saleh attempted to break out of the stereotypes and conventions that were normal and expected in an Orientalist painting. The break-out, however,

---

7   See Viljoen (2000).

can only be witnessed if the observer looks beneath the surface. Saleh's use of the "language of the oppressor" leads to a rejection of a binary East-West position. Saleh was himself emersed in a Western aesthetic sensibility but at the same time painted against the colonizer. This critique is subtle and only recognizable if the observer makes the journey, as Kraus did, from the *zahir* to the *batin*. It is ironic, although typical, that the memory of colonial forms lives in Raden Saleh's painting to the extent that he adopted a European style. As mentioned above, however, it is the form rather that content that makes *Die Gefangennahme des javanischen Häuptlings Diepo Negoro* an Orientalist work.

A more critical and nuanced approach to the art and thought of Raden Saleh is likely to develop in years to come as more and more Indonesian as well as Western scholars become critical of Orientalism and Eurocentrism in the arts and humanities and develop sympathy for the project of the decolonization of knowledge or decoloniality.

Conclusion

Orientalism is not merely a feature of the distant or recent past. The assignment of qualities such as weakness and fraudulence to the Orient meant that the Orient was not only subjugated physically, but that its modes of knowing were marginalized and made irrelevant. Although it has been recognized that "vernacular" artists in the colonies had an impact on Western practitioners of Orientalist art, it cannot be denied that the rise of modern science and its introduction globally eventually displaced pre-modern modes of knowing that included dialectics, rhetoric and poetics. It is not that these modes are unknown in modern education. The teaching of dialectics, rhetoric and poetics, however, tends to be restricted to course in philosophy, logic and literature. This chapter has tried to show that pre-modern methods ought not to be confined to certain fields in the humanities but must be cultivated by anyone who wishes to gain an understanding of history and society, the purview of the social sciences. The modern social sciences restrict their methods to demonstration, that is, deduction and induction. But, social scientists have much to learn from using methods such as dialectics, rhetoric and poetics. This chapter illustrates how the consideration of art as poetics complements the sociological study of ideologies such as Orientalism. Other works on the two paintings have been published. This chapter, however, through a discussion of these paintings makes both a case for methodological pluralism as well as a counter-Orientalist discourse through art.

FIGURE 1.1   *The Submission of Prince DipoNegoro to General De Kock, Nicolaas Pieneman (c. 1830–35). The Rijksmuseum, Amsterdam, Netherlands.*

FIGURE 1.2   *The Arrest of Diponegoro. Raden Saleh (1857). Istana Negara, Jakarta, Indonesia.*

References

Bachtiar, Harsja W. (1978). Raden Saleh: Aristocrat, Painter and Scientist. In A. Day and A. Lapian (Eds.). *Papers of the Dutch-Indonesian Historical Conference held at Noordwijkerhout, the Netherlands, 19 to 22 May 1976.* (pp. 46–63). Leiden & Jakarta: Bureau of Indonesian Studies.

Beaulieu Jill & Roberts, Mary. (2002). *Orientalism's Interlocutors: Painting, Architecture, Photography.* Durham, NC. Duke University Press.

Brown, Richard H. (1977). *A Poetic for Sociology: Toward logic of discovery for the human sciences.* Cambridge: Cambridge University Press.

Brown, Richard Harvey. (1978). Symbolic Realism and Sociological Thought: Beyond the positivist-romantic debate. In Brown, Richard Harvey & Lyman, Stanford M. (Eds.) *Structure, Consciousness and History.* (pp. 13–37). Cambridge: Cambridge University Press.

Carey, Peter B. R. (1982). Raden Saleh, Dipanegara and the Painting of the Capture of Dipanegara at Magelang (28 March 1830). *Journal of the Malaysian Branch of the Royal Asiatic Society*, 55(1), 1–25.

Carey, Peter B. R. (2007). *The Power of Prophecy: Prince Dipanagara and the End of an Old Order in Java, 1785–1855.* Leiden: KITLV Press.

Carey, Peter B. R. (2012). *Kuasa Ramalan; Pangeran Diponegoro dan Akhir Tatanan Lama di Jawa, 1785–1855,* 3 volumes, Jakarta: Kepustakaan Populer Gramedia. Translation of Carey, *The Power of Prophecy.*

Carey, Peter B. R. (2014a). *Destiny: The Life of Prince Diponegoro of Yogyakarta 1785–1855.* Oxford: Peter Lang.

Carey, Peter B. R. (2014b). *Takdir; Riwayat Pangeran Diponegoro (1785–1855).* Jakarta: Buku Kompas. Indonesian translation of Carey, *Destiny.*

Eaton, Natasha. (2013). *Mimesis across Empires: Artworks and Networks in India, 1765–1860.* Durham, NC: Duke University Press.

Gouldner, Alvin W. (1962). Anti-Minotaur: The Myth of a Value Free Sociology. *Social Problems*, 9(3), 199–213.

de Graaf, H. J. (1978). Raden Saleh's leertijd in Holland. *Moesson*, 22(1), 14–15.

James, Jamie (2012, Jun 13). Orientalism Inverted, *The Wall Street Journal.* Retrieved from http://www.wsj.com/articles/SB10001424052702303768104577460802152339094.

de Jong, C. (2003). Leipoldt en Diponegoro. *South African Journal of Cultural History*, 17(2), 69–77. (in Afrikaans)

Ibn Khaldun, 'Abd al-Rahman. (2005). *Al-Muqaddimah,* 5 Vols., 'Abd al-Salam al-Shaddadi [Abdesselam Cheddadi], Casablanca: Bayt al-Funun wa al-'Ulum wa al-Adab. (in Arabic)

Ibn Khaldûn. (1967). *Ibn Khaldun: The Muqadimmah—An Introduction of History,* 3 vols., translated from the Arabic by Franz Rosenthal. London: Routledge & Kegan Paul.

Kraus, Werner. (2005). "Raden Saleh's Interpretation of the Arrest of Diponegoro: an Example of Indonesian 'proto-nationalist' Modernism," *Archipel* 69(1), 259–294.

Leipoldt, C. Louis. (1932). *Uit my Oosterse dagboek.* (From my Oriental Diary), Cape Town: Nasionale Pers Beperk. (in Afrikaans)

Lemaire, Gérard-Georges. (2001). *The Orient in Western Art.* Cologne: Könemann.

Lie, John. (1996). Sociology of Contemporary Japan. *Current Sociology*, 44(1), 1–95.

Maharani, Shinta. (2013, November 30). "Lukisan Parodi Penangkapan Diponegoro Dipamerkan," *Tempo Seleb* 30. Retrieved from https://seleb.tempo.co/read/news/2013/11/30/114533567/lukisan-parodi-penangkapan-diponegoro-dipamerkan. (in Indonesian)

Mahdi, Muhsin. (1957). *Ibn Khaldûn's Philosophy of History*, London: George Allen & Unwin.

Marasutan Baharudin. (1973). *Raden Saleh 1807–1880. Perintis Seni Lukis di Indonesia. The Precursor of Painting in Indonesia.* Jakarta: Dewan Kesenian.

Nursi, Bediuzzaman Said. (1995). *The Flashes Collection.* Istanbul: Sözler.

Ricklefs, M. C. (2008). *A History of Modern Indonesia since c. 1200,* 4th ed. Houndmills: Palgrave Macmillan.

Said, Edward. (1979). *Orientalism.* New York: Vintage Books.

Said, Edward. (1980, April 26). Islam Through Western Eyes. *The Nation.* Retrieved from https://www.thenation.com/article/islam-through-western-eyes/.

Shahab, Alwi (2002, December 22). Itu Merupakan Sebuah Karya Lukis yang Revolusioner dan Antipenjajahan., *Republika.* (in Indonesian).

Sidell, Daniel. (2012, August 30). The Poetics of Painting: Part One—Pigments on a Canvas. *Patheos.* Retrieved from http://www.patheos.com/blogs/goodletters/2012/08/poetics-pt1/.

Sidell, Daniel. (2012, October 16). The Poetics of Painting: Part Two—Beyond the Image. *Patheos.* Retrieved from http://www.patheos.com/blogs/goodletters/2012/10/the-poetics-of-painting-part-two/.

Sidell, Daniel. (2012, November 19). The Poetics of Painting: Part Three—Standing before a Painting. *Patheos.* Retrieved from http://www.patheos.com/blogs/goodletters/2012/11/the-poetics-of-painting-part-three/.

Soekanto. (1951). *Dua Raden Saleh. Dua Nasionalis Abad ke-1 9. Suatu Halaman dari Sedjarah Nasional.* Djakarta: N.V. Pusaka Asli.

Stevens, Mary Anne (Ed). (1984). *The Orientalists: Delacroix to Matisse: European Painters in North Africa and the Near East.* Exhibition catalogue. London: Royal Academy of Arts.

Viljoen, Louise (Leipoldt and the Orient: a Reading of C. L. Leipoldt's Travel Writing in the Context of Orientalist Discourse, in Prins, Brandt & Stevens, Shannon (Eds.) (2000). *The Low Countries and the New World(s): Travel, Discovery, Early Relations.*

Lanham, MD: University Press of America, pp.199–213. Retrieved from https://www
.researchgate.net/publication/265824227_Leipoldt_and_the_Orient_A_Reading
_of_CL_Leipoldt%27s_Travel_Writing_in_the_Context_of_Orientalist_Discourse.
Wright, Astri. (2001). Hendra Gunawan: Styles, Themes and Visions. In Agus Dermawan
T. and Astri Wright, (Eds.), *Hendra Gunawan: A Great Modern Painter.* (pp. 39–67).
Jakarta: Ciputra Foundation.

CHAPTER 2

Images of the Prophet Muhammad: Brief Thoughts on Some European-Islamic Encounters*

Christiane Gruber

Introduction

On February 7, 2015, a massacre took place in the Paris offices of *Charlie Hebdo*. While the French satirical magazine mocks all politicians, races, and creeds with equal irreverence, in recent years it became best known for its series of raucous cartoons satirizing Islam and the Prophet Muhammad. During their attack, the gunmen who assassinated staff members at *Charlie Hebdo* exclaimed that they had avenged the Prophet, leading to widespread speculation that this horrific incident was intended to punish those who produce images insulting to the Prophet. And yet it remains unknown whether such images were indeed *the* major reason for the attack.

In the wake of the massacre that took place in the Paris offices of *Charlie Hebdo*, I was called upon as a scholar specializing in Islamic paintings of the Prophet to explain whether images of Muhammad are banned in Islam (Gruber, 2009; Gruber and Shalem, 2014).

Although admittedly curt and skirting nuances, the short and simple answer is no. The Qur'an does not prohibit figural imagery. Rather, it castigates the worship of idols, which are understood as concrete embodiments of the polytheistic beliefs that Islam supplanted when it emerged as a purely monotheistic faith in the Arabian Peninsula during the seventh century. Moreover, the *Hadith*, or Sayings of the Prophet, present us with an ambiguous picture at best: at turns we read of artists daring to breathe life into their figures and, at others, of pillows ornamented with figural imagery ('Isa, 1995; and Ghabin, 1998).

In addition, there does not exist a single expressively stated and universally accepted "ban" on images in Islamic legal texts. It is only in the year 2006 that a reactionary Saudi Sunni-Salafi *fatwa* against "blasphemous" caricatures was issued as a direct response to the Danish cartoons of the Prophet Muhammad.

---

* The present essay is a synthesis and expansion of three earlier articles published in Newsweek in response to the Charlie Hebdo attack (see http://www.newsweek.com/user/16692).

© KONINKLIJKE BRILL NV, LEIDEN, 2018 | DOI 10.1163/9789004357013_004

While this decree might be accepted and followed by some individuals of austere Sunni inclinations, other Muslims of more moderate or secular Sunni or Shi'i leanings do not consider figural representations of the Prophet necessarily problematic as long as Muhammad is depicted respectfully.

This essay thus aims to give a brief account of Islamic traditions of depicting the Prophet Muhammad, evidence of such images' legal standing within historical and contemporary Islamic jurisprudence, and contemporary pictorial images produced primarily in Iran during the aftermath of 2005 publication of satirical images of the Prophet in the Danish newspaper *Jyllands-Posten* (Klausen, 2009; Cohen, 2009). In so doing, I aim to interrogate dominant discourses on the prohibition of prophetic imagery, much as the contributors to this volume on the "Seen and Unseen" collectively agitate against a kind of "visual imperialism" that presupposes and hence fossilizes singular and immutable meanings for works of art and visual culture within global Islamic contexts.

Images of the Prophet in Islamic Traditions

While Islam has been described as a faith that is largely aniconic—i.e., that tends to avoid images—figural imagery has nevertheless been a staple of Islamic artistic expression, especially in secular, private contexts (and today, Muslim majority countries are saturated with images, dolls, and other representational arts). Indeed, a variety of Muslim patrons commissioned illustrated manuscripts replete with figural and animal imagery from the thirteenth century onward. Among them are images of animals, humans, and saintly figures.

Over the past seven centuries, a variety of historical and poetic texts largely produced in Turkish and Persian spheres—both Sunni and Shi'i—include depictions of the Prophet Muhammad. These many images praised and commemorated the Prophet. They also served as occasions and centerpieces for Muslim devotional practices, much like celebrations of the Prophet's birthday (*mawlid*) and visitations to his tomb in Medina.

As a result, the visual evidence clearly undermines the premise that images of Muhammad are strictly banned in Islamic law and practice, thereby providing us with a less ideologically divisive and more fact-based way to speak about a subject that has grown increasingly contentious ever since 2005.

Representations of the Prophet in Islamic traditions have varied over time, and they have catered to different needs and desires. During the fourteenth century, a number of Persian drawings and paintings depict Muhammad as an enthroned leader surmounted by angels and surrounded by his companions (Figure 2.1). These images show the Prophet as a human messenger

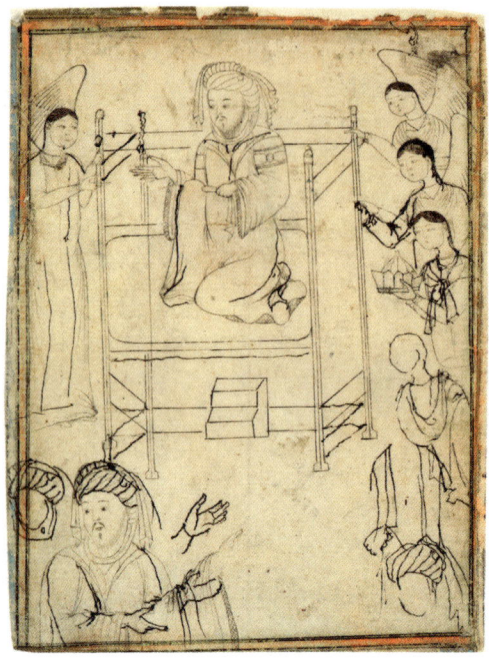

FIGURE 2.1
*Black-ink sketch of the Prophet
Muhammad enthroned, possibly
Tabriz, 14th century CE.
Staatsbibliothek zu Berlin—
Preussischer Kulturbesitz,
Orientabteilung, Diez A, fol. 72,
page 2, no. 2.*

entrusted with divine revelation through the angelic figures that protect and accompany him.

At other times, medieval paintings depict Muhammad alongside other Abrahamic prophets, the latter represented in fourteenth-century universal histories and sixteenth-century illustrated copies of popular texts concerned with explaining the lives and tales of the prophets (*qisas al-anbiya'*) (Milstein, 1999). In some instances, Muhammad is accompanied by Jesus Christ, who is revered as the Prophet 'Isa in Islamic traditions.

In other narratives, especially those dedicated to narrating and illustrating the Prophet's heavenly ascension (*mi'raj*) from Mecca to Jerusalem and onward through the celestial spheres, Muhammad is depicted surrounded by the Abrahamic prophets as he sits in the Dome of the Rock in Jerusalem (Figure 2.2). In these medieval paintings, which were commissioned around 1317–35 by the Sunni Persian ruler Abu Sa'id, Muhammad is praised as the leader of his faith community, as the bearer of divine revelation, and as a messenger belonging to a long and respected line of monotheistic prophets (Gruber, 2010).

After 1500, a major shift in representations of the Prophet occurs in both Persian-Shi'i and Ottoman-Sunni lands. Muhammad's facial features become covered by a white veil while his body is engulfed by a large gold aureole, visual

FIGURE 2.2 *The Prophet Muhammad sits with other prophets in
Jerusalem as he undergoes the "testing of the cups,"
anonymous, Mi'rajnama (Book of Ascension), Tabriz,
ca. 1317–30 CE. Topkapı Palace Library, Istanbul, H. 2154,
folio 62r.*

devices that doubly stress his unseen, numinous qualities (Figure 2.3). While
these more abstract depictions of the Prophet certainly show an emerging tendency to shy away from figural representation, they also praise the Prophet as
a secret, unseen mystery. This metaphorical language, which was translated
pictorially, is a hallmark of Sufi (mystical) traditions found in both Sunni and
Shiʻi spheres.

While images of the Prophet have waned since 1800, there nevertheless exist
a number of modern and contemporary representations that reveal a rather
unsteady, and thus not cohesive or uniform, approach to the production of
Muhammad-centered imagery. While "blessed icons" of the Prophet made in
Iran during the nineteenth and twentieth centuries show Muhammad in his
full corporeal form and touched by God through the symbol of the golden halo

FIGURE 2.3

The Prophet Muhammad receives revelations at Mount Hira, al-Darir, Siyer-i Nebi (The Prophet's Biography), Istanbul, 1003 AH/1595–96 CE. Topkapı Palace Library, Istanbul, H. 1222, folio 158v.

FIGURE 2.4

Blessed Icon of the Prophet Muhammad, Iran, 19th century, Imam Ali Museum of Religious Arts, Tehran, icon no. 11267.

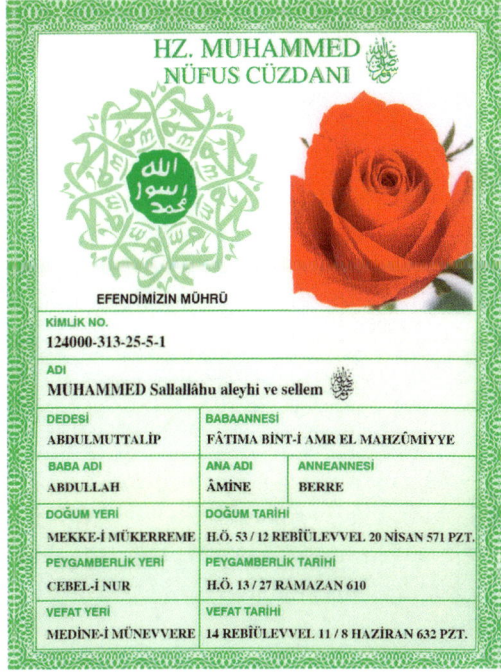

FIGURE 2.5
State ID card of the Prophet
Muhammad, Istanbul, Turkey, 2014.
Card in author's collection.

(Figure 2.4), depictions in Sunni and especially Arab lands remain largely abstract and show a clear preference for textual representations describing his physical attributes. Known as *hilya*s, these aniconic icons have been printed in Turkey in the format of a state ID card in recent years (Figure 2.5).

The contemporary ID card of the Prophet highlights a number of issues that are of particular concern today. First, in 2015 these laminated *hilya*s were used as invitation cards for celebrations of the Prophet's birthday in Turkey. At exactly the same time, ISIS (the Islamic State in Iraq and Syria) suppressed all *mawlid* celebrations in Iraq ("ISIS Blocks," 2015), and recently a document has revealed that Saudi Arabia has discussed plans to exhume the Prophet's remains from his tomb in Medina, supposedly in order to prevent his worship (Spillett, 2014).

Taken altogether, these images, sites and celebrations have one thing in common: namely, a very contemporary urge to erase various forms of devotion to the Prophet within discourses emanating from conservative and Salafi spheres. Such discourses, which present themselves as representing a "true Islam," have been loudly disseminated in the public sphere. With increasing frequency, this type of rejectionary rhetoric also has penetrated and altered discussions pertaining to the permissibility of depicting the Prophet Muhammad within and outside of Islamic traditions. As in other spheres of political life, an extreme position has incrementally moved to the center, thereby altering what is perceived as Islamic "normativity" within a global setting.

The So-Called "Ban" on Images of Muhammad

In the wake of the attack on *Charlie Hebdo*, a flurry of articles have explored whether images of the Prophet Muhammad are "banned" in Islam. While some Muslim voices are adamant that this is strictly the case in Islamic law, others (both Muslim and non-Muslim) have cautioned that it is not so.

Most public discussions of this so-called "ban" have explored verses in the Qur'an and *Sayings* by the Prophet, neither of which yields decisive results. What has been lost in the mix, however, is an exploration of the evidence found within Islamic law. Indeed, if one is to speak of a "ban," then one must canvas a variety of Islamic jurisprudential sources in order to determine the legality or illegality of representing the Prophet in Islamic traditions. And if one carefully mines the sources, the results become much clearer—and much more nuanced and complex than one might anticipate (Touati, 2015).

There exist many handbooks of Islamic law that compile opinions on a number of matters. In regard to image making, the earliest and most synthetic source is the medieval law book of Ibn Qudama (died 1223), a towering Sunni theologian of the medieval period. In his handbook, Ibn Qudama discusses the various possible "abominations" that can occur at wedding ceremonies, including the playing of music and backgammon, the consumption of liquor, and the presence of images. As for the legality of images, he notes that the question is complicated because it depends on what the images depict and where they are situated. He thus concludes that images are not prohibited *per se*; rather, their legality depends on content and context (Cook, 2000, pp. 145–146).

A century later, the staunchly Sunni theologian Ibn Taymiyya (died 1328)— who exerted great influence on today's ultraconservative Wahhabi and Salafi theological movements—penned a hefty number of legal opinions. In his collection of *fatwas*, Ibn Taymiyya warns that images should not be used as a way to get closer to God, to seek His intercession, or to request a favor from Him. He also notes that Muslim practices must be differentiated from Christian ones, the latter defined by the prolific presence and use of images in churches.[1]

---

1 See his *fatwas* on "images" (*tamathil*) available online at: http://moamlat.al-islam.com/
   Loader.aspx?pageid=522&Words=+%D8%AA%D9%8E%D9%85%D9%8E%D8%A7%D8
   %AB%D9%90%D9%8A%D9%84%D9%8F&Level=exact&Type=phrase&SectionID=7.

As a consequence, in even this most conservative collection of medieval *fatwas*, there does not exist a single expressly stated "ban" on images. The crux of the matter, rather, is that images of saints should not be used for requests and when seeking intercession, as is the case in Christian religious traditions. In addition, no mention whatsoever is made of images of the Prophet Muhammad.

Moving forward through the centuries, the next major summary of legal opinions about images can be found in an essay-long *fatwa* written by Muhammad 'Abduh (died 1905), best known as the reformist chief jurist (*mufti*) of modern Egypt. In his treatise titled *Images and Representations: Their Benefits and The Opinions About Them* (ca. 1899–1905), Muhammad 'Abduh argues that the safeguarding of images and paintings represents a preservation of Islamic cultural heritage and knowledge. In addition, he stresses that, if images are not used in idolatry, then portraying people, plants, and trees is not forbidden (Ramadan, 2013).

He goes even further, stating that: "None of the legal scholars (*'ulama*) has ever opposed it. There is no opposition against the benefits of images in the abovementioned case." With defiant gusto, he goes on to state that: "You cannot convince a jurist (*mufti*) that the image has been, in all cases, an object of idolatry!" He then concludes that Islamic law (*shari'a*) is "far from calling one of the greatest means of knowledge illegitimate, once it is ensured that it is not a threat to religion in either belief or practice. Indeed, Muslims are not keen to forbid themselves from something with obvious benefit" ('Abduh, 1344/1925, vol. 2, pp. 498–502).

In sum, during the second half of the nineteenth century, this reputed grand jurist proclaimed in no uncertain terms that images and paintings were both beneficial and educational.

Muhammad 'Abduh's exposé was likely composed as a response to the spread and multiplication of images via the newly emergent printing press in Egypt. By far and large, before the nineteenth century, images were not publicly available, since they were embedded in rare luxury manuscripts and therefore restricted to a very small elite. With the onset of the mass media, however, new anxieties arose around the production and consumption of images. For these reasons, new forms of control over prophetic representations began to emerge in the form of legal decrees.

Among them is a 1926 *fatwa* that was issued by the Sunni clerics at al-Azhar University in Cairo, which banned a film about Muhammad that was financed by the secular Turkish Republic. Fifty years later, the cinematographer Moustapha Akkad faced similar difficulties when he set out to film his biopic about Muhammad titled *The Message* (Bakker, 2006; El Khachab, 2011). Although he received permission to produce the movie from the Sunni clerics at Al-Azhar, the Muslim World League—which is funded by Saudi Arabia and follows a strict Salafi interpretation of Islam—refused to approve the film even though Muhammad is never shown on screen (the movie is shot from the Prophet's point of view). In the case of these two twentieth-century movies, Egyptian and Saudi Arabian Sunni clerical bodies dissented on the manner in which Muhammad can be portrayed in film. This disagreement evidently did not fall along Sunni-Shiʿi sectarian lines.

Moving forward a couple decades, the legal landscape and the wrangling over images of Muhammad become much more muddled from the 1990s onward. While earlier debates on the subject can be found, it appears that the year 1997 was a watershed in this regard.

At this time, the Council on American-Islamic Relations (CAIR) wrote to Chief Justice William Rehnquist to request that the sculpted representation of the Prophet Muhammad in the north frieze inside the Supreme Court of the United States be removed or sanded down (Figure 2.6) (Bjelajac, 2014). Included among the great lawgivers of history and standing between Justinian and Charlemagne, the turbaned Muhammad is shown holding the Qurʾan— the source of Islamic law—and a sword—a symbol of justice within the Supreme Court's pictorial program.

FIGURE 2.6

The Prophet Muhammad holding the Qurʾan and a sword while standing between Charlemagne (left: holding the globe of Christendom) and Justinian (right: holding the "Corpus Juris Civilis," or body of civil laws). Great Lawgivers of the Middle Ages, north wall frieze (designed by Adolph Weinman), Supreme Court of the United States, Washington, D.C., 1931–32.

PHOTOGRAPH COURTESY OF THE COLLECTION OF THE SUPREME COURT OF THE UNITED STATES.

Around the time that Rehnquist rejected CAIR's request (as physical injury to an architectural feature in the Supreme Court building is unlawful), a *fatwa* on the matter was issued in 2000 by Taha Jaber al-Alwani, who at the time served as a professor of jurisprudence in Saudi Arabia and as the chairman of the Islamic Jurisprudence Council of North America. With his *bona fides* firmly established, al-Alwani sets out to argue through traditional forms of Islamic legal argumentation that, first, there exist no firm prohibitions on images in Islam and, second, that the depiction of Muhammad in the Supreme Court is nothing but praiseworthy. He thus arrives at the following conclusion:

> What I have seen in the Supreme Courtroom deserves nothing but appreciation and gratitude from American Muslims. This is a positive gesture toward Islam made by the architect and other architectural decision-makers of the highest Court in America. God willing, it will help ameliorate some of the unfortunate misinformation that has surrounded Islam and Muslims in this country.
>
> AL-ALWANI, 2000–2001, PP. 27–28

Put simply, in the year 2000 one of the highest-ranking legal scholars who was then based in Saudi Arabia and also served as the chairman of the principal council on Islamic law in America judged a sculptural representation of Muhammad in the nation's capital both permissible and laudable.

But then 9/11, the U.S.-led invasion of Iraq, and the Danish cartoons of 2005 happened. The derogatory *Jyllands-Posten* caricatures of Muhammad became enmeshed in the complex geopolitics, the shifting European demographic landscape, and the Middle Eastern wars of the post-9/11 period. Understood as an attack and an affront to the Islamic faith, these cartoons were denounced by Saudi imams as sacrilegious in 2006 ("Imaams Denounce"). It is at this very moment that we suddenly see the more precise statement that "Islam considers images of prophets disrespectful and caricatures of them blasphemous" ("Imaams Denounce"). Along with this brand new legal proclamation, Saudi companies and organizations launched a boycott against Danish goods, including medicine, dairy products, and Lego toys. Flexing its monetary muscles to the tune of billions of dollars, Saudi Arabia's counterblow resulted in hefty financial losses for Denmark. Thus, this relatively recent Saudi *fatwa* against images of Muhammad also shows how loudly money talks.

Since 2005, Islamic law has evolved with contemporary circumstances and further *fatwas* against images of Muhammad have emerged. A number of these are easily accessible because they are available online as electronic fatwas (or *e-fatwas*). Two representative examples reveal that the legality or illegality of representing Muhammad remains an unresolved and ever-evolving issue within the Islamic world.

For instance, the Salafi position remains utterly uncompromising: images of the Prophet and his companions are not permissible whatsoever.[2] On the other hand, Ayatollah al-Sistani, the supreme Shi'i legal authority in Iraq, opines that representations of the Prophet are acceptable as long as they show due deference (*ta'zim*) and respect (*tabjil*).[3]

It thus should come as no surprise that today reverential depictions of the Prophet can be found in Shi'i-majority areas, especially Iraq, Iran and Lebanon (Figure 2.7). Indeed, there exists a lively market for these kinds of devotional pictures, objects, and even rugs, which are purchased by many Muslims who do not tread the Salafi line.

FIGURE 2.7
The Prophet Muhammad holding the Qur'an, which emits flickers of radiant light, as he points his index finger to the proclamation of the faith (shahada), reading: "There is no god but God and Muhammad is His Messenger," postcard, Tehran, Iran, 2001.
POSTCARD IN AUTHOR'S
COLLECTION.

2 See Shaykh Muhammad Saalih al-Munajjid's ruling on art and acting, which includes a discussion of filmic depictions of the prophets (http://islamqa.info/en/158232).
3 See al-Sistani's ruling on the subject at http://www.sistani.org/english/qa/01282/ (English) and http://www.sistani.org/arabic/qa/0384/ (Arabic).

In these latest disagreements between Sunni-Salafi and Shi'i scholars of Islamic law, it is easy to see how some might argue that the divergence in legal opinion falls along the sectarian divide. While this certainly rings true today, this was not the case before the Danish cartoons of 2005.

Indeed, in the year 2000, the Sunni legal scholar al-Alwani praised and expressed gratitude for the depiction of Muhammad in the Supreme Court while, during the twentieth century, Sunni legal bodies disagreed with one another as they turned to tackling the emergence of public images of Muhammad precipitated by the printing press and the motion picture industry.

Before then and stretching back to the twelfth century, scholars of Islamic law, among them famous Sunni luminaries, did not expressly forbid images, including representations of Muhammad. So the notion of a long-standing and immutable Islamic "ban" on images of the Prophet is nothing if not a contemporary innovation, catalyzed by the mass media, accelerated by insulting cartoons, and propelled throughout the world via the seismic influence of Saudi petrodollars.

Visually Reclaiming the Prophet in Today's Iran

An Iranian film about the Prophet Muhammad had its debut in the immediate aftermath of the *Charlie Hebdo* massacre. Directed by Majid Majidi and entitled *Muhammad: The Messenger of God*, the 2015 biopic's cost exceeded $30 million, making it the most expensive Iranian movie shot to date. Well before its release, the film was the subject of criticism due to the physical presence of Muhammad on screen. Although the Prophet's facial features are camouflaged through light and shade strategies, the Sunni clerics at al-Azhar in Cairo nevertheless attempted to halt its release so that "an undistorted image of the Prophet can be preserved in the minds of Muslims" (Dehgan, 2015).

This latest disagreement over filmic portrayals of Muhammad reveals ongoing anxieties regarding visual representations of the Prophet in the Islamic world. However, such divergences do not appear to be based on a sectarian reading of the Prophet's biography, as the movie covers Muhammad's childhood until the age of twelve. Sunni and Shi'i debates over the life of the Prophet tend to revolve around the events of his adulthood, especially whether he appointed 'Ali, his cousin and son-in-law, as his rightful successor. As Majidi himself has noted, the film purposefully skirts these sectarian debates over the life of the Prophet in order to present a positive and united presentation of Muhammad to international movie audiences.

This new Muhammad film does not emerge out of thin air. In addition to earlier movies (like Akkad's *The Message*) and others still in the making (by

Qatar), Majidi's large-scale project is part of a larger effort to visually reclaim the Prophet and his legacy in Iran that has been under way since the Danish cartoons of 2005 (Child, 2013). While reactions to the cartoons in some Arab, Sunni, and especially Salafi quarters included the issuing of decrees stipulating that "images of prophets are disrespectful and caricatures of them blasphemous," a vastly different response has unfolded within Iran over the past decade. Instead, Iran has launched a number of artistic, educational, and public relations projects since 2006, itself dubbed by Ayatollah Khamenei "The Year of the Noble Prophet."[4] As a result, celebratory depictions of the Prophet have emerged in full force, with Majidi's film the latest outcome of these officially sanctioned endeavors (Gruber, 2016).

Among them, one of the most visible Iranian responses to the Danish cartoons is a colorful mural depicting Muhammad's celestial ascension, which was painted in 2008 on a five-story building located on a major thoroughfare in central Tehran (Figure 2.8) (Gruber, 2013). Sponsored by Tehran's municipality, the mural beautifies the capital city's urban space much like the vibrant and sometime surreal compositions by Iranian artist Mehdi Ghadyanloo. Notably

FIGURE 2.8 *Five-story mural depicting the Prophet Muhammad's celestial ascension, Tehran, Iran, 2008.*
PHOTOGRAPH BY AUTHOR.

---

4 See Ayatollah Khamenei's New Year (2006) speech at http://farsi.khamenei.ir/message
-content?id=208.

missing here are portraits of Ayatollahs Khomeini and Khamenei, as well as Palestinian and Iranian martyrs. In their stead appears a pictorial eulogy of the Prophet based on several paintings included in a fifteenth-century Turco-Persian manuscript illustrating Muhammad's night journey and ascension (Séguy, 1977). While the original illustration shows Muhammad's facial features, the contemporary mural renders his face as if a blank slate. This erasure of the Prophet's facial features most likely is because the image appears in the public domain instead of tucked inside a private manuscript. It also partially results from the more reactionary Muslim responses to images of Muhammad in the wake of the Danish cartoon controversy.

Besides this large-scale mural, a number of other Prophet-centered products have been made for the Iranian market since 2006. Targeting a juvenile audience in particular, a series of illustrated books written in simple prose and verse aims to teach children about Muhammad's life and miracles. These books include images of the Prophet, who often is depicted with a veiled face and solar halo, as can be seen in one image in which he is shown extending his arms to receive revelations at Mount Hira (Figure 2.9). The text that accompanies the colorful illustration informs its young readers that Muhammad was like the summer sun and the full moon, emitting both light and enlightenment into the world.

FIGURE 2.9
The Prophet Muhammad receives revelations on Mount Hira, children's book entitled "Greetings, Rose of Muhammad," Tehran, 2006.
IMAGE SCANNED FROM THE CHILDREN'S BOOK IN AUTHOR'S COLLECTION.

Just like these Iranian children's books, Majidi's film takes up the question of childhood. The film's major scenes reiterate some of the more famous episodes of the Prophet's youth, including his highly auspicious birth and his being recognized as a prophet by the Christian monk Bahira. Visually depicting these pivotal moments of Muhammad's early life is by no means a new phenomenon in Persian lands. Indeed, from 1300 onward a number of manuscript paintings represent Muhammad's birth as a luminous, angelic event (Gruber, 2009). The texts that buttress these images inform us that, when he was born, Muhammad illuminated the entire world with his cosmic radiance, which rose upward to set the heavens and stars alight.

Persian illustrated histories and biographies also depict Muhammad's foretelling as a prophet at the tender age of twelve, when he visited the city of Busra in Syria. It is at this time that the Christian monk Bahira recognized the signs of the young boy's future prophethood through a series of natural phenomena (such as the bending of a tree's branches and/or a cloud providing him with shade) as well as the "seal of prophecy" mark imprinted on Muhammad's body (Figure 2.10) (Talbot Rice, 1976, 66, cat. no. 30). The latter episode belongs to a corpus of Islamic narratives that relate that the Prophet was announced and foretold as a prophet by a Christian holy man, who had read about his coming in the Bible.

The story of the young Muhammad's "seal of prophecy" remains a popular tale across Islamic lands until today. Over the course of the twentieth century, a number of mass-produced images of the young Muhammad—composed in a wide array of creative variants—were made in Iran. These appeared in

FIGURE 2.10   *The Christian monk Bahira recognizes the young Muhammad as a prophet, Rashid al-Din, Jami' al-Tawarikh (Compendium of Chronicles), Tabriz, 714 AH/1314–15 CE. University of Edinburgh Main Library, Special Collections Or. Ms. 20, folio 43v.*

banners, posters, postcards, carpets, and stickers until their production was curtailed in 2008. While the recent Iranian shunning of these images is in response to the Danish cartoon controversy, it also emanates from the discovery of its original pictorial source: an early twentieth-century Orientalist photograph of a young and rather effeminate Arab boy (Grabar and Natif, 2003; Centlivres-Demont, 2005).

Not shying away from depicting this pivotal moment in the Prophet's youth, Majidi in his biopic shows the young Muhammad arriving at Bahira's monastery (Figure 2.11). In this film still, the adolescent protagonist walks down the main aisle of a church as a burst of sunlight streams in from the open doors. This radiance symbolic of Muhammad's future prophecy floods into the interior space and overwhelms his facial features. This carefully designed visual strategy allows the Prophet to be both seen and unseen—represented and unrepresented—all at once.

These paintings, murals, children's books, and films about the Prophet that have been made in Iran since 2006 are illuminating in several ways. First, they show that traditions of representing Muhammad are still well and alive in some areas of the Muslim world. These still and moving images aim to commemorate the Prophet, present his status and legacy in a positive light, and teach a variety of audiences about his life and miracles.

FIGURE 2.11   *The young Muhammad enters a monastery, where*
                he is recognized as a prophet by the Christian monk
                Bahira, film still, Majid Majidi, Muhammad Rasul
                Allah (Muhammad, the Messenger of God), Iran, 2015.
                IMAGE FROM: HTTP://WWW.IFILMTV.COM/
                DEFAULT/DETAILS/222713.

Unlike in Sunni-Salafi spheres, in which recent responses to the Danish and *Charlie Hebdo* cartoons have largely comprised a flurry of obdurate injunctions, the response in Iran has been markedly different. Rather than shying away from or banning images of the Prophet, Iranian leaders, artists, and filmmakers have harnessed the creative arts to recover and restore the image of Muhammad in the public domain.

Such images serve as powerful reminders that there is no universally accepted "ban" on the figural arts in Islam and that traditions of prophetic representation still continue to flourish in Iran today. Above all, they highlight the fact that in Islamic lands there exist two diametrically opposed reactions to defamatory European cartoons: while some actors engage in censorship and suppression, others actively seek the promulgation of the Prophet Muhammad by reasserting the positive power of picture-making.

Conclusion

In sum, when one ignores (or suppresses) historical evidence and speaks of a "ban" of images of the Prophet in Islam, the negative repercussions are many. First, all doors to constructive dialogue on the topic are closed *a priori*, thus precluding a nuanced and apolitical discussion of historical Islamic images freed from the polarizing ideological narratives of today. In addition, such images effectively become further endangered as a form of artistic heritage if merely speaking of and illustrating them is seen as a subversive, rather than a productive and reconstructive, act. It is therefore now more than ever that concerned individuals—scholars, students, and the public at large—must labor to preserve the rich and textured pictorial traditions of Islam, which constitute a major contribution to our shared global artistic patrimony.

Last but not least, it is important to keep in mind that representations of Islam stemming from both Euro-American and Middle Eastern lands have been subjected to a variety of assumptions and simplifications. Over the centuries, Euro-American discourses have been all too keen to focus on Islam's "differential" character—that is, what makes it putatively "other." Within such a framework, an overemphasis on the notion that images of Muhammad do not exist or are banned strengthens age-old Oriental discourses, which have tended to couch Islamic civilizations as devoid of or actively adverse to images. As for their part, contemporary Salafi narratives about the same topic meet at exactly the same juncture, the latter presumption reinforcing the former, and vice versa. What gets lost in this loudly mediatized Oriental-Salafi echo chamber, however, is the creativity of Islamic cultures and arts, which over the centuries have proved remarkably diversiform as well as embracing of devotional representations of the Prophet Muhammad in various times and places.

References

'Abduh, M. (1344/1925). *Ta'rikh al-ustadh al-imam al-Shaykh Muhammad 'Abduh*. Cairo: Manar Publisher.

Al-Alwani, T. J. (2000–2001). Fatwa concerning the United States Supreme Courtroom frieze. *Journal of Law and Religion*, 15(1–2), 1–28.

Bakker, F. (2006). The image of Muhammad in *The Message*, the first and only feature film about the prophet of Islam. *Islam and Christian-Muslim Relations*, 17(1), 77–92.

Bjelajac, D. (2014). Masonic fraternalism and Muhammad among the lawgivers in Adolph A. Weinman's sculpture frieze in the United States Supreme Court (1931–1935). In C. Gruber & A. Shalem (Eds.). *The prophet between ideal and ideology: A scholarly investigation*. (pp. 357–381). Berlin: De Gruyter.

Centlivres-Demont, P. & M. (2005). Une étrange rencontre: La photographie orientaliste de Lehnert et Landrock et l'image iranienne du Prophète Mahomet. *Etudes Photographiques*, 17, 5–15.

Child, B. (2013, March 15). Qatar and Iran on rival missions to make films about Prophet Muhammad. *The Guardian*, Retrieved from https://www.theguardian.com/film/2013/mar/15/qatar-iran-films-prophet-muhammad.

Cohen, P. (2009, August 12). Yale University bans images of Muhammad in new book. *The New York Times*, Retrieved from http://www.nytimes.com/2009/08/13/books/13book.html?_r=0.

Cook, M. (2000). *Commanding the right and forbidding the wrong*. Cambridge: Cambridge University Press.

Dehgan, S. K. (2015, January 30). Iranian film on Prophet Muhammad set for premiere. *The Guardian*, Retrieved from http://www.theguardian.com/world/2015/jan/30/iranian-film-prophet-muhammad-premiere.

El Khachab, W. (2011). Muhammad au cinéma. La destruction des idols dans un média iconodule ou la politique de la verticalité comme mediation. In O. Hazan & J-J. Lavoie (Eds.). *Le Prophète Muhammad: entre le mot et l'image*. (pp. 65–94). Quebec: Fides.

Ghabin, A. (1998). The quranic verses as a source for legitimacy or illegitimacy of the arts in Islam. *Der Islam*, 75(2), 193–225.

Grabar, O. & Natif, N. (2003). The story of the portraits of the Prophet Muhammad. *Studia Islamica*, 96, 19–38.

Gruber, C. (2016). Prophetic products: Muhammad in contemporary Iranian visual culture. *Material Religion*, 12(3), 259–293.

Gruber, C. (2013). Images of Muhammad *in and out* of modernity: The curious case of a 2008 mural in Tehran. In idem & H. Haugbolle (Eds.). *Visual culture in the modern Middle East: Rhetoric of the image.* (pp. 2–31). Bloomington: Indiana University Press.

Gruber, C. (2010). *The Ilkhanid book of ascension: A Persian-Sunni devotional tale.* London: I.B. Tauris.

Gruber, C. (2009). Between logos (*kalima*) and light (*nur*): Representations of the Prophet Muhammad in Islamic painting. *Muqarnas*, 26, 1–34.

Gruber, C., & A. Shalem (Eds.). (2014). *The prophet between ideal and ideology: A scholarly investigation.* Berlin: De Gruyter.

Imaams denounce Danish & Norwegian newspapers in cartoons row (2006, January 28). *Fatwa-Online*, Retrieved from http://www.fatwa-online.com/imams-denounce-danish-and-norwegian-newspapers-in-cartoons-row/.

'Isa, A. M. (1995). Muslims and *taswir. The Muslim World*, 45(3), 250–268.

ISIS blocks celebrations of the Prophet Muhammad's birthday (2015, January 3). *Middle East Monitor*, Retrieved from https://www.middleeastmonitor.com/news/middle-east/16136-isis-blocks-celebrations-of-prophet-muhammads-birthday.

Klausen, J. (2009). *The cartoons that shook the world.* New Haven: Yale University Press.

Milstein, Rachel et al. (1999). *Stories of the prophets: Illustrated manuscripts of the qisas al-anbiya.'* Costa Mesa, CA: Mazda Publishers.

Ramadan, D. (2013). 'One of the best tools for learning': Rethinking the role of 'Abduh's fatwa in Egyptian art history. In G. Salami & M. Blackmun Visonà (Eds.). *A companion to modern African art.* (pp. 137–153). Malden, MA: John Wiley & Sons.

Séguy, M.-R. (1977). *The miraculous journey of Mahomet.* New York: George Braziller.

Spillett, R. (2014, September 1). Will Saudi Arabia move the remains of the Prophet Muhammad? *Daily Mail*, Retrieved from http://www.dailymail.co.uk/news/article-2740307/Controversial-plan-calls-Saudis-tomb-Prophet-Muhammad-Fears-idea-stoke-religious-divisions.html.

Talbot Rice, D. & B. Gray (Eds). (1976). *The illustrations to the 'World History' of Rashid al-Din.* Edinburgh: Edinburgh University Press.

Touati, H. (2015). Le régime des images figuratives dans la culture islamique médiévale. In idem (Ed.). *De la figuration humaine au portrait dans l'art islamique.* (pp. 1–30). Leiden and Boston: Brill.

PART 2

Unseen Reality

∴

Nightmarish Visions? Shifting Visual Representations of the 'Islamic' Terrorist Throughout the 'War on Terror'

Jared Ahmad

Introduction

Since the end of the Cold War, and in particular following the attacks of September 11th 2001, news media coverage of Islam within Britain has increasingly centered upon issues concerning violence, terrorism, fundamentalism and religious extremism (See Poole & Richardson, 2006; Flood et al., 2012, for example). While this narrowing of the news agenda has resulted in a number of worrying social and political developments, not least a growing suspicion of Muslim communities across the United Kingdom (See Pantazis & Pemberton, 2009), one of the more visible consequences of such coverage has been a powerful resurgence, and rearticulation, of the figure of the 'Islamic' terrorist within mainstream news discourse. From the highly publicised photographs of individuals such as Osama bin Laden and Ayman al-Zawahiri to the grainy footage of masked, anonymous militants engaging in aggressive training activities in places such as Iraq and Afghanistan, the visually arresting, yet seemingly elusive, figure of the 'Islamic' terrorist has dominated the landscape of the 'war on terror.' Crucially, these mediated images have formulated a key point of access for ordinary citizens by providing insight into various aspects of the social, cultural, gender and ethnic make-up of those who comprise this complex, multifaceted phenomenon. But rather than objectively depict the 'Islamic' terrorist, they have also served to constitute the very reality of this subject, often depicting a shallow, one-dimensional figure who has been constructed from a limited range of visual components. Despite a tacit level of scholarly attention (See Mitchell, 2011; Nashef, 2011; Dixit, 2016 for example), few studies have sought to consider the different ways in which the 'Islamic' terrorist has been visually depicted, and, importantly, how these representations have shifted throughout the course of 'war on terror' period.

What is of particular concern in this chapter, therefore, is the *visual production* of the 'Islamic' terrorist across key sites of the British news media, and the way in which this contradictory figure has been made both visible and invisible

© KONINKLIJKE BRILL NV, LEIDEN, 2018 | DOI 10.1163/9789004357013_005

for news audiences more generally. Its central argument rests on the belief that news media visual representations of the 'Islamic' terrorist both draw upon and challenge the simplified, Orientalist-inspired modes of representation and depiction that are considered typical of 'Western' news coverage (See Said, 1987, pp. 88–89), which makes the terrorist seen in highly specific, yet increasingly diverse ways. As such, Orientalized depictions function to contain the 'Islamic' terrorist within a foreign, yet strangely familiar, and instantly recognizable mode of representation, thus preventing other, more nuanced ways of seeing the threat possible, while more contemporary forms of representation free the terrorist from such cliché-ridden portrayals, but make him/her increasingly visible within society. Here, the 'Islamic' terrorist becomes embodied within a seemingly concrete and tangible form, as opposed to an abstract stereotype, thus generating greater levels of fear and uncertainty with regard to who the terrorist is and, crucially, where the threat can be located.

The chapter begins by considering how a particular understanding of Islam has taken shape in the West, and how recent structural and technological developments in the contemporary media landscape can be said to facilitate a broader range of images and visual representations of 'Islamic' terrorist groups. A subsequent section outlines the analytical and methodological tools used in this investigation and points towards visual discourse analysis as a useful approach for studying how images encourage particular ways of seeing the political world (Rose, 2001). This is then followed by the analysis of three dominant modes of visual representations from across the opening stages of the 'war on terror' period (2001–2005). The key aim here is not to cover the total range of images and visual representations that have been made available, but rather to analyze the changing ways in which the 'Islamic' terrorist has been made (in) visible during this historical timeframe. A final section summarizes the argument and discusses the political and cultural consequences that can be said to arise from adopting particular modes of representation.

It should be noted, however, that in contrast to other chapters in this collection, the images analyzed here focus mainly on visual representations of men rather than women. Although women play a central role in organized political violence (See Sjoberg & Gentry, 2011), part of the reason for this focus is because, as we shall see, the phenomenon of terrorism has traditionally been viewed through highly gendered lenses. In concentrating on images of male terrorists, therefore, the chapter provides a unique perspective on the modes of visual representation discussed elsewhere in this book, and, perhaps more crucially, shows how forms of visual imperialism occur both within and across a variety of sites of meaning.

Orientalism, 'Islamic' Terrorism and the Contemporary Media Landscape

As Richard Jackson has pointed out, "[d]espite its sudden ubiquity in the public arena, the notion of "Islamic terrorism" actually has a long history and is
already deeply embedded within the broader cultural, institutional and discursive structures of Western society" (Jackson, 2007, p. 397). Perhaps most notable in this regard is the work of Palestinian-American critic Edward W. Said
(See Said, 2003). Despite focusing mainly upon literary and academic, as opposed to visual, representations, Said highlights the way 'the East' has been
traditionally portrayed within Western culture as a place of "romance, exotic
beings, haunting memories and landscapes"; a mode of thought he refers to as
'Orientalism' (Ibid., p. 1). Drawing on the work of Michel Foucault, Said suggests that Orientalism functions discursively, by imposing limits on the way
people see and speak about the East, reducing its inhabitants into a mass of
stereotypical figures and locales. As a consequence, he argues that this process functions to powerfully constitute the identity of the West, with these
reductive and idealized images being incorporated into Western culture as a
means to have an 'Other' against which the 'Self' can be conceived (Hurd, 2003,
pp. 36–39). As he asserts,

> [t]he general basis of Orientalist thought is an imaginative and yet drasti-
> cally polarized geography dividing the world into two unequal parts, the
> larger, "different" one called the Orient, the other, also known as "our"
> world, called the Occident or the West.
>
> SAID, 1997, P. 4

With the end of the Cold War, however, there appears to have been a subtle
shift in Orientalist discourse; with a movement away from an exotic and sensual understanding of the East towards a more monolithic and threatening
image. Here, the dangers posed by 'Islamic' fundamentalism are now, according to Said, understood to have replaced the threat posed by Communism and
the Soviet Union (Said, 1997). As Karim H. Karim has observed, it is during this
period that the 'Islamic' terrorist came to be "a major figure in the typology
of characters who perform in Western dramaturges about Muslim societies"
(2006, p. 121). Indeed, a series of hijackings and kidnappings of European and
American hostages by groups such as the Palestinian Liberation Organisation,
Islamic Jihad and Hizbollah throughout the late 1980s and early 1990s served
to confirm this view, with the figure of the fanatical and bloodthirsty 'Islamic'

terrorist being placed firmly on the news media agenda. While the heightened visibility of this figure can be partially attributed to the increased availability and affordability of video recording equipment during this period (el Houri & Saber, 2010, p. 73), the adoption of official, State-coined definitions and labels within 'Western' news reporting of terrorist incidents further served to delegitimize the actions of these groups, removing them from the various political and historical contexts from which they had emerged (Said, 1987, p. 89). As David L. Paletz et al. noted at the time,

> [t]he underlying objectives of the violence are rarely explained, almost never justified. When tactics are emphasised without discussions of motives, objectives, goals or precipitating social conditions, then context is discarded, and political justifications are denied. The terrorists are identified with criminal violence and seen simply as bent on terror.
>
> 1982, P. 162

Visually, the 'Islamic' terrorist also began to assume a number of highly discernable features during this period, such as the ubiquitous appearance of the *keffiyeh* scarf and the Kalashnikov assault rifle, and he, for this individual was most often gendered, was almost always pictured in a dusty, 'Oriental' setting (Lederman, 1992, p. 176). A set of institutionalized routines, not to mention spatial and economic constraints, also stood to powerfully impact upon the visual nature of these representations, something that led journalists and news producers to often select images that reproduced time-worn, cliché-ridden stereotypes about the East, Islam and religious extremism (Shoemaker & Reese, 1996). Outside of the news media, moreover, this figure also received considerable attention in the mainstream cinema of the day, with highly jingoistic films such as *Delta Force* (1986), *Navy Seals* (1990) and *True Lies* (1994) serving to add further flesh to the bone of these simplistic portrayals (see Shaheen, 2009).

Since the attacks of September 11th 2001 and the subsequent 'war on terror,' however, a number of important shifts have taken place within the contemporary media landscape; something that, moreover, can be understood to be slowly challenging the discursive boundaries and embedded knowledge structures that separate the East from the West, or the Self from the Other. Despite the continued presence of Orientalist-inspired stereotypes (See Featherstone et al., 2010; Lewis, 2013; Ahmad, 2016 for example), a growing number of critical analyzes have shown how the globalized, post-Cold War media environment can be understood to facilitate a broader range of visual and verbal discourses concerning the Islamic Other, with news media visual and verbal representations exhibiting a variety of tensions and overlapping, hybridized identities (See Poole, 2002; Flood et al., 2012; Chuang & Roemer, 2013, for example). Perhaps most significantly, Said's belief that the Oriental subject is simply contained within a dominant representational framework devised by Western elites has found significant opposition (Ahmad, 1992, p. 172), with groups such as al-Qaeda, Hizbollah and Islamic State creating their own media outlets with which to produce and disseminate a series of powerful self-representations. These representations often knowingly appropriate and subvert Orientalist-inspired stereotypes, capitalizing on the fear and uncertainty engendered by such ways of seeing and speaking about 'Islamic' terrorism.

In this regard, Nathan Roger (2013) has shown how recent advances in telecommunications equipment and the increased interconnectedness of the contemporary (new) media landscape has enabled groups like al-Qaeda to harness the power of mediated imagery, employing them as a form of strategic 'weaponry' that can be used to simultaneously communicate with sympathetic audiences, while also striking fear in the hearts and minds of enemies. For example, the series of grizzly beheading videos produced by Abu Musab al-Zarqawi during the occupation of Iraq were skilfully manipulated by al-Qaeda to both shock its enemies *and* recruit more fighters. Although it is important to bear in mind that these images are is still subject to the same institutionalized patterns of selection and omission as described above, with news producers and editors focusing on the most immediate, 'newsworthy' aspects of terrorist communiqués (see Hoskins & O'Loughlin, 2011), in the years after the September 11th 2001 attacks political communications scholarship has become increasingly aware of the fact that it is difficult to prevent the production and global circulation of media images (O'Loughlin, 2011, p. 73).

Such a view necessarily entails that the news media can no longer be regarded as merely an outlet for the most dominant discourses within society, as emphasized by Said, but rather as a complex, shifting terrain upon which a range of competing images and representations can be seen in conflict, or even in cooperation, with each other (Kellner, 1995, p. 4). As Gadi Wolfsfeld makes clear, although political elites enjoy considerable advantages in the realm of the news media, by enjoying a more legitimate political status or having greater access to resources, "[t]heir inability to maintain full control over the political environment provides considerable opportunities for challengers to make significant inroads into the political process and the news" (1997, p. 25). As we shall see, despite the continued presence of reductive, Orientalist-inspired images, these cultural and structural shifts can be understood to be slowly challenging the simplified modes of representation that have been traditionally characteristic of Western news media coverage of 'Islamic' terrorism, giving rise to new, more complex ways of seeing this phenomenon.

Analyzing News Images of the 'Islamic' Terrorist

Given the focus on news visuals then, before turning to the analysis of images of the 'Islamic' terrorist, it is first necessary to briefly outline a number of analytical strategies that will help us gain clearer insight into the various ways news images *speak* to audiences. As David Shim and Dirk Nabers have noted (2013, p. 295), in order to fully analyze mediated imagery "it is important to expose their productive effects, representational patterns, and recurring visual key themes. That is, to reveal the ways in which visual representations enact subjectivities by positioning the viewer in relation to the viewed." In this regard, one of the most useful methods for analyzing contemporary forms of mediated imagery is visual discourse analysis (Rose, 2001, pp. 141–171). In the words of Rose, this form of analysis is "interested in how images construct accounts of the social world," and how particular modes of visual representation are privileged at the expense of others (Ibid., p. 146). Indeed, although we should be clear that images are sites of contestation, and are always open to interpretation and negotiation (See Hall, 1993; O'Loughlin, 2011), studies into both print and broadcast news have shown that audiences respond to, and recall, visual content much more readily than verbal or narrative imperatives, particularly if those visuals draw upon violent, negative imagery (Grabe & Bucy, 2009, p. 17), or, moreover, if they are personalized through a focus on individual figures (See Fahmy et al., 2006: 7; Bleiker et al., 2013, p. 399).

In order to analyze images of a particular cultural or political phenomenon, therefore, Rose suggests that it is necessary to draw upon a broad range of sources in order to establish a corpus of visual materials. As she asserts, "[t]his eclecticism is demanded by the intertextuality of discourse," because the meaning of certain images and visual representations are shaped by their relationship to other images and texts (Rose, 2001, p. 149). This is especially the case when looking at the news media, because news is inherently reflexive in nature; feeding off, and generating, its own representations and narrative conventions (Hoskins, 2006, p. 455). With this in mind, although references will be made to recent portrayals, the following analysis focuses on images taken from the period covering 2001 to 2005, a time frame in which fears surrounding the threat posed by terrorism were at their highest in Britain (Goodwin et al., 2005). These images range from print sources, such as *The Daily Mail*, *The Independent*, *The Guardian*, and *The Sun*, and news broadcasts from the likes of the BBC and ITV. Despite being taken from a range of different contexts, not to mention 'medias,' these contrasting forms of visual representation will provide insight into the way the figure of the 'Islamic' terrorist has been made concurrently visible and invisible for news audiences, and, importantly, will shed light on the way these images either reinforce or challenge the kinds of simplified, Orientalist-inspired discourses outlined above.

The analysis proceeds by paying close attention to the site of the image itself, and, in particular, its semiotic and compositional elements. This means investigating the presence of dominant visual themes in news media portrayals of the 'Islamic' terrorist, such as the use of real-world settings or backdrops, the appearance of certain forms of clothing, bodily expression or religious symbolism, or the use of particular camera angles or the recurrent presence of certain colors. Investigating these discursive features provides clearer insight into the way the figure of the 'Islamic' terrorist has been organized and categorized within news media discourse throughout this period, and, importantly, helps to show how certain images are privileged at the expense of others.

In addition, the analysis will also pay close attention to the way images powerfully reproduce forms of identity and subjectivity by 'positioning' the viewer in relation to the viewed. According to Rose, all images and visual representations offer a particular position to viewers, inviting spectators and audiences to adopt a certain point of view (2001, p. 46). While this is often carried out on a purely spatial level, locating the spectator 'outside' of an image, it can also be powerfully accomplished on a discursive level, by encouraging particular ways of looking at, and identifying with, those depicted. Crucially, this relates back to the compositional elements of the image and the presence of certain visual features, such as dress or bodily expression. Here, different forms of clothing function symbolically to embody and enact a specific subject position or category, leading audiences to identity with one or the other. As Elspeth Van Veeren has observed, clothing or other forms of bodily appearance "work as symbols and inscribe meaning into bodies, and in doing so, help to create categories and boundaries" (Van Veeren, 2016, p. 134). Particularly important here is the way still or moving images are situated within the media text. For example, how certain images are placed alongside others within a news article, or the way footage of the 'Islamic' terrorist is sequenced in relation to other on-screen participants, such as newsreaders and journalists. These forms of subject positioning can powerfully impact upon audience perceptions and should, therefore, be central to the analysis.

Dominant Patterns of Representation

In light of these analytical and methodological considerations, the chapter now turns to the analysis of a select number of images that have emerged over the course of the 'war on terror' period. As highlighted above, the central argument is that news media visual depictions of the 'Islamic' terrorist both draw upon and challenge Orientalist-inspired stereotypes, making the terrorist seen in highly specific, yet increasingly diverse ways. It is important to point out, however, that on closer inspection many of the newspaper articles and television broadcasts analyzed for this chapter can be understood to present their audiences with far greater levels of textual information than can conceivably be discussed here, with depictions shifting not simply over time, but also in relation to different political contexts and news genres. Nevertheless, the key aim is to assess the *visual production* of the 'Islamic' terrorist, namely, the way this figure has been made simultaneously visible and invisible for British news audiences, and how these representations have shifted over the course of the opening stage of this conflict.

Terror Chiefs, Ideologues and the Figure of the Bearded, Finger-Wagging 'Fanatic'

Despite pre-dating the 'war on terror' by several centuries, one of the most prominent modes of representation to emerge in the aftermath of the September 11th 2001 attacks has been the cliché-ridden figure of the bearded, finger-wagging 'fanatic'; as seen in visual representations of individuals such as Ayman al-Zawahiri, Abu Bakr al-Baghdadi, Abu Hamza al-Masri, Abu Qatada, Mullah Omar, Mokhtar Belmoktar, and, of course, Osama bin Laden (See Figure 3.1). Visually echoing the one-dimensional portrayals of historical characters such as Hassan-i-Sabbah and Salah ad-Din, this potent image has come to be imbued with a considerable level of symbolic appeal in recent years, functioning to individualize the threat posed by a number of loose, disparate terror groups and also contain the 'Islamic' terrorist within a seemingly familiar, Orientalist-inspired figure. Indeed, this category of representation has served to foreground the non-Western, specifically Arab and Middle Eastern, nature of the terrorist threat, something that has subtly worked to visually demarcate the boundaries between the foreign terrorist 'Other' and the more familiar Western 'Self,' thus, making other ways of seeing this complex, multifaceted figure much more difficult to comprehend.

Key to this mode of representation has been the culturally significant presence of the turban and the long, flowing, typically silver-flecked, beard. While for some the bearded and turbaned appearance of the 'Islamic' terrorist might signal religious piety or a near-clerical status (See Gunaratna, 2002, p. 41), for those unfamiliar with such attributes this can be more readily interpreted as connoting backwardness or religious extremism. As Karen Culcasi and Mahmut Gokmen have noted, although beards feature prominently in all world religions, they have 'been equated with backward or non-Western peoples for centuries' and are now viewed as "a defining symbol of the dangerous other, and even more specifically as a symbol of Islamic extremism" (2011, pp. 87–88). While it is important to point out that this is form of appearance that has been consciously adopted by such figures, the seemingly 'traditional,' religious appearance of the 'Islamic' terrorist can be interpreted as symbolizing an irrational, antiquated world-view, something that, on a more subtle level, can work to powerfully depoliticize the various aims and grievances of movements like al-Qaeda in the eyes of Western news audiences. Indeed, though this is not to suggest that viewers will all see this mode of representation in the same manner, but rather its sheer presence within media portrayals serves to obscure other ways of viewing the 'Islamic' terrorist.

Similarly, an equally important feature of this mode of representation is the visually arresting, and highly-symbolic, gesture of the raised index finger. As Andrew Hoskins and Ben O'Loughlin have noted, when sequences from terrorist propaganda communiqués appear within mainstream Western news media reports there seems to be a "consistent selection of visual moments in the video productions when the speaker looks angry and raises his index finger defiantly" (2011, p. 208). Such forms of representation often serve to underscore the violent threats issued in these propaganda statements, and, again, work to reinforce the reductive notion that 'Islamic' terrorists are driven, not by rational political ideals, but by an archaic, violent and intolerant system of beliefs. In this regard, Jürgen Streeck has suggested that when used in political speechmaking the embodied gesture of the raised index finger is often construed as being a pedagogical or hierarchical gesture (2008, p. 179); for example, when an adult scolds or berates a child. As Streeck asserts, the repeated use of a raised index finger "displays the speaker's claim that what he is saying is important, instructive and new" and "is predicated on and assertive of an asymmetry of knowledge," leading viewers to interpret the speaker as patronising or condescending (Ibid., p. 181). Indeed, although this sign has become an important symbolic gesture in the visual rhetoric of 'Islamic' terrorist propaganda, using the raised index finger in order to symbolise monotheism and allegiance to God, and thus emulating the body language of influential Jihadi ideologues such as Abdallah Azzam and Safar al-Hawali, as with the other elements discussed here, these gestures often function to subtly render other ways of seeing and understanding the terrorist more difficult.

While this mode of representation has been witnessed across the visual landscape of the 'war on terror,' and still continues to appear in the pages of British newspapers, moreover (See *The Guardian*, June 6th 2012; *The Independent*,

June 7th 2012; *The Mirror*, July 5th 2014, for recent examples), the features identified here find themselves epitomised in the news media depictions of Osama
bin Laden that surfaced in the immediate aftermath of the September 11th
2001 attacks. Pictured in *The Guardian* newspaper the day after these events
(See figure 3.1), the image of bin Laden stands to contain the looming threat
posed by al-Qaeda, and the phenomenon of 'Islamic' terrorism more generally,
by centring the viewers' attention onto his visually compelling, yet seemingly
antiquated, image. Here the persuasive combination of bin Laden's beard, 'traditional' appearance and raised index finger functions to subtly communicate
the idea that the threat is confined to an easily identifiable, and highly visual,
minority of terrorists, something that, furthermore, works to prevent other,
more diverse and complex ways, of seeing and speaking about the 'Islamic' terrorist possible. Indeed, this notion can be seen to be more effectively conveyed
when bin Laden's image is inadvertently positioned alongside other subjects
and objects appearing in such news texts. Here, his bearded, 'traditional' appearance can be seen to be unwittingly contrasted against the, typically white,
clean-shaven and conventionally-dressed journalists, news presenters and in-
terviewees who appear in the newspaper and television reports following the
September 11th 2001 attacks.

In one BBC 'News at Ten' broadcast, for example, an interview with a Western
security analyst is immediately followed by grainy footage of Osama bin Laden
(See BBC, 'News at Ten,' September 11th 2001; See also Ahmad, 2016, for further analysis). The contrast between these two figures is particularly stark,
with the security analyst pictured on his own in a modern, urban setting and
wearing a grey suit and tie, and a bearded and ascetically-dressed bin Laden
emerging out of a mud-bricked building into a chaotic scene of masked, heavily armed fighters. Despite the presence of a number of key accoutrements
of modern warfare, here, bin Laden's beard and non-Western dress function
discursively as visual markers of his backwardness and fanaticism, something
that, more importantly, works to produce a series of powerful subject positions (Westerner/non-Westerner, terrorist/non-terrorist, Self/Other, etc.) that
serve to police and maintain these discursive boundaries. Although they might
equally reject such forms of positioning, in this short visual sequence the BBC's
audience members are invited to identify with the modern, well-dressed security analyst, with bin Laden's dull, out-of-date clothing signifying his similarly
antiquated world view.

It should be noted, however, that outside of the 'closed' discourse of news
and current affairs this reductive category of representation has also passed
into the realm of caricature and self-parody; with the 'war on terror' providing
several notable examples of resistance to, and comedic subversion of, this form

FIGURE 3.1
Osama bin Laden pictured in
The Guardian (September 12th 2001).
SOURCE: AFP/GETTY IMAGES.

of imagery. Thus, the figure of the bearded, finger-wagging 'Islamic' terrorist has also made a less-threatening appearance in a number of films, comedy sketches, political cartoons and television advertisements. In particular, Chris Morris' acclaimed black comedy *Four Lions* (2010) is perhaps most notable in this regard, in which several scenes seek to directly spoof the self-representations and propaganda statements of figures such as bin Laden and al-Zawahiri. Nevertheless, although the 'Islamic' terrorist has been at its most visible when pictured in the form of the bearded, finger-wagging 'fanatic,' this figure has also been seen in a much more veiled and less-identifiable mode that finds itself manifested in a series of propaganda images featuring unknown numbers of masked, shadowy terrorists.

Terror Clones, Suicide Brigades, and the Figure of the Masked, Shadowy Militant

Echoing W. J. T. Mitchell's claim, that the 'war on terror' has often appeared to be a conflict fought against an endless 'array of faceless, anonymous, homogenous warriors' (2011, p. 17), the second mode of representation to emerge during this period has been the image of the masked, shadowy terrorist. Drawing on a long history of cultural representations of non-state terrorism, from black-and-white newspaper images of the 1972 Munich Olympic attack to the grainy footage of members of the Provisional Irish Republican Army that appeared on British television screens during the 1980s, within this set of images the 'Islamic' terrorist continues to be contained within a similarly familiar, albeit unsettling, category of representation. However, this time the tension between what is the seen and unseen is further played out in the fact that the black, anonymizing mask renders this figure as one that is simultaneously visible *and* invisible. Here, the focus on the black-masked terrorist, therefore, functions to obscure the fact that beneath the veil this figure might look like someone from one of Britain's diverse, multi-ethnic Muslim communities. In addition to this, rather than simply Orientalize the 'Islamic' terrorist, as some have suggested (Karim, 2006), here, it is important to emphasise that the news media's visual representations of this figure find themselves inadvertently implicated in the propaganda aims of the terrorist group itself; with the image of the masked, shadowy terrorist deliberately *appropriating* the discursive power of Orientalism, whilst at the same time furthering the fear that there is a sinister network of operatives and sleeper cells lying in waiting across the United Kingdom.

Key to this representational mode is the veiled and anonymous appearance of the 'Islamic' terrorist; a powerful strategy that functions to make the terrorist simultaneously visible and invisible for British news audiences. Although in practical terms the use of masks and balaclavas hinders terrorist identification, particularly important when trying to evade the authorities, in a more targeted sense their use functions to powerfully engender fear and uncertainty in the civilian population by de-individualizing the identities of the fighters and providing an abstract canvas on which a range of fears and identities can be projected. This is a strategy that groups such as al-Qaeda, al-Shabaab, Hamas, Hizbollah and Islamic State have powerfully capitalized upon, with each of these groups making extensive use of facial coverings in their propaganda releases, something that has featured heavily in recent news reporting of the Islamic State phenomenon (See *The Guardian*, October 9th 2013; *The Sun*, September 22nd 2014; *The Independent*, December 14th 2014, for examples). According to Tish Stringer, 'the mask foregrounds a collective rather than an individual identity,' a strategy that works to powerfully convey an image of a singular, uniform threat (2013, p. 329). Indeed, over the course of the 'war on terror,' British news audiences have become increasingly familiar with grainy footage of scores of masked, *keffiyeh*-wearing gunmen, often pictured marching in unison or engaged in a series of aggressive training activities, or slick propaganda images of veiled, anonymous militants issuing chilling messages to those watching.

As noted with regard to the image of the bearded, finger-wagging 'fanatic,' moreover, the communicative power of this category of representation also lies in the forms of clothing and bodily appearance of the 'Islamic' terrorist. Here, a hybrid uniform of military-style combat fatigues, Western and 'non-Western' clothing, such as the *keffiyeh* scarf, the *salwar kameez*, or the *shahadah*-inscribed headband, have become sartorial signifiers that symbolise the modern 'Islamic' terrorist. By way of explanation, Michael Semple has suggested that 'Islamic' terrorists often adopt similar forms of dress in order "to symbolise their belonging to an army," albeit an imagined one, that draws together groups and individuals that are spread out across the Muslim world (2015). In doing so, groups as disparate and disconnected as al-Qaeda, al-Shabaab, Boko Haram and Islamic State imbue their propaganda releases with a continuity that belies their conflicting ideological stances and local grievances. Indeed, while it has been suggested that Western news coverage of Islam-related incidents are often accompanied by visual representations of large groupings of anonymous, de-individualized masses (Said, 2003, p. 87), it is important to make clear that such deliberate and calculated forms of self-representation work on a broader level to harness the discursive power of Orientalism—that is, of the East as a looming, monolithic and conspiratorially-spreading threat—in order to further engender fear in the minds of British and Western news audiences. Thus, rather than be contained within a representational framework that has been simply established by a number of powerful Western elites, here, the 'Islamic' terrorist can be understood to knowingly take possession of, indeed actively perform, the discourse of Orientalism, using it to tap into existing fears and further their own propaganda aims.

A particularly salient example of this mode of representation can be witnessed during the news coverage of the trial and sentencing of those involved in the infamous 2003 'ricin' plot, Britain's most notorious 'al-Qaeda'-related terror conspiracy (See Archer & Bawdon, 2010, for an overview). Both BBC and ITV 'News at Ten' reports surrounding this event each featured extensive training sequences cut from al-Qaeda's slick *State of the Ummah* (2001) propaganda video, in which scores of masked, identically-dressed fighters can be seen engaged in violent synchronized training activities deep in the Afghan hinterland (See Figure 3.2). Indeed, although such sequences comprise only a small portion of the overall video, they formulate a key part of the visual narrative of these news reports. Here, the figure of the masked 'Islamic' terrorist functions to flatten erase the differences that exist between al-Qaeda's numerous cells, operatives and local franchises, helping to maintain an image of uniformity and coherence, and also obscure the truth that those involved in the alleged plot had very little connection to the core leadership (See BBC1, 'News at Ten'

FIGURE 3.2
Still image from Al-Qaeda's State of the Ummah
propaganda feature as pictured in BBC1 *and* ITV,
'News at Ten' (April 13th 2005).
SOURCE: PUBLIC DOMAIN.

April 13th 2005; ITV, 'News at Ten' April 13th 2005, for example). Rarely mentioned is the fact that many of those featuring in this propaganda release were in actual fact 'rented mujahideen,' drawn from the local militias and private armies of wealthy Afghan warlords (Wright, 2006, p. 270). Rather, this footage serves to conceal the fear that that beneath these masks the 'Islamic' terrorist might look like any other member of Britain's multicultural and diverse society.

It should also be noted, however, that in addition to fulfilling the propaganda aims of groups like al-Qaeda the figure of the masked, shadowy terrorist has gone on to become a mode of representation that has been central to legitimising the State's narratives surrounding the 'war on terror,' something that has lent credibility to a whole set of extraordinary and invasive security measures (See Oborne, 2007, for example). Nevertheless, while it is evident that such images has served a variety of strategic aims during this period, it is important to point out that the veiled and elusive nature of the masked, anonymous terrorist has served to foreshadow a much more prosaic and everyday mode of representation.

Lone-wolves, Jihobbyists and the Emergence of the 'Home-grown' Extremist

Challenging the reductive, Orientalized-inspired nature of the images outlined above, the final mode of representation pictures the 'Islamic' terrorist, not as an externalized, stereotypical monster, but, more ominously, as a series of seemingly 'normal,' 'ordinary' British citizens. Although they do not appear with the same level of frequency as those analyzed above, as the strategies adopted by groups like al-Qaeda have adapted, and, indeed, as new forms of image-based media have become more widely available, news audiences are increasingly presented with images and visual representations of people who would appear to formulate an integral feature of British, multicultural society. Thus, from police mug-shot images and Facebook 'selfies,' to high-school and family portrait photography, more and more the figure of the 'Islamic' terrorist is made manifest through a series of images that appear to show 'typical,' British teenagers in everyday social settings and engaged in the kinds of 'ordinary' activities that can be identified with by a range of audience members, regardless of their own, unique cultural backgrounds. Importantly, while very little critical attention has been paid to this emergent mode of representation, images of the 'lone-wolf' or 'home-grown' terrorist are of increasing significance due to the fact that they render the 'Islamic' terrorist to be highly visible within mainstream society, presenting news audiences with a tangible, as opposed to abstract and cliché-ridden, figure who can seamlessly blend in within Britain's multicultural communities.

Central to this mode of depiction is the seemingly normal, everyday nature of the 'Islamic' terrorist, something which allows this figure to stand outside of the powerful, culturally constructed frameworks through which the distant, radical 'Other' has conventionally been understood. Here, rather than be contained within a threatening, albeit familiar, image of the stereotypical terrorist monster, the 'Islamic' terrorist becomes the 'Other-as-Self': That is, the person sat next to you on the bus, the friendly neighbor across the street, or the 'innocent'-looking schoolboy playing football in the park. Thus, despite the increased visibility of this figure, paradoxically, within this mode of representation, the 'Islamic' terrorist becomes much harder to identify and, thus, much more difficult to apprehend. Indeed, this is an ambiguity that Deborah Jermyn (2003) has noted with regard to the use of conventional portrait photography in television representations of criminality and deviance. Jermyn suggests that visual representations of normality and deviance fulfil a deep cultural need to manage and fix 'difference,' something that functions to maintain and manage a fragile status quo. As she explains, while most popular media representations of crime and criminality typically employ CCTV and mugshot-style imagery, sometimes the images used fall into the domestic and idyllic category of family portrait photography, something that 'makes them more fascinating, more shocking, than the "mugshot," since it places the "deviant" in the realm of the ordinary' (Ibid., p. 181). Here, within Britain's liberal, multicultural, multiethnic landscape, the seemingly hard boundary between the internal Self and the externalized, terrorist Other collapse, and it becomes increasingly difficult to separate the two.

In particular, studies have consistently shown how those who seek to carry out acts of violent terror or affiliate themselves with terrorist groups come from an extraordinarily diverse range of ethnic, cultural, social and ideological backgrounds (Devji, 2005, p. 25), thus contradicting the culturally construct-ed image of the socially-isolated fanatic (Travis, 2008). According to Marc Sageman, for example, the typical home-grown 'Islamic' terrorist is someone who is well educated, is likely to have lived a relatively normal, settled life, embedded within a broad, multi-ethnic social network, and, perhaps most im-portantly, is a person who has very little understanding, or prior knowledge, of religion and politics (2008, p. 51). A study carried out by MI5's Behavioral Science Unit into the phenomenon of 'radicalization,' moreover, also con-cluded that those who carry out acts of home-grown terrorism "are a diverse collection of individuals, fitting no single demographic profile, nor do they fol-low a typical pathway to violent extremism" (See Knapton & Gardham, 2008). Indeed, it is here where we can appreciate *why* this mode of representation does not appear with as much frequency within news media depictions of the 'Islamic' terrorist, as such an understanding can be seen to powerfully desta-bilise and undermine Britain's delicate social fabric, destroying the deep, cul-turally embedded discourses that serve to distinguish 'normal' from 'deviant,' 'citizen' from 'terrorist.' As Rose has suggested in regard to the perpetrators of the July 7th 2005 bombings, the real strangeness and anxiety surrounding such forms of visual representation "is not only that we can never be sure who they are, but, as a consequence, we can never be sure who we are" (2010, p. 103).

Perhaps the most significant example of this mode of representation from the period under analysis can be seen in the emergence of Shehzad Tanweer's high-school portrait photograph in the aftermath of the July 7th 2005 bomb-ings (See Figure 3.3). At the time of its first appearance in *The Sun* newspaper's July 13th 2005 edition, Tanweer's image stood in stark contrast to conventional visualization of al-Qaeda, and the phenomenon of 'Islamic' terrorism more broadly, as an external, distant and seemingly foreign threat. With his head tilted slightly to the left, a gesture known as 'head-canting' (Goffman, 1976), Tanweer affects a stereotypically 'submissive' pose common in secondary-school portrait photography and is often understood to signify stereotypically 'feminine' forms of non-verbal bodily communication (Ragan, 1982, p. 42). The school uniform, edited out of some of the images used in *The Sun* and BBC's 'News at Ten' coverage (See 'News at Ten,' July 13th 2005), further serves to un-derscore the normal, everyday background of the Aldgate Station bomber, drawing upon culturally embedded notions of 'innocence' and 'purity.' In ad-dition to this, and as remarked above, while all images and visual representa-tions function to position audiences relationally, subtly inviting spectators to adopt a particular perspective of point of view (Rose, 2001, p. 46), with regard to Tanweer's image, although his ethnic identity might lead some viewers to adopt an oppositional reading, the familiar, culturally resonant nature of his

FIGURE 3.3
Shehzad Tanweer's school portrait photo as pictured in The Sun
(July 13th 2005).
SOURCE: ROSS PARRY PICTURE AGENCY LTD.

portrait photograph, such as its clearly identifiable semiotic and iconograph-
ic qualities, can be said to act against such straightforward forms of subject
positioning. Here, British audiences might be expected to identify with the
Aldgate Station bomber, recognizing an aspect of themselves or their own experiences in the schoolboy's image. On a more controversial level, and perhaps
more problematically, Tanweer's photograph would also not look out of place
if placed alongside the multicultural and ethnically-diverse images of the victims of the July 7th 2005 bombings, with this image drawing on the same culturally constructed notions of normality and familiarity called upon to make
sense of those killed in the attacks.

Finally, while the 'Islamic' terrorist has traditionally been viewed through
highly gendered lenses, this final mode of representation functions to further
extend the discursive boundaries surrounding those who can carry out acts
of violent terrorism; with the figure of the lone-wolf or home-grown terrorist
including both male and female operatives within its shifting ranks. Indeed,
in recent years, British news audiences have witnessed an increasing number
of incidents perpetrated by female 'Islamic' terrorists, such as Aafia Siddiqui,
Roshonara Choudhry, Muriel Degauque, Sadija al-Rishawi and, perhaps the
most notorious of which, Samantha Lewthwaite, the elusive 'White Widow'
(See *The Sun*, December 23rd 2013, for example). Although women are often
marginalized within news accounts, either as passive victims or as individuals
who lack agency and, thus, act under the influence of their male counterparts
(Brown, 2011, p. 707), the forms of visual representation engendered within
this, home-grown, mode of representation function to imbue these individuals with a level of power that is often lacking in textual accounts.

Conclusions

Despite the sheer levels of media and political attention heaped upon the
'Islamic' terrorist, it is somewhat surprising that few studies have sought to consider the various ways in which this figure has been visually represented over

the course of the 'war on terror' period. Indeed, although the findings discussed here support the tacit levels of analysis made elsewhere (See Macdonald, 2003; Hoskins & O'Loughlin, 2011; Nashef, 2011, for examples), this chapter shows how the 'Islamic' terrorist has been represented through an increasingly diverse range of images and visual representations, thus providing much needed insight into the shifting ways in which this complex, multifaceted figure has been presented for British news audiences. Perhaps most notably, it has tried to reveal the tensions that emerge between what becomes seen and unseen when the news media privilege one mode of representation over and above another. Thus, while Orientalised modes of representation have sought to control and contain the threat, making this figure at once both visually arresting and highly identifiable for British citizens, such images of bearded, bescarved, or masked, anonymous terrorists has merely functioned to obscure other, more nuanced ways of seeing the 'Islamic' terrorist. Similarly, the gradual emergence of a number of more contemporary forms of imagery has served to free the terrorist from such simplified, cliché-ridden modes of representation, but at the same time has made this figure much more visible within mainstream society and, paradoxically, much harder to fully identify. Indeed, it would seem that, as François Debrix has noted, the power of the terrorist image lies in the fact that "it can never be captured or located" (1995, p. 279).

With the analysis in mind, therefore, the final section of this chapter will consider some of the social and political consequences that have emerged from such various modes of representation during the opening stages of the 'war on terror.' Although this is not to suggest that British news audiences have passively accepted the various images discussed here, it is important to recognize the fact that media representations help to establish the discursive and ideational conditions in which particular understandings of the 'war on terror' have been made possible. Indeed, by focusing on the seemingly foreign and religious nature of the 'Islamic' terrorist, as seen in some of the modes of representation discussed here, such forms of imagery can be said to have had a severe impact upon Britain's 2.7 million Muslims during the course of this conflict, helping to cement a series of associations between Islam and violence that may take years to redress. Broader research into the news media's representations of Muslims and Islam during this period also stands to confirm this notion, with a number of studies highlighting the way in which the focus on 'Islamic' terrorism is further supplemented by coverage centring on violence, conflict and cultural difference (Poole, 2011, pp. 53–59). One opinion poll, for example, noted a significant hardening in public attitudes towards Muslims in Britain, with the proportion of citizens perceiving this religion to be a threat to Western, liberal democracy rising steeply from 32% in 2001 to 52% in 2006 (Field, 2007, p. 465). Here, the visual emphasis on the 'traditional,' overtly religious, appearance of the terrorist has served to further perpetuate baseless associations between Islam, terrorism and violence, thus linking Muslims to a threat that they too are often the victims of.

With the emergence of a set of more conventional, home-grown images and visual representations, the belief that the terrorist is not simply a distant, foreign Other, but also a more familiar-looking 'enemy within,' is something that has also had lasting consequences for Britain's social, political and legal landscape. Indeed, though often orientated towards Britain's various Muslim communities (See Choudhury & Fenwick, 2011), the development of an increasingly pervasive security apparatus that can be directed towards any citizen, regardless of their ethnic or religious origin, has profoundly impacted upon civil liberties in the United Kingdom. From the unprecedented broadening of state definitions 'terrorism' and the criminalization of certain forms of behavior, to the creation of new surveillance powers and the gradual removal of the right to protest, the 'war on terror' has seen a complete overhaul of Britain's legal system, removing a series of rights and constitutional privileges that have taken centuries to secure (See Atkins, 2007). While this is not to suggest that images such as those analyzed here are directly responsible for these developments, but rather that the shifting understandings of the 'Islamic' terrorist that have developed over the course of this 'war,' something, in part, made possible through media representations, has served to engender the conditions for a series of more repressive and far-reaching legal and policy responses. As noted, while these security measures are most often directed towards Britain's Muslim communities, it is important to keep in mind that such exceptional practices can be used against *any* citizen, regardless of their religious, cultural or economic background.

To briefly conclude, despite focusing on a limited range of images, this chapter has sought to provide much needed insight into the various shifting modes of visual representation that have been used to depict the 'Islamic' terrorist for British news audiences during the past fifteen years or so. And, even though it is clear that this figure is most often depicted in ways that foreground the foreign, distant, very much '*Islamic*,' nature of the terrorist, it is increasingly the case that these images and visual representations are reflecting the diversity and complexity that exists within today's globalized, multicultural societies. Indeed, as this analysis has sought to make clear, far from simply reflecting the reductive binaries and forms of knowledge that produce discourses such as Orientalism, the image of the 'Islamic' terrorist is increasingly an image of ourselves.

References

Ahmad, A. (1992). *In Theory: Classes, Nations, Literatures*. London: Verso.

Ahmad, J. (2016). A Shifting Enemy: Analysing the BBC's Representations of "Al-Qaeda" in the Aftermath of September 11th 2001. *Critical Studies on Terrorism*, 9(3), 433–454.

Archer, L. & Bawdon, F. (2010), *Ricin! The Inside Story of the Terror Plot that Never Was*. London: Pluto Press.

Atkins, C.; Bee, S. & Button, F. (2007). *Taking Liberties: Since 1997*. London: Revolver Press.

Bleiker, R.; Campbell, D.; Hutchison, E. & Nicholson, X. (2013). Visual Dehumanisation of Refugees. *Australian Journal of Political Science*, 48(4), 398–416.

Brown, K. (2011). Muriel's Wedding: News Media Representations of Europe's First Female Suicide Terrorist. *European Journal of Cultural Studies*, 14 (6), 705–726.

Choudhury, T., Fenwick, H. (2011). The Impact of Counter-Terrorism Measures on Muslim Communities. *International Review of Law, Computers and Technology*, 25 (3) 151–181.

Chuang, A. & Roemer, R. C. (2013). The Immigrant Muslim American at the Boundary of Insider and Outsider: Representations of Faisal Shahzad as "Homegrown" Terrorist. *Journalism and Mass Communication Quarterly*, 90 (1), 89–107.

Cloud, D. (2004). "To Veil the Threat of Terror": Afghan Women and the 'Clash of Civilization' in the Imagery of the U.S. War on Terrorism. *Quarterly Journal of Speech*, 90 (3), 285–306.

Cottle, S. (2006). *Mediatized Conflict: Developments in Media and Conflict Studies*. Maidenhead: Open University Press.

Culcasi, K. & Gokmen, M. (2011). The Face of Danger: Beards in the U.S. Media's Representation of Arabs, Muslims and Middle Easterners. *Aether: The Journal of Media Geography*, 8, 82–96.

Debrix, F. (1995). Simulated Terrorism. *Peace Review: A Journal of Social Justice*, 7 (3), 275–281.

Devji, F. (2005). *Landscapes of the Jihad: Militancy, Morality, Modernity*. London: Hurst & Co.

El Houri, W. & Saber, D. (2010). Filming Resistance: A Hezbollah Strategy. *Radical History Review*, 106, 70–85.

Engel, K. (2007). The Face of a Terrorist, *Cultural Studies—Critical Methodologies*, 7(4), 397–424.

Fahmy, S. (2004). Picturing Afghan Women. *Gazette: International Journal for Communication Studies*, 66(2), 91–112.

Fahmy, S. et al. (2006). Visual Agenda Setting After 9/11: Individuals' Emotions, Image Recall and Concern with Terrorism. *Visual Communication Quarterly*, 13(1), 4–15.

Featherstone, M. et al. (2010). Discourses of the War on Terror: Constructions of the Islamic Other after 7/7. *International Journal of Media and Cultural Politics*, 6(2), 169–186.

Field, C. (2007). Islamophobia in Contemporary Britain: the Evidence of the Opinion Polls, 1988–2006. *Islam and Christian Relations*, 18 (4), 447–477.

Flood, C. et al. (2012). *Islam, Security and Television News*. Hampshire: Palgrave Macmillan.

Goffman, E. (1976). Gender Advertisements. *Studies in the Anthropology of Visual Communication*, 3(2), 69–154.

Goodwin, R. et al. (2005). Terror Threat Perception and its Consequences in Contemporary Britain. *British Journal of Psychology*, 96(4), 389–406.

Grabe, M. & Bucy, E. (2009). *Image Bite Politics: News and the Visual Framing of Elections*. New York: Oxford University Press.

Gunaratna, R. (2002). *Inside Al-Qaeda: Global Network of Terror*. London: Hurst & Co.

Hall, S. (1993). Encoding/Decoding. In Simon During (Ed.), *The Cultural Studies Reader*. (pp. 507–517). London: Routledge.

Hoskins, A. (2006). Temporality, Proximity and Security: Terror in a Media-Drenched Age. *International Relations*, 20 (4), 453–466.

Hoskins, A. & O'Loughlin, B. (2011). Remediating Jihad for Western News Audiences: The Renewal of Gatekeeping? *Journalism*, 12 (2), 199–216.

Hoskins, A. & O'Loughlin, B. (2007). *Television and Terror: Conflicting Times and the Crisis of News Discourse*. Hampshire: Palgrave Macmillan.

Hurd, E. S. (2003). Appropriating Islam: The Islamic Other in the Consolidation of Western Modernity. *Critique: Critical Middle Eastern Studies*, 12 (1), 25–41.

Hutchings, S. & Miazhevich, G. (2009). The Polonium Trail to Islam: Litvinenko, Liminality and Television's (Cold) War on Terror. *Critical Studies on Terrorism*, 2(2), 219–235.

Jackson, R. (2007). Constructing Enemies: "Islamic Terrorism" in Political and Academic Discourse. *Government and Opposition*, 42(3), 394–426.

Jackson, R. (2005). *Writing the War on Terrorism: Language, Politics and Counter-Terrorism*. Manchester: University of Manchester Press.

Jermyn, D. (2003). Photo Stories and Family Albums: Imaging Criminals and Victims on *Crimewatch UK*. In Paul Mason (Ed.), *Criminal Visions: Media Representations of Crime and Justice*. (pp. 175–191). Devon: Willan Publishers.

Karim, K. (2006). American Media's Coverage of Muslims: The Historical Roots of Contemporary Portrayals. In Elizabeth Poole & John Richardson (Eds.), *Muslims and the News Media*. (pp. 116–127). London: I.B. Tauris.

Keith, S. & Schwalbe, C. (2010). Women and Visual Depictions of the U.S.-Iraq War in Print and Online Media. *Visual Communication Quarterly*, 17(1), 4–17.

Kellner, D. (1995). *Media Culture*. London: Routledge.

Knapton, S. & Gardham, D. (August 21st 2008). 'MI5: Terrorists not Frustrated Religious Loners,' *The Telegraph*, Retrieved from: http://www.telegraph.co.uk/news/uknews/2593626/MI5-Terrorists-not-frustrated-religious-loners.html (Accessed January 5th 2015).

Lederman, J. (1992). *Battle Lines: The American Media and the Intifada*. New York: Henry Holt & Co.

Lewis, J. (2012). Terrorism and News Narratives. In Des Freedman & Daya Kishan Thussu (Eds.), *Media and Terrorism: Global Perspectives*. (pp. 257–270). London: SAGE.

Macdonald, M. (2003). *Exploring Media Discourse*. London: Arnold.

Machin, D. (2007.) Visual Discourses of War: Multimodal Analysis of Photographs of the Iraq Occupation. In Adam Hodges & Chad Nilep (Eds.), *Discourse, War and Terrorism*. (pp. 123–142). Philadelphia: John Benjamins Publishing Co.

Mitchell, W. J. T. (2011). *Cloning Terror: The War of Images, 9/11 to the Present*. Chicago: University of Chicago Press.

Morris, C. (2010). *Four Lions*. United Kingdom: Film 4/Warp Films.

Nashef, H. (2011). The Blurring of Boundaries: Images of Abjection as the Terrorist and the Reel Arab Intersect. *Critical Studies on Terrorism*, 4 (2), 351–368.

Oborne, P. (2007). The Use and Abuse of Terror: The Construction of a False Narrative on the Domestic Terror Threat. In George Kassimeris (Ed.), *Playing Politics with Terrorism: A User's Guide*. (pp. 101–138). New York: Columbia University Press.

O'Loughlin, B. (2011). Images as Weapons of War: Representation, Mediation and Interpretation. *Review of International Studies*, 37 (1), 71–91.

Paletz, D. L.; Ayanian, J. Z. & Fozzard, P. A. (1982). Terrorism on Television News: The IRA, the FALN, and the Red Brigades. In William C. Adams (Ed.), *Television Coverage of International Affairs*. (pp. 143–165).Norwood: Ablex.

Pantazis, C. & Pemberton, S. (2009). From the "Old" to the "New" Suspect Community: Examining the Impacts of Recent UK Counter-Terrorism Legislation. *British Journal of Criminology*, 49 (5), 646–666.

Poole, E. (2011). Change and Continuity in the Representation of British Muslims Before and After 9/11: The UK Context. *Global Media Journal—Canadian Edition*, 4 (2), 49–62.

Poole, E. (2002). *Reporting Islam: Media Representations of British Muslims*. London: I. B. Tauris.

Poole, E. & Richardson, J. (Eds.). (2006). *Muslims and the News Media*. London: I. B. Tauris.

Ragan, J. M. (1982). Gender Displays in Portrait Photographs. *Sex Roles*, 8 (1), 33–43.

Roger, N. (2013). *Image Warfare in the War on Terror*. Hampshire: Palgrave Macmillan

Rose, G. (2010). *Doing Family Photography: The Domestic, the Public and the Politics of Sentiment*. Farnham: Ashgate Publishing.

Rose, G. (2001).*Visual Methodologies: An Introduction to the Interpretation of Visual Materials*. London: SAGE.

Sageman, M. (2008). *Leaderless Jihad: Terror Networks in the Twenty-First Century*. Philadelphia: University of Pennsylvania Press.

Said, E. (2003). *Orientalism*. London: Penguin.

Said, E. (1997).*Covering Islam: How the Experts and the Media Determine How We See the Rest of the World*. London: Vintage.

Said, E. (1997) (1987). 'The MESA Debate: The Scholars, the Media and the Middle East,' *Journal of Palestine Studies*, 16 (2), 85–104.

Semple, M. (January 16th 2015). 'Black Flags and Balaclavas: How Jihadis Dress for Imaginary War,' *The Conversation*, Retrieved from http://theconversation.com/black-flags-and-balaclavas-how-jihadists-dress-for-imaginary-war-36152.

Shaheen, J. (2009). *Reel Bad Arabs: How Hollywood Vilifies a People*. Northampton: Olive Branch Press.

Shim, D. & Nabers, D. (2013). Imaging North Korea: Exploring its Visual Representations in International Politics. *International Studies Perspectives*, 14 (3), 289–306.

Shoemaker P. & Reese, S. (2nd Eds.). (1996). *Mediating the Message: Theories of Influences on Mass Media Content*. New York: Longman.

Sjoberg, L. & Gentry, C. (Eds.). (2011). *Women, Gender and Terrorism*. Athens: University of Georgia Press.

Streeck, J. (2008). 'Gesture in Political Communication: A Case Study of the Democratic Presidential Candidates during the 2004 Primary Campaign,' *Research on Language and Social Interaction*, Vol. 41, No. 2, pp. 154–186.

Stringer, T. (2013). Is This What Democracy Looks Like? In Jeffrey S. Juris & Alex Khasnabish (Eds.), *Insurgent Encounters: Transnational Activism, Ethnography and the Political*. (pp. 318–341). Durham: Duke University Press.

Travis, A. (2008, August 20). 'MI5 Report Challenges Views on Terrorism in Britain,' *The Guardian*, Retrieved from http://www.theguardian.com/uk/2008/aug/20/uksecurity.terrorism1.

Van Veeren, E. (2016). Orange Prison Jumpsuit. In Mark Salter (Ed.), *Making Things International 2: Assemblages*. (pp. 122–136). Minneapolis: University of Minnesota Press.

Wolfsfeld, G. (1997). *Media and Political Conflict: News from the Middle East*. Cambridge: Cambridge University Press.

Wright, L. (2006). *The Looming Tower: Al-Qaeda's Road to 9/11*. London: Penguin.

Primary Sources: Television Broadcasts and Newspaper Articles

Ahmed, A.; Ackerman, S. & Smith, D. (2013, October 9). 'How the US Raid on al-Shabaab in Somalia Went Wrong,' *The Guardian*, Retrieved from https://www.theguardian.com/world/2013/oct/09/us-raid-al-shabaab-somalia-navy-seals

Boone, J. & Burke, J. (2012, June 6). 'Drone Attack Kills al-Qaida Number Two,' *The Guardian.*

Childs, M. (June 7th 2012). 'Abu Yahya al-Libi: Libyan Militant Who Rose to Become Second-in-Command of Al-Qa'ida,' *The Independent.*

Endley, B. (2014, July 5). 'ISIS Leader Abu Bakr al-Baghdadi Breaks Cover and Tells Followers "We Like Killing our Enemies,"' *The Mirror.*

Easton, M. (2005, April 13). 'News at Ten,' BBC1.

Eykyn, G. (2001, September 11). 'News at Ten,' BBC1.

Gillan, A. (2001, October 8). 'Bin Laden Appears on Video to Threaten US,' *The Guardian*

Hills, S. (2013, September 9). '"I'm Ready to Become a Suicide Bomber": Chilling Words of 7/7 Bomber's Widow on Worlds Most Wanted List,' *The Daily Mail.*

Hughes, S. & Hall, A. (2013, December 23). 'Brit 7/7 Widow "Plotted Station Horror"; Terror Bomb Failed,' *The Sun.*

MacAskill, E. (2001, September 12), 'Finger of Suspicion Pointed at Saudi Dissident Osama bin Laden,' *The Guardian.*

Pollard, C., & Mayer, C. (2014, September 22) 'Inside Islamic State Terror Camps,' *The Sun.*

Rivers, D. (2005, April 13) 'News at Ten,' ITV.

Sharp, A. (2014, August 23). 'SAS and US Special Forces Forming Hunter Killer Unit to "Smash Islamic State,"' *The Daily Mirror.*

Sullivan, M. (2005, July 13). 'The Brit Bomber,' *The Sun.*

Withnall, A. (2014, December 14). 'Hamas Anniversary Parade sees Militants Display Heavy Rockets and Heavy Weapons as they Vow to Destroy Israel,' *Independent.*

CHAPTER 4

Oil and Women: Invisibility as Power in Nawal El-Saadawi's *Love in the Kingdom of Oil*

Layla Hendow

Introduction

At first glance, there is something unsettling about the exterior of Nawal El-Saadawi's novel *Love in the Kingdom of Oil*, published by Saqi Books in 2001. The back cover and the front image provide readers with the first visual representations of El-Saadawi's interior, literary message. However, the title's juxtaposition of 'love' and 'oil' is unusual. Secondly, the cover painting by Thuraya Al-Baqsami shows a woman, unveiled, with large eyes and flowing black hair. Behind her is a painting of a man. There is disturbing irony here in the apparent reversal of the masculine gaze. Normally a painting of a woman, this cover uses the common Victorian trope of the hanging portrait but shows the painting of a man being seen by a woman. Moreover, when turning to the back cover, readers are informed that the novel is about the "issues and questions surrounding a woman's role and position in a repressive, patriarchal order." Although this is what we might expect to find in a novel from Nawal El-Saadawi, the controversial female-rights activist, it jars with the novel's idealistic title and its cover image—not to mention the interior plot, which confuses readers with endless flash-backs and flash-forwards, blurring and blending of characters, and magic realism. In short, such a simplified reading, as offered on the back cover, does not seem to be possible.

At the onset, El-Saadawi challenges the Western constructed image of a woman wearing a veil. By doing this, she is already attending to the negative representation of visual imperialism connected with this specific form of Muslim identity. Therefore, when this study examines the politics of the seen and unseen in *Love in the Kingdom of Oil*, it does not aim to solely provide an account of El-Saadawi's political and social position on women's emancipation from male dominance, including the precariousness of the veil. This chapter examines how El-Saadawi, an Egyptian novelist writing in English, challenges the limited perspective of western visual imperialism through the media of literature, similar to the way in which contemporary women reclaim the agency of the veil in the use of media such as Facebook pages, as shown in chapter 5.

Like Raihanah M. M., I explore a narrative of a woman who actually wears the veil, and creates her own sense of self-identification from it.

Furthermore, like Chapter 3, which examined the Western visual representation of the foreign Other in the realm of terrorism, this essay looks at the visual representations of veil through a type of foreign Other. The action of the novel takes place on an unknown island away from the protagonist's home. Although the place is similar to where she has come from, she is still in a foreign Other. It is between spaces. *Love in the Kingdom of Oil*, too, is between spaces. A Middle Eastern narrative, it is written in English and sold by a London publisher; it is meant for Western bookshelves and Western eyes. I argue that El-Saadawi attends to a dual purpose: at once challenging perceptions of negative images of the veil and positioning this endeavor through the wider Western enterprise of oil. Oil—a substance included in the title but brushed over as a means to disguise the name of El-Saadawi's fictional island—is arguably the key to the attitude of both the male dominance and the politics of visibility within the novel. It forces the reader to accept a different side to their contemporary affluence brought to them by oil. And, in the same light, the contemporary Muslim woman behind the visual production that has been constructed by the West.

Women's rights, in this novel, are read through the growing environmental concerns surrounding oil. Nawal El-Saadawi does this by finding a connection between oil and women as two entities caught up in a patriarchal power struggle. They are paradoxically driven into the unseen on a public level, but also are subject of a male, voyeuristic gaze. Why does El-Saadawi do this, and what is the larger message? Is El-Saadawi using oil to make a political statement about women's rights, or using the already established opinions on women's rights to make a statement about the new and emerging oil world? The history of the emancipation of women in Egypt and other Middle Eastern countries is very old, but the history of oil is a largely modern phenomenon, and El-Saadawi is doing something unique in bringing them together. *Love in the Kingdom of Oil*, then, is a novel about resistance and the ability to use the unseen as simultaneously a symbol of freedom and repression.

This paper utilizes theories of visual representation and its relation to power to aid in the understanding of El-Saadawi's novel and its possible engagement in a wider Islamic debate. It also looks at the symbol of the veil as a source of visual control and representation in itself. With this in mind, this chapter makes use of Michel Foucault's work on the gaze, power and the notion of the panopticon as a tool to discuss the relationship between visibility and power. The theory of the panopticon is based on a prison designed by Jeremy Bentham, which ensures complete and total observation of prisoners. Foucault famously states that "visibility is a trap" (2004, p. 554). He is referring to the way in which people in the panopticon system are unable to escape the repression of observation. Applying these ideas to a novel about power struggles and what it means to be seen and unseen poses interesting questions about women's sense of imprisonment but, also, the ability of oil to escape such observation. There has been little work done on Foucault's theory and its impact on Islamic feminist literature; therefore this is unique ground to cover.

This chapter is structured into two parts: 'Value and Shame' and 'Surveillance and Escape.' The first section examines the role of the patriarch in the novel, who dictates the first kind of unseen—the 'forced' unseen. It will look at the use of the veil in comparison to the treatment of oil as two Western archetypes that have been reclaimed and rewritten by El-Saadawi. The second section will look at the flipside: the use of surveillance and the gaze to monitor the invisible subject. I will use work by Foucault to help unravel issues of power, but also surveillance in relation to the negative attitude to Muslim women that El-Saadawi, as a feminist and activist, is also keen to uncover. In the end, I view the novel as having a heroic trajectory when placed against modern, Western standards; the "woman," the unnamed protagonist, consistently fights against the repression placed upon her. However, there are problematic consequences of this fight, and El-Saadawi leaves the ending of the novel open to interpretation; hinting at the fact that the protagonist may not progress at all, but remain exactly where she began: "a wife of oil" (2001, p. 72). If this is the case, what does this say about El-Saadawi's opinion about the progressing oil world and its relation to female emancipation?

Value and Shame

This section explores the relationship between oil and women within the Islamic, male dominating world. Through their juxtaposition, El-Saadawi is able to make a larger comment about the seemingly opposing emotions of value and shame, which are powered by visibility and invisibility. We would imagine that objects of value would desire to be seen, while those associated with shame are unseen. El-Saadawi complicates this binary, although the decision-making always lies at the hands of patriarchy. From the beginning of the novel, we are aware that to be seen or unseen/invisible is determined by men. Readers learn in the first lines that a "woman goes on leave and does not return" (2001, p. 5). The protagonist, an unnamed female archaeologist who is only referred to as "woman," has vanished from her hometown, running away to escape her repressive life and take up excavation work on a strange island. Running away is classed as illegitimate invisibility, as we are in a world where "women do not go on leave" without their husband's permission (2001, p. 6). In other words, to vanish or become unseen *without* the permission of the patriarch is forbidden. By comparison, we find legitimate invisibility through the act of veiling. The protagonist goes against both by vanishing illegitimately, and, we learn, by not wearing a veil in public.

Gender differences in *Love in the Kingdom of Oil* go beyond the societal and religious discriminations that El-Saadawi has reacted against in previous work. In this novel, as I have suggested, gender is seen through the lens of the highly politically and financially-driven oil world. For El-Saadawi, it is clear that not only is the world controlled by the various male figures, such as the King, the protagonist's husband, or the police officer, it is the world of oil, specifically, that is a masculine arena. Oil oozes patriarchy, and El-Saadawi is not alone in this diagnosis. From Upton Sinclair's 1927 novel *Oil!* to Abdul Rahman Munif's *Cities of Salt* (1984), the oil world is one portrayed as being male orientated, insofar as the extraction, selling and politics of oil is conducted solely by men. Moreover, the writers themselves are male, showing that the majority of writers engaging in what Amitav Ghosh would label the GAON (Great American Oil Novel) are men. Except male authorship, the same is true for El-Saadawi's novel: the oil industry is controlled by men. When the woman runs away she is imprisoned by a variety of different 'husband' figures who force her to enter the oil world instead of pursuing her excavation work. They are all authority figures: policemen, employers, husbands. The man she lives with is "not her husband, nor a police commissioner," and his real identity is never known (2001, p. 79). From one prison to another, the protagonist finds she is unable, at the same time, to escape the cyclical work dictated by the unknown, male figures, and the cyclical world of oil, where "the land was changing as the oil changed" (2001, p. 42).

I am connecting oil and women primarily through their connection to the overarching male patriarch and the dichotomy of value and shame that they both possess. The idea that both oil and women are worth controlling comes from the fact that both hold a unique value. In *Love in the Kingdom of Oil*, women are loving wives, with "a mother's compassion" (2001, p. 51). Significantly, the value of the mother and wife is connected both with their desire to be showcased and seen, and their need to be unseen through the use of the veil. This is revealed in the literature surrounding the wearing of the veil:

> And tell the believing women to reduce [some] of their vision and guard their private parts and not expose their adornment except that which [necessarily] appears thereof and to wrap [a portion of] their headcovers

over their chests and not expose their adornment except to their husbands, their fathers, their husbands' fathers, their sons, their husbands'
sons ... (24:31)

Without giving legitimacy to the concept, I include this extract, from the
Quran, to disclose that the reason for veiling is somewhat due the value and
possession of the female body, foregrounded with the repetition of 'adornment.' Although my purpose here is not to engage with the vast array of literature concerning the veil, I mention the Quran here only to point out that the
veil, as well as symbolizing repression, also symbolizes the value of the female
form. In this instance, the woman is controlled by the man through family and
marriage, and this becomes her value to society. Religious scripture feeds into
Islamic literature and into El-Saadawi's other work, for instance, *The Nawal
El-Saadawi Reader*, which addresses the inequality of gender as being down to
the 'Islamic fundamentalist movement' (1997, p. 95). She further argues that:

> I have come to see more and more clearly that religion is more often used
> in our day as an instrument in the hands of economic and political forces,
> as an institution utilized by those who rule to keep down those who are
> ruled. In this it serves the same purpose as juridical, educational, police
> and even psychological systems used to perpetuate the patriarchal fam-
> ily, historically born, reinforced and maintained by the oppression of
> women, children and slaves. (1980, p. 3)

For El-Saadawi, religion and the politics surrounding the economic and political world cannot be seen separately—this is perhaps why the way the veil
is utilized in the novel is similar to the way oil is utilized—as a way to disguise women and space, rather than being used as a tool for self-identification.
El-Saadawi, therefore, disagrees with Michael Ross' argument (which I will
expand on below) that "the persistence of patriarchy in the Middle East has
relatively little to do with Islam" (2008, p. 120). It is the forces of religion which
coerce women into staying in the home, rather than the inability to work.
Through this, El-Saadawi forms a compelling trilogy of "politics, religion and
sex," which she plays out in her novel *Love in the Kingdom of Oil* (1980, p. 4). It
is not that we must either blame religion or oil. El-Saadawi offers us a system
in which these two concepts are linked together in the way they uphold the
patriarchal value of invisibility.

   In the article "Oil, Islam, Women," Ross reveals that the connection between
oil, women and labor is not, in fact, a new one. Ross also recognizes that there

is a link between gender and oil, and he maintains that oil is the reason behind the inequality between men and women in the Middle East. Furthermore, he argues that:

> Women have made less progress towards gender equality in the Middle East than in any other region. Many observers claim this is due to the region's Islamic traditions. I present evidence that oil, not Islam, is at fault; and that oil production has caused women to lag behind in many other countries. Oil production reduces the number of women in the labor force, which in turn reduces their political influence. As a result, oil-producing states are left with atypically strong patriarchal norms, laws, and political institutions. (2008, p. 107)

Ross blames oil for female repression because of the consequences to labor. This is a convincing argument, and enters into the same issues that El-Saadawi attends to regarding value. Like oil, women have a valued status in society. What's more, just as Ross suggests oil dictates a decline in value of women, in *Love in the Kingdom of Oil*, the initial status of the wife is replaced by an oil-powered "new type of machine" (2001, p.96). It is a machine that performs all the roles of the woman that are valued, and in some way acts to justify the woman's disappearance, as, to some extent, she is no longer needed. This passage comes at the beginning of the novel:

> The machine did not have a mouth like a woman to eat, nor a tongue to talk with. Moreover, it wrote in a clear hand. And if it was not writing, it stayed in place without moving. If it became decrepit with time, it could be exchanged, and it would be possible for him to do without the woman entirely.
> "It's a new type of machine, with buttons for writing and buttons for reading, buttons for brushing and buttons for wiping ..."
> "And who will cook for you?"
> "There's a white button which you press on and ask for any food you want. It'll give you a piping hot meal, along with salads, pickles and everything else." (2001, p. 96)

The role of the wife is one that can be transferred completely to a commodity that provides a service—because the labor of most women is not in industry, but in the role of wife. This means that the job of the wife in this novel is also a commodity, like oil, that can be purchased and has monetary, as well as symbolic, value. El-Saadawi continues this argument in *The Hidden Face of Eve*, which, although written in 1980, may still hold some truth in the twenty-first century. She argues that in Islam, "the norms of buying and selling are the ones applied to marriage" (77–78). El-Saadawi suggests that this leads to the status of a woman becoming an "unpaid servant to her husband" (144). The very same phrase is used in *Love in the Kingdom of Oil*, twenty-one years later, when she is trapped with the unknown new husband:

> The man's voice pierced her ears. An imperative tone, completely natural when a man addresses his wife. An unpaid servant. Wasn't he her husband? She didn't know exactly when he had married her. Probably he had married her in her absence and the marriage contract had been prepared without her being present. The woman didn't attend her marriage ceremony anyway, and the formalities could be completed without her existence. (2001, p. 49)

The protagonist does not remember the marriage, and feels like she is a kind of slave in an unauthorized matrimony. As well as this, though, the woman is also a slave in labor. She becomes aware of the fact "from the day she had come, she had received nothing. She never held any money in her hands" (2001, p. 41). This shows how the apparent power that she gains through her occupation is destabilized. In *Love the Kingdom of Oil*, there is no room for archaeologists. Her talents are first reassigned to carrying jars of oil because the "bowels of the earth" where the goddess lies is also the "only place" oil is found (2001, p. 24). She is placed, yet again, in a position of powerlessness and is the property of her husband, not dissimilar to the oil she carries. Therefore, could it be possible that even through the woman's status as property and commodity, she could gain a unique power? I believe it is significant to note that in *Love in the Kingdom of Oil*, the woman is associated with more than one husband. Reversing the stereotype, it is the woman who has multiple husbands, rather than the man having multiple wives. Furthermore, by belonging to many different men, the woman compromises what it means to be possession. On the one hand, being owned by many different men heightens her repression, but, on the other hand, it does the opposite, allowing her a sense of freedom normally only associated with men.

However, it is important to remember that the protagonist of this novel is not solely a wife. As aforementioned, she is, first and foremost, an archaeologist who is working on the discovery of goddesses. I would like to suggest that part of the woman's value is down to her occupation as well as her status as a woman. Her boss tells her "this department only accepts males. The work we do, I mean digging up the ground, is not suitable" (2001, p. 23). Indeed, it is no coincidence that the woman takes on an occupation of "discovering remains of old civilizations by digging up the ground" (2001, p. 8)—the same job, is it not, as the oil worker who digs up the slow, pressurized hydrocarbon from under the earth's surface? Her attempts to discover the 'ancient goddess' is mirrored throughout the novel to the discovery of oil, and, therefore, the job of men. The value of this work, like the value associated with uncovering oil, allows El-Saadawi to give the woman a sense of value only ever assigned to men, as she is in control of actively creating, instead of passively being created.

The same can be said of oil, which leads me onto the notion of oil as a valuable subject both in the Middle East but also through the Western representation of its power. This is something less surprising; less in need of validation due to its monetary value. But most accounts of oil's value in the petrofiction world comes from Western, masculine literature. This is largely because, I would argue, the Western world imports its oil from Saudi Arabia and other oil-rich nations. To show the other side of the oil process is to show its extraction, its visibility, instead of its usage in a first-world setting, where oil doesn't just have an equivalent price tag and is not only known for its ability to be used as fuel. In its raw form, oil is something dangerous but also magical—and the politics of value and shame similarly apply here. The unnamed island in *Love in the Kingdom of Oil* is a supernatural space where "everything is dreamlike" (2001, p. 34). When describing the village for the first time, El-Saadawi writes:

> On the horizon was the top of a hill. The village stretched out below it. Massive pipes tore through it, gushing with what looked like black water. There were also wide-mouthed wells from which flowed a liquid resembling mercury; there was the smell of gas mixed with that of human beings. (2001, p. 12)

El-Saadawi attacks all of the reader's senses in this scene to paint a picture of the new village and the strange attitude to oil through sound, smell, and sight. El-Saadawi goes onto say that "the one definite movement was the movement of oil. A strange movement, which appeared to be the opposite of any other movement" (2001, p. 34). Here we are like Alice peering with wide eyes through the Looking Glass, amazed to find that with every tentative step forward we go only one step backwards. It sets up the fact that rather than running invisibly underground, the opposite happens on this island, and oil runs freely over ground, which I will attend to in more detail below. Stranger than this, however, is the characters' reaction to the oil they are in. Like Alice, they are not frightened, but this is not due to a placid suspension of disbelief, but the brainwashing from powerful officials. This makes the men believe what should be water is actually oil. When the sky rains down oil droplets, they are told "the sky gives what it wants boundlessly like a religion blessing" (2001, p. 24). Oil is a religious God, live-giving, mysterious and nourishing—and, in fact, even better than water, as it "induces greater tranquillity" (2001, p. 70).

The comparison between water and oil is particularly intriguing and goes back to the initial quote, above, of the first description of the new village. The women, at first, thinks the oil is 'black water,' not oil. Then, as we proceed, water is actually replaced by oil and given similar value status. Toby Jones, in his essay "Saudi Alchemy," broaches the same subject of the alteration of water into oil, but through a unique lens. Jones reveals how the Gulf in Saudi Arabia is a space with an abundance of oil on the one hand, and a scarcity of water on the other. "The kingdom possesses one-fifth of the world's oil reserves," according to Jones, but at the same time "has no natural lakes or rivers" (2010, p. 24). In marketing oil for water, "Saudi Arabia has effectively been turning oil into water for the last four decades" (2010, p. 25). On the reverse, by "using the region's water resources to pressurise local oil fields, pumping water in to force crude oil out," Saudi Arabia has also been turning water into oil (2010, p. 25).

The movement of water into oil we see in *Love in the Kingdom of Oil*, however, has an undoubtedly religious stimulus rather than a technological or economic. Possibly acknowledging her Western audience, El-Saadawi engages with seemingly Christian metaphors. First is a modern-day Jesus turning water into oil instead of wine, and, secondly, a more frightening version of Noah's flood, where oil "seeps through the ceiling" (2001, p. 49). Both small and large scale transformations have religious implications. In fact, these are more frightening due to the fact that, although the oil seems like water, it is still a thick, black liquid which has the ability to drown people, and, furthermore, alter its form from liquid to solid, so villagers can walk on it easily. Acting as one last biblical reference, we are shown the glimpses of a world where men can walk on oil instead of water.

This is what gives the novel elements of magic realism. Oil holds mythical qualities that extend from the black and sticky fluid all the way to the electrical energy produced by oil power stations. It is not a new concept. Michael Watts claims that "petroleum is a commodity ... saturated in the mythos of the rise of the industrial West" (2001, p. 189). The use of the word 'mythos' brings to light the mystical nature of oil that is often forgotten in lieu of the "fundamental building blocks of twentieth-century hydrocarbon capitalism" (2001, p. 189). But, in my opinion, the use of the words 'mythos' and 'saturated' together is interesting. Saturated is an ambivalent term, heavy with oil-connotations which imply undesirable abundance. The mythos of oil in *Love in the Kingdom of Oil* is equally negative despite the oxymoronic association with mythos (a commonly positive notion). Ryszard Kapuscinski's book, *The Shah of Shahs*, gives a similarly supernatural insight into Arab oil, suggesting that:

Oil creates the illusion of a completely changed life, life without work, life for free, the concept of oil expresses perfectly the eternal human dream of wealth achieved through lucky accident. In this sense oil is a fairy tale and like a fairy tale a bit of a lie.

(QUOTED IN WATTS, 2001, PP. 203–4)

The 'fairy tale' that Kapuscinski identifies is not lost or shown to be a lie in El-Saadawi's work. It is for this reason that the effect of oil is even more concerning. In *Love in the Kingdom of Oil*, for instance, oil is a lifeline, keeping the island afloat, providing fluid for hydration and technology which can "perform the work of four wives at least" (2001, p. 111).

With the visibility of oil, the novel must address also the aspects of oil that need to be covered up: the problems with importing and exporting and the wars that take place due to this. El-Saadawi writes:

The battle to control oil resources and raw materials and the fight to open new consumer markets for US commodities (material and cultural) in the Third World take place through information, who controls it, who analyzes it and who is capable of counteracting it with a flow of false counter information disguised as truth. (1997, p. 181)

Here, El-Saadawi is talking about the 1991 Gulf War. The problem with the desire for countries to control and possess oil (perhaps similar to the desire to control and possess women?) is that oil does not restrict itself to country borders or barbed wire fences. It runs freely underground and under the sea, out of sight until it is brought up to the earth's surface. The value alters depending on whether it is underground or over the ground, and, furthermore, the perception of it alters depending on what state it is seen in. By this, I mean that in its transformed form as fuel, it is valuable and desired, but in its raw form, oil carries association of shame as well as affluence due to its destructive qualities. In this light, can oil really belong to a land, a company or a person, purely because of geography? If not, claiming possession of oil, or a country claiming possession of an oil-rich land, becomes subject to debate, and, inevitably, war. Oil blurs geographical boundaries (literally and metaphorically), and this is something that affects its value status. Graeme MacDonald sees it occurring in all oil literature:

Questions of oil's visibility and configuration in national literary histories ... needs to be reconceptualised on at least two fronts: geographic and generic. What constitutes an American (or indeed a British, Nigerian,

Iranian, Trinidadian, Russian etc) oil text in an age where the circularity
of literature grows increasingly international? (2012, p. 7)

Macdonald picks up on the relative 'visibility' of oil as precarious. To have a
purely American oil novel is impossible in petrofiction when both the circulation of literature and of oil is international. It is difficult to assign oil a geographical status—the USA, for instance, imported around forty percent of the
oil it consumed in 2012 (EIA). The oil then, that I consider as the feminized
object, is extracted, possessed, sold and transported all over the world, regardless of where it came from. *Love in the Kingdom of Oil* reverses this observation. Rather than oil flowing secretly beneath the earth's surface, it is painfully
visible, and the new island that the woman finds herself on is not an Elysium
of promise but a suffocating and blackened pool. Here, the blurred visual representation of oil and women in the Middle East is reattributed by El-Saadawi
in the literal blurring of the visual representation of oil itself. Instead of being
hidden; oil hides everything else.

When it comes to the shame associated with oil and women, I have suggested that this is based on its visibility, whether this is for religious or environmental motivations. However, they are two very different types of shame.
The first is the shame of the object, the women, for not making herself unseen.
The second is the shame of the subject, the shame of man for the evidence
of the destruction of the environment. The shame associated with the veil has
a long history, and I will not retell it here. Suffice to say that women in El-
Saadawi's novel are expected to wear veils; to hide as a form of religious modesty; to "conceal [their] face completely" to avoid shame (2001, p. 66). Similarly,
when talking about the veil in *The Hidden face of Eve*, El-Saadawi states that
a woman's "thigh is a source of evil, a taboo that must be hidden from sight.
From a young age, a girl is made to feel like her body is something impure,
obscene and must remain invisible, unseen" (1980, p. 46). This is very different
from the reasons given in the Quran—instead of a woman's body being something sacred, it is something impure and dangerous.

For the purposes of this paper, this debate has interesting comparisons with
oil: at once a valued substance, but seen as dangerous and shameful to encounter in its raw, veiled form. By this, I mean that when we encounter oil,
it is in a guise—whether this is in the form of plastics, fuel or electricity. Oil
also produces shame due to the environmental impact it has on the planet.
Oil spills, like the Gulf War Oil Spill, is a heightened act of shame because it is
documented as an example of the oil crisis. With the advent of documentaries
came the televised accounts of oil spills. On a daily basis, the twentieth-century human is likely to have utilized oil in one form of another. Is it not shocking,

then, that we never see it? The shame of oil means that it is made invisible, in exactly the same way as women's 'adornments' are made invisible by the veil. According to Amitav Ghosh, oil is "a matter of embarrassment verging on the unspeakable, the pornographic" (2002, p. 75), difficult to both see and speak about. The use of the word pornographic is unusual—humanizing the visibility of oil and likening it not simple to the visibility of flesh, but the sexual visibility of flesh. Like Muslim women, oil has undergone the process of negative visual imperialism.

Following Islamic conventions, the first woman to come across the protagonist exclaims, "Why don't you veil your face? Have you no shame?" (2001, p. 17). Following this encounter, the woman learns to hide her face due to the association with shame—such a crucial part of Muslim women's identity because of its religious association with Eve and the shame of Original Sin, but also due to the act of being seen. David Morgan sheds light on this desire to hide from other's gaze. In *An Embodied Eye*, he argues that "one looks away from the sight of others as if to cancel vision and become unseen" (2012, p. 23), but this is impossible. It is something El-Saadawi's hero does not understand:

> She slipped her hand under the bed and took out her shoes. They were full to the brim with oil. She emptied them and beat them against one another. She placed the chisel in the bag, along with the map. She put the strap over her shoulder and made off before any eye could notice her. She closed her eyelids as she ran as if closing her eyes would conceal her from other's eyes. (2001, p. 66)

The protagonist wrongly assumes that by closing her own eyes, she will not be seen by others. It is worth pointing out here that, paradoxically, by closing her eyes the woman imitates the lack of sight that is produced by the veil. Recall the quote from the Quran, which first demanded that women 'reduce some of their vision'. Wearing the veil reveals only the eyes, but obscures some of the wearers peripheral vision. By closing her eyes, the woman does submit to one of the veil's purposes, even if she cannot hide her own face. Furthermore, the heavily repeated image of eyes in the novel highlights the importance of surveillance as well as visibility. The woman is not simply under orders to veil herself, she is under constant supervision which adds to the dyad of shaming and ashamed. As Morgan points out, 'shaming is a visual procedure, a way of looking, and being ashamed is a way of being seen, a way of appearing' (2012, p. 3). The woman in *Love in the Kingdom of Oil* does not have the power to look back, as she "never used to look at other men" (2001, p. 117). She can only be looked at, only be ashamed.

This takes us back to the discussion of the front cover of the novel. Although the image seems to reverse the dialogue of the masculine gaze by having a man's picture hanging on the wall, it is somehow compromised. It is significant that the woman has her back to the painting, and is not subjecting the man to her feminine gaze. This means that, in fact, the only gaze that is occurring is that of the man in the painting onto the woman—thereby returning the hierarchy back to normal. Furthermore, her flowing black hair is evocative of the flowing oil that permeates the novel. It thereby also symbolically establishes the man's authority on the world of oil. The fact that the man's painting is hung on the wall, on account of this, makes it seem less like the woman's property and more like an important figure who is surveying his surroundings. The woman is literally and metaphorically unveiled, as is the world of oil. Sanaz Fotouhi's analysis in *Changing the Cover Page* concerning the shifting imagery of book covers is crucial here. Fotouhi marks a shift from the unveiling of women to the unveiling of the mystery of the city. In this case, it is the mystery and potential of oil that provides the new source of 'unveiling.' Fotouhi's observations in the concluding chapter are helpful in understanding the links between the cover page and the growing misinterpretation of Muslim women in the West.

Surveillance and Escape

In a special issue of *Imaginations*, "Sighting Oil," Andrew Pendakis and Sheena Wilson cleverly point out that there are different levels of visibility concerning oil. They claim: "sight, site, cite: sighting oil requires this triple passage through vision, space and discourse" (2012, p. 4). All three of these passages are examined in *Love in the Kingdom of Oil*. Sight: what we can see and what is kept from view; site: how oil is located in space and how the women are located in (and, of course, restricted to) space; cite: how El-Saadawi writes oil into the pages of a book and how oil is documented through writing.

As briefly mentioned above, as well as living with forced invisibility under the masculine gaze, the woman is also subject to constant surveillance. It is this surveillance that comprises her ability to escape even more than her subjection to the veil. Where the first section looked at the object, this section looks at the *subject*, the viewer, and how the gaze and surveillance are inflicted upon the subject to gain authority. I turn now to the novel's setting, the island, which is heightened masculine surveillance. It becomes reminiscent of the modern day CCTV and 'big-brother' phenomenon, as it is not long before the protagonist "realised she was under observation, that their ears could hear her voice" (2001, p. 61). El-Saadawi writes "the surveillance was masterly" (2001,

p. 63). This insinuates the power and control associated with surveillance, but also the machismo with the word 'master.' What is interesting about the surveillance in *Love in the Kingdom of Oil* is that the woman suffers from both visual and audio surveillance. The novel steps over the boundary of visual documentation such as CCTV, and enters into a more personal surveillance through what Western readers might associate with phone-tapping. And, even more unsettling, is somehow the surveillance can attend to speech before it is even verbalized. We are told that the watcher "could hear her voice even if it had not emerged from her mouth" (2001, pp. 61–2). El-Saadawi is hinting that, in this world, even freedom of thought is stifled. We know that freedom of speech is something important to our author, and something that was taken away from her when she was imprisoned for publishing a feminist magazine in 1981 called *Confrontation*. In her writings, El-Saadawi often dwells on the notion of observation. When El-Saadawi was put on the 'death list' from 1988 to 1993, she remarked how "at one time the enemy was visible, we could see him wearing a uniform, carrying a gun, occupying our land"; the enemy "had a name and all of us knew it. But this hidden face, unknown to us, without a name, how could one fight against it?" (2002, pp. 16–7) This fear and paranoia, I would argue, is mirrored in her novel through the use of surveillance.

From the moment the woman leaves her home, she is subject to surveillance. It turns the island into a construction similar to Michel Foucault's model of the panopticon. The panopticon is an architectural circular structure that is based on Jeremy Bentham's nineteenth-century design for a new type of institution to house peripheral members of society. These buildings included prisons, hospitals and asylums. The design is founded on the notion of visibility and power dynamics that are determined by being seen or unseen. Instead of through violence, power is gained through observation. In Bentham's model, a man resides in a central watchtower, encircled by prisoners who are individually caged. Foucault writes how the panopticon is a "segmented, immobile, frozen space. Each individual is fixed in his place" (2004, p. 551). And, like in *Love in the Kingdom of Oil*, "the gaze is alert everywhere" (Foucault, 2004, p. 551). The guard's power comes from location and height—in his ability to see everything without ever being seen by the prisoners. Similarly, the woman, for the majority of the novel, does not realize she is being constantly watched, and neither do the other women on the island. Despite being covered by a veil; they are still watched at all times. Equally, prisoners are encased in four walls but are still able to be seen by the man in the watchtower. It is the way to maintain social control and policing those who need policing. Foucault's panopticon goes further than Bentham's design, as the people in the prison cells are unable to see the watchtower—they are blackened out so there is always the potential for surveillance. In this way, the prisoners begin to monitor their own behavior;

"the inmates should be caught up in a power situation of which they are themselves the bearers" (Foucault, 2004, p. 555). We may be able to find parallels in
the way that in *Love in the Kingdom of Oil*, it is the women in the novel who
actually enforce the protagonist's wearing of the veil, not the men. When she
is first encountered, it is a woman who asks her: "Why don't you veil your face?
Have you no shame?" (2001, p. 17).

In this way, sight in the panopticon is not only about observation, but also
about the way the observations are then utilized to inflict repression and alter
behavior. The beginning lines of the novel make my point perfectly clear:
"women do not go on leave" without their husband's permission (2001, p. 6).
The observation through the panopticon is not done in isolation, but then requires restrictions in terms of space and actions, and thus leads to changes
in the way discipline is handled. The woman, eventually, conforms to societal
expectations and begins to wear a veil—without the patriarchal forces having
to tell her to do so. However, I want to complicate Foucault's model here. The
panopticon metaphor that Foucault describes does not take into account the
woman's movement in space, which is so important to this novel. Foucault's
model relies on institutions such as prisons and asylums, but the woman does
not always remain in these spaces. She is, first and foremost, the woman who
ran away from home. Her discipline, arguably, is her own choice. She begins to
wear the veil not because she has altered her behavior as Foucault imagines,
but because she recognizes that she is able to use it to her advantage:

> However, a new idea came into her mind. She could hide her face com-
> pletely from people's view, without anyone seeing her face. It was a wom-
> an's right to conceal her face completely without anybody pursuing her.
> However, in her case the situation was different. She was a bare-faced
> woman. The newspapers had published her picture and her full name
> and address.
>
> (EL-SAADAWI, 2001, P.66)

The veil, then, becomes a way to hide from observation at the same time as
being something repressive and restricting. I believe that this adds hope in
the novel because it offers the chance of escape: both from surveillance and a
life of repression. This is something Foucault does account for: invisibility as
power, but not for the prisoners—for the person in the watchtower. In this way,
the woman undergoes a category transfer, whereby she chooses to embrace
invisibility as a prisoner, but with the power associated with the man in the
watchtower (who, it is important to recognize, does not even need to be in the
tower for the surveillance to work. He can be invisible, like the woman under
the veil, and both can hide their identity and, as such, escape surveillance).

Therefore, the woman in El-Saadawi's novel learns that she can use the veil to make herself invisible, hide her face so that she can escape the confines of her panopticon and the surveillance of the men around her. The double-constriction (surveillance and veiling) actually act to cancel each other out. If the men in Foucault's watchtower were all wearing the same outfits and had their faces covered, the system would collapse as they would not be able to distinguish from one to the other. In other words, there are two ways to make the self invisible. You can either become invisible, or you can blind the observer. Rather than "challenging the west by hiding [her] hair or face behind a veil", as El-Saadawi accuses modern women of doing, the protagonist challenges her own surveillance by adopting a disguise (1997, p. 96). Subsequently, the walls of the panopticon break down in *Love in the Kingdom of Oil*.

By utilizing the black coat of oil *and* the veil, the woman seems to succeed in using invisibility as a form of power. She is even able to reverse the role of surveillance "to hear [her husband's] opinion of her in her absence" (2001, p. 71). However, as the novel is persistent in its desire to challenge its readers, its ending is no exception. When we reach the end of the novel, a flip occurs and we are taken back to the beginning, given the information we have known all along, that "the woman went on leave" (2001, p. 132). The narrative returns us to the very first newspaper headline, which immediately gives the impression of failed progress. Have we come no further than where we started from? The speaker lingers on the phrase, slowly highlighting its cryptic definition:

> "As you see, the woman went on leave."
>
> "Yes, these cases have become totally commonplace. One in three women goes on leave like this."
>
> "It is a new illness?"
>
> "Yes. In psychiatry, we call it schizophrenia."
>
> [...]
>
> "Do you mean a dual personality?"
>
> "No. With a dual personality, the woman and the other person are two who are forced to accompany one another. With schizophrenia, the woman and herself and that other man become one person." (2001, pp. 132–3)

This sheds doubt on the reliability of the whole novel, as seen through the eyes of the woman. If readers were unsure what episodes were real and what were imaginary, now we are even more so. By giving the woman potential schizophrenia at the last page, the distorting of male characters (such as her second husband) is no longer a female reaction to the oppression of men but symbolizes a new condition whereby all blurring occurs on a psychological level rather than El-Saadawi's narrative licence.

Conclusion

If the woman in El-Saadawi's novel does have schizophrenia, although this may simply be another excuse given by the patriarchal forces in order to rationalize her behavior, it is possible that she never left the bed we find her in at the end of the narrative. Her escape from the ties of patriarchy could be entirely imaginary, as the novel ends with her contemplation that "as long as he has the ability to laugh, there is no call to runaway, at least not tonight. She can go on sleeping and tomorrow she will try again" (2001, p. 134). The act of running away is one that we have already seen her do, so it is possible that this is a flashback to the beginning of her journey. Equally, it is possible that the second life is her real life after all, as half-way through the novel it is suggested that "perhaps she had been born here and she didn't have another life" (2001, p. 41).

However, complicating matters further, the meaning changes depending on whether we assume she is with her first or second husband. If she is with the second, then she is planning her *second* escape and the claim of schizophrenia is unfounded. If it is the first, however, then the previous point stands: she is suffering from an illness that makes her believe she has run away and acquired herself a new husband, a new life, and a new found freedom in invisibility. The novel obscures all men together in a way which makes it impossible to offer a clear answer to this question, and this is arguably part of the problem that El-Saadawi is revealing. Is the woman sick, is she a victim or a hero, or is she like every other Muslim woman attempting to gain a sense of vision and end repression?

Nonetheless, *Love in the Kingdom of Oil* ends with the woman re-embraced in the prevailing panoptical powers, which have emerged in a different guise. An exchange takes place from the prison to mental hospital, housing another group of people eligible for the panopticon. The protagonist in *Love in the Kingdom of Oil*, then, despite the advancements made through the powers of the unseen, remains in a space of surveillance, and trapped in the identity and visual representation of the Muslim woman that El-Saadawi has spent her life fighting against. However, internally, she is free: the schizophrenia actually allows her to escape surveillance *and* become unseen through her changing identities. The visual imperialism, then, is challenged by El-Saadawi in one final rejection of the West: the power of the unconscious beneath the visual.

References

The Quran.

El-Saadawi, N. (1980). *The Hidden Face of Eve.* New York: Zed Books.

El-Saadawi, N. (1997). *The Nawal El-Saadawi Reader.* New York: Zed Books.

El-Saadawi, N. (2001). *Love in the Kingdom of Oil.* London: Saqi Books.

El-Saadawi, N. (2002). *Walking through Fire.* London: Zed Books.

Foucault, M. (2004). Discipline and Punish. In Rivkin, J. & Ryan, M. (Eds), *Literary Theory: An Anthology*, 2 edition. (pp. 549–566). Malden: Blackwell Publishing Ltd.

Ghosh, A. (2002). *The Imad and the Indian.* New Delhi: Ravi Dayal.

Jones, T. (2010). Saudi Alchemy: water in oil, oil into water. *Middle East Report, 254,* 24–29.

MacDonald, G. (2012). Oil and World Literature: Special "Petrofiction" Issue. *American Book Review, 33*(3).

Morgan, D. (2012). *The Embodied Eye.* London: University of California Press.

Pendakis, A. & Wilson, S. (2012). Sight, Site, Cite: Oil in the Field of Vision. *Imaginations, 3*(2).

Ross, M. (2008). Oil, Islam and Women. *The American Political Science Review, 102*(1), 107–123.

Watts, M. (2001). Petro-violence: community, extraction and political ecology of a mythic community. In Peluso, N. L. (Ed), *Violent Environments.* (pp. 189–212). London: Cornell University Press.

CHAPTER 5

'World Hijab Day': Positioning the *Hijabi* in Cyberspace*

Raihanah M. M.

Introduction

This chapter sets out to investigate how *hijabis* are positioned in cyberspace; *hijabis* used in this essay is defined as Muslim women who use the head covering as part of their outer garment when in public or in the company of non-familial male members. In addition, it also sets out to examine how *hijabis* are using digital media to promote greater presence as practicing Muslim women in the current globalized age while raising awareness of *hijab* as a tool for self-identification and self-documentation.

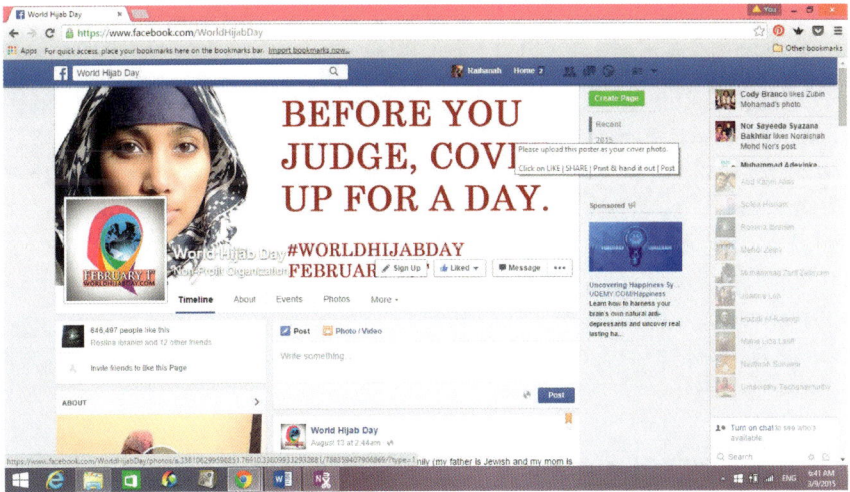

FIGURE 5.1   *The facebook page of 'World Hijab Day' (WHD).*

*   This writing of this chapter was funded by a grant investigating the psycho-social climate of vulnerability in popular culture provided by Universiti Kebangsaan Malaysia. [GUP-2014-024]

For the purpose of discussion, I have chosen the Facebook page 'World Hijab Day' as a case study. The Facebook page was set up by a Bangladeshi migrant, Nazma Khan who experienced continuous verbal and physical discrimination as a schoolgirl in the Bronx, United States. As she admits, her turbulent years of growing up in the Bronx as a *hijabi* left her in a constant state of fear and self-doubt: "At one point, students literally kicked me and spat at me both inside and outside the school ... I was so scared that I used to enter the school from the boys' entrance instead of the girls." (Nazma Khan, 2014) Her "lowest point," she says, was when an English teacher in middle school in the Bronx joined in and "made fun of the way [she] dressed." (ibid.) Being a college student in New York post 9/11 further exacerbated her situation, as she endured verbal abuses which were more political in nature with taunts of "Osama Bin Laden" and "terrorist". In an 11-minute emotional video on YouTube, she explains the genesis of the website and Facebook page as "a support system where Muslim women could share their *hijab* experience." She also draws out her vision of how the 'World Hijab Day' website and Facebook page can be a tool to promote greater awareness and an exercise on empathy for the dignity of being a *hijabi*: "I thought if I could invite women of all faith, Muslim and non-Muslim, to walk in my shoes, just for one day, perhaps ... things would change." Her exercise at positioning her private narrative within the larger non-Muslim context has gained tremendous support as the Facebook site has received over seven hundred thousand followers. (See screenshot above)

Through a study of first-person brief "testimonies" (Jones, 2014, p. 21) submitted by participants of the World Hijab Day Facebook page (thereafter, WHD), this chapter investigates the positioning of veiling as a "micro-narrative" (Rettberg, 2014, p. 35) within the current macro-narrative of the Islamophobic world. My focus is to show that despite the grave misrepresentation today regarding *hijab* and its purpose, the *hijabis* are endowed with clarity of voice and online presence to exercise their sense of self agency in the act of veiling as seen from their testimonies and selfies.

Of *Hijab, Haya'* and the Politics of Positioning

The current politics associated with being a Muslim minority in a majority non-Muslim context informs us that nothing is apolitical and nothing is sacred. From the near violent act of burning 2998 copies of the Islamic holy book by the Florida Pastor in 2013 as a demonstration against the 9/11 atrocities (*Aljazeera America*, 2013), to the distasteful and insensitive caricature of what is supposed to be the prophet of Islam published in *Charlie Hebdo*, the

French magazine in 2014, and the threat to Arizona Muslim worshippers by armed bikers in front of the Arizona Mosque in 2015 (Hanrahan, 2015), Muslim minorities continue to be subjected to damaging and distorted public misrepresentation in the western world. Charles Taylor's (1994, p. 25) forewarning of the consequences of misrecognition warrants attention: "a person or group of people can suffer real damage, real distortion, if the people or society around them mirror back to them a confining or demeaning or contemptible picture of themselves." Hence the kind of misrecognition imposed on the Muslim minorities today creates a climate of an "oppressive [and] imprisoning" (ibid.) consequence.

Similar damaging and distortive misrepresentation is also experienced by the minority Muslim *hijabi*. As seen in the 2015 case of Tahera Ahmad, a Muslim Chaplain for North Western University, Muslims with *hijab* can be subjected to scrutiny for their continued choice of attire. Tahera was verbally abused by a United Airlines flight attendant and refused an unopened can of Coke least she "use[s] it as a weapon" (Rummana Hussin, 2015). The unsaid in the way she was treated is based fundamentally on her attire. She was judged as a threat and the poor service she received on flight illustrates the othering that she was subjected to because of her *hijab*. This overt declaration of faith in the form of veiling opens the *hijabi* to be "publicly targeted as a threat to people." (ibid.)

The *hijab* today has become such a contested aspect of a Muslim woman's sense of public image that the politics associated with the piece of cloth goes against the fundamentals of veiling. From being labelled as "second class citizen" and 'offending' "feminist" for our choices (Braybooke, 2011: 10), to being viewed as a product of "cultural inferiority" (Gabriel, 2011, p. 12) and "a symbol of the oppression of women in Islam" (Gabriel & Hannan, 2011, p. 2; Contractor, 2011), *hijabis* continue to be scrutinised for their choices, or, lack of. Albeit the "unveiling of women has been part of the general social metamorphosis" (Gabriel & Hannan, 2011, p. 1) of the Western world, the continued veiling of women which has historical and religious foundation should remain normalized. It should be "a matter of women's human rights to wear what they want" (Asser, 2006, p. np).

In the current context, the veil has entered the public domain within the discourse of multiculturalism and has become a tool for the detractors of Islam to misrecognize the *hijabi* as lacking freedom and self-empowerment. In 'Visual Discourses of (Un)veiling: Revisiting Women of Allah' in this volume, Zeiny demonstrates how Shirin Neshat's veiled women in her photography have been misinterpreted as silent, passive and victim. However, using the lens of multiculturalism, the discussion of the *hijab* needs to take into consideration the politics of positioning which denote, "the notion that since our understanding of the world and ourselves is socially constructed, we must devote special attention to the differing ways individuals from diverse social backgrounds construct knowledge and make meaning." (Kincheloe & Steinberg, 1997, p. 206). In other words, politics of positioning must take into account both external and internal forces that continue to create a tension in the individual and/or minority group's public identity construction (Raihanah, 2009). The former, i.e. external forces, includes the hegemony imposed on the individual from without by the powers that be, thus robbing the individual/minority of her rights. The latter, i.e. internal force, signals the attempts at self-positioning made by the individual/minority which subsequently signifies the availability of social and political agency as a member of a minority, and her actions must be read within the "differing ways" (ibid.) she constructs her public image. This chapter expands the discussion on the latter and investigates the mechanism that the *hijabi* is endowed with to create such internal force of change.

Within the context of Muslim veiling, the politics of positioning plays a crucial role in the escalating tension between the public misrecognition as seen in today's digital media and the personal/private demand by the *hijabi* for greater acceptance and recognition of her rights to dress accordingly. Examples of the latter can be seen in the two court cases in 2015 where *hijabis* from Germany and America, respectively, won their rights to use the *hijab* in their workplace (See Smale 2015; Liptak 2015). In both cases, the *hijabis* chose to adorn the head scarf and demanded that their respective employer respected their choice. However, in March 2017 European Union Court of Justice ruled against two other Muslim women, one in France and the other in Belgium, who were dismissed by their respective employers for wearing the *hijab* (Aljazeera, 2017). The court of justice states that companies can ban their employees from wearing all forms of "visible religious symbols" provided the company has an internal rule banning the wearing of "any political, philosophical or religious sign" (El Aabedy, 2017). The latter move by the EU Court of Justice draws criticism from various religious minorities including the Jewish and Muslim organizations (Amrani, 2017).

Within the Islamic tradition, veiling is included in the notion of *haya'*[1] which takes into consideration notions of "self-respect, modesty, bashfulness

---

1   As narrated by Abu Hurairah (r.a.), Prophet Muhammad (peace and blessings be upon him) said, "Faith (Belief) consists of more than sixty sub-divisions or branches (i.e. parts). And *al-haya'* (this term *al-haya'* covers a large number of concepts which are to be taken together; amongst them are self-respect, modesty, bashfulness, and honor etc.) is a part of faith." (In Muhammad Muhsin Khan, 1997, p. 59) The hadith, or sayings from Prophet Muhammad (peace and blessings be upon him) quoted is from an authentic narration in which he

and honour" (In Muhammad Muhsin Khan, 1997, p. 59). As echoed by Akhtar (2011, p. 149), "despite revolutionising fashion trends and cultural norms, the basic essence of modesty encouraged by the Islamic religion remains the underpinning philosophy behind observing the *hijab*." *Hijab* then is both the tool to exercise one's faith in public and the means to demonstrate a greater sense of *haya'* or modesty within the parameters of Islam. Thus, *haya'*, within the context of veiling, is the governing principle for the way a *hijabi* chooses to dress in public as prescribed in the Quran.[2] It denotes the public act of positioning oneself within the boundaries of the faith. It's not an act that challenges the social and cultural convention of a land or people as argued in many western contexts. (See Smale 2015; Liptak 2015; Secor 2005). In identifying the verse from which the act of veiling is described in the holy Quran, the sacred text for Muslims, Khola Hasan (2011, p. 115) identifies a more pressing issue, the availability of public space for the *hijabi*.

----

identified two ideas. Firstly, the notion of "faith" or belief in Islam is broad ranging and has many parts. Secondly, one of the "parts" of a believer's belief system is *al-haya'* which can be loosely defined as a manifestation of positive characteristics including modesty, bashfulness and, being aware of one's self respect, dignity and honor. The unsaid in this hadith is that when one practices a sense of *haya'* one is also practicing one's "faith" as a Muslim. Scholars discussing the notion of *haya'* also consider the awareness of God's presence in our lives: "Once the believer realizes that Allah (SWT) is watching us all the time and we will have to answer to every move we make in this *dunya* (world), he would not neglect any order from Allah or His Messenger (saws). The stronger this sense of *haya* becomes, the more it motivates one to make sure that Allah (SWT) doesn't see him doing anything prohibited". (The Islamic Bulletin, p. 21)

2   There are two important verses in the Quran regarding the issue of veiling. The requirements came in the 17th year of prophethood: The first is as follows: "O Prophet, tell your wives and your daughters and the women of the believers to bring down over themselves [part] of their outer garments. That is more suitable that they will be known and not be abused. And ever is Allah Forgiving and Merciful" (33:59); the second is this: "And tell the believing women to reduce [some] of their vision and guard their private parts and not expose their adornment except that which [necessarily] appears thereof and to wrap [a portion of] their headcovers over their chest and not expose their adornment except to their husbands, their fathers, their husbands' fathers, their sons, their husbands' sons, their brothers, their brothers' sons, their sisters' sons, their women, that which their right hands possess, or those male attendants having no physical desire, or children who are not yet aware of their private aspects of women. And let them not stamp their feet to make known what they conceal of their adornment. And turn to Allah in repentance, all of you, O believers, that you might succeed." (24:31). This essay does not set out to problematize the validity of the *hijab* rule on contemporary Muslim women. Rather the essay investigates how *hijabis* position themselves in the cyberspace both through their choice of profiling and short write up as seen on the 'World Hijab Day' Facebook page.

Hijab as the Muslim woman's public dress is referred to twice in the Quran, but as *Khimar* (head scarf) and *jilbab* (shawl or cloak). I see these verses as normative commandments, instructing women how to dress in public. But I also see these verses as providing implicit permission for women to enter the public sphere freely and confidently, and in the context of modest clothing, decency and prudent conduct in public.

At this juncture, the point raised by Khola Hasan (2011) warrants attention. The issue of entrance into "the public sphere freely and confidently" (ibid.) for the *hijabi* signifies the availability of public space and public role for the Muslim women in society which validates public engagement for Muslim women within the parameters of Islam. An ethnographic study by Julie Billaud (2009, p. 121) likewise, illustrates how Afghan women's use of *chadari* to create public visibility, for instance, has simultaneously allowed them to "become legitimate actors in public sphere." The current discussion extends the investigation into the visibility of *hijabis* by focusing on another public domain, cyberspace.

There are numerous articles in the digital media today that deal with the politics of veiling in the western context and each one, most times, shows the *hijabi* being "spoken for more often than she speaks for herself" (Lewis, 2009, p. 70), and is accompanied by a provocative and misleading image of a woman clad in a full-face veil as a two-dimensional illustration of a *hijabi*. Consider the article by Stephen Hume (2015), the *Vancouver Sun*'s columnist. Albeit championing equality for Muslim women in Canada in the face of the former Prime Minister Stephen Harper's controversial statement about the *niqab* as "the product of a culture that is 'anti-women,'" (Bryden, 2015), Hume's article equates *niqab* with *hijab* using an image of a woman in *niqab*. This can be seen from the caption underneath the image that states: "Any threat to the Canadian way is not from Muslim women wearing veils, Stephen Hume writes." (See Photo at http://www.vancouversun.com/news/Stephen+Hume+Woman+hating+culture+column+provokes+explosive+response/10900508/story.html).

To begin with, despite face veiling or *niqab* being permissible in Islam, veiling or *hijab* as used in the Sunni Muslim context denotes the covering of the Muslim's hair and body, except for face and hand (See Sayed Khalil Tabatabai, 2012). Hume's article, while attempting to present a more positive discussion of the issue, fails through his choice of image. By placing a picture of a woman in full face veil and captioning it as "veiling", he has homogenized all discussion of veiling to the *niqab*. This type of grave misrepresentation in the digital world, especially when read by non-Muslims who have very limited access to actual *hijabi* can lead to the damaging effect of misrecognition as forewarned by Taylor (1994). In the current discussion, through the testimonies and selfies by *hijabis* on 'World Hijab Day', the heterogeneity of veiling will be explored.

An image that has gone viral, has more currency than the truth. A case in point can be seen in the best photograph of the day for the 7th of May 2015 on *The Guardian* online newspaper which included among others the picture of a person in yellow neon *burqa*. Known as the "High Visibility Burqa" by Marco Biagini which was seen at the 2015 Venice Biennale, the yellow neon outfit resembles a fireman's uniform. This type of provoking misrepresentation of the face veiling is anything but apolitical. As Noah Feldman (2015, p. np) writes in *Bloomberg View* about the work:

> First, it's worth imaging the piece as a statement warning against Islam and criticizing immigration, views that aren't hard to find in contemporary Europe. According to this interpretation, the piece is meant to draw emergency attention ("Danger, Danger") to the phenomenon of European Muslim immigration. The piece would then be noting that traditionally dressed Muslims are highly visible, and warning that their presence shouldn't be normalized.

Such a curation of the image of veiling, albeit face veiling, speaks to the heart of the politics of othering and marginalization. As Reina Lewis (2009, p. 70) argues, the continued objectification of the Muslim veiled women also functions as an orientalist "cipher for the mysteries and threats of Islam." Furthermore, this kind of Islamophobic perspective in understanding the issue of the veil continues to damage the sanctity of an otherwise purposeful and sacred act of servitude.

As stated earlier, *hijab* or the veil within Islam is an "outer wear ... that preserves modesty between the sexes when outside the gender-secluded space of the Islamically structured home (or when non-familial men are present in the domestic space ...)." (Lewis, 2009, p. 74). This piece of clothing functions as a means of ensuring privacy for the *hijabi* to live her public life to the fullest. What needs to be kept in mind is that the issue of modesty or *haya'* is not sacrosanct to the Muslim community. All Abrahamic religions including Christianity, Judaism and Islam emphasize on the importance of modesty in everyday life. In a recent article in the *Catholic Herald*, Mary O'Regan (2015) writes about the value of veiling for the Catholics: "When a woman covers her hair, she is obscuring her crowning glory, and when a whole congregation of women do so they are voluntarily covering their beauty so that we are better placed to adore the glory of Our Lord in the Most Holy Eucharist." The image accompanying this article shows a young woman in a mantilla at mass.

(See image at http://www.catholicherald.co.uk/commentandblogs/2015/04/14/
women-need-to-embrace-the-empowering-veil-again/) Unlike the lady with a
lovely lace cloth covering her head, the images of the veiled Muslim woman in
the digital media, as illustrated in Hume's (2015) article, is largely politicised for
the disempowerment and disenfranchisement that she apparently is subjected
to by the patriarchal and "anti-woman" culture she is raised in. Similarly, on
their first trip overseas on May 20, 2017, President Trump and his wife visited
Saudi Arabia where she refused to cover her head but four days later in Vatican
she covered with a black lace cover. Here, her choice to wear the veil at the
Vatican is not seen as forced but if she were to wear it in Saudi Arabia, it is
forced, and would be considered as an imposition. Hence, the hegemonic misrepresentation of *hijabi* in current digital media deepens the schism between
minority Muslim *hijabi* and mainstream society. The latter, mainstream society, relies largely on today's media for their mis/understanding of Islam and
the world of the *hijabi*, and the former, *hijabi*, continues to struggle for greater
public recognition.

At this point, it is crucial to acknowledge the many societies that continue
to subjugate and victimize their women in the name of Islam.[3] The issue between personal choice as an act of faith and societal enforcement of the faith
is real in many Muslim contexts. In some Muslim majority countries, Muslim
women experience acute subordination by the patriarchal tradition which
imposes veiling as a mandatory act (See Shirazi, 2001). Such imposition is in

---

3   Consider Mahboba Rawi, the diasporic Afghani Australian who as a teenager had to leave her
    homeland in secrecy in a burka or a complete head, and body covering, to save herself from
    being prosecuted for speaking up against the atrocities of the Taliban. Her moving account
    captured in her memoir *Mahboba's Promise* illustrates the extent Muslim girls must endure
    to survive in this world (Raihanah et al., 2012). Another teenager who faced a more gruesome
    treatment in the hands of the Taliban, is the Nobel Prize nominee, Malala Yousafzai. In her
    memoir I am Malala, the young lady recounts the attempted assassination on her life and
    the lives of her parents by the Taliban. She did not denounce her faith in the name of the
    brutality she and her family were subjected to in their hometown in Swatvalley, Northwest
    Pakistan. Rather she acknowledges the ignorance and cowardly actions of her perpetrator,
    and promises to strive on. The images of both *hijabis* on the social media as beautifully veiled
    Muslims whose faces are not hidden from the public and whose public presence continue to
    serve a higher purpose, of education and equality for women and children in the world. The
    cheerful faces of the two survivors of Taliban abuse clad in colorful *hijab* seen in the digital
    media are a constant reminder that firstly, more needs to be done to ensure the image of the
    hijabis in the 21st century media remains positive, despite the atrocities committed by minor-
    ity groups in the name of Islam. Secondly, continued efforts need to be made to ensure *hijabis*
    living in non-Muslim contexts are given the public rights to position themselves within the
    contours of *haya'*.

contradiction to the basis of Islam which represents 'submission' with awareness. This chapter does not set out to investigate the various social and cultural environments that continue to subordinate Muslim women in the name
of faith. Nor does it explicate the numerous websites that celebrate women's
choice to not put on the *hijab*. Suffice to say, when Muslim women are not
given the choice to veil, the act then does not represent their true submission
to the governing principles of the faith as they perform the act to merely please
their fellow country men and women.

Today, researches on being a *hijabi* in the globalized world take into account
a more dynamic perspective of the tension and challenges we experience in
the highly fluid digital landscape where one's sense of public self can be misrepresented as the truth and broadcasted into the cyber world within seconds.
In such a digital ecosystem, the physical manifestation of the truth is not given
as much attention as the curation of an image. Faegheh Shirazi's (2001: p. 180)
investigation into the representation of hijab in modern culture best sums the
many signifiers that are associated with the *hijab*:

> On the one hand, the veil is a simple garment that millions of women
> deal with in their daily lives as a matter of habit, ... On the other hand, the
> veil is enormously important symbol, as it carries thousands of years of
> religious, sexual, social and political significance within its folds.... Some
> people think of the veil as erotic and romantic, others perceive it as a
> symbol of oppression, still others consider it a sign of piety, modesty or
> purity.... The various connotations it has, the many emotions it arouses,
> testify to its continuing, perhaps even growing, significance in the mod-
> ern world.

In the explication of the testimonies and selfies on WHD, we are given a firsthand account into how *hijabis* choose to describe and position themselves,
both as individuals with a distinct personality and fashion sense, and as a
member of the Muslim collective.

'World Hijab Day': Positioning a Counter Narrative

The participants for WHD come from 140 countries including many non-Muslim
majority countries such as Angola, Bhutan, Comoro Islands, Ecuador, Greece,
Haiti, Italy, Japan, Korea, Latvia, Mexico, Norway, Philippines, Suriname,
Trinidad and Tobago, and Vietnam. The testimonies are from both Muslims
and non-Muslims. The former are *hijabis* while the latter are non-Muslims who

identified themselves as the following: Catholic, Mennonite and Mormon, devout Christian, Jewish, Atheist, Agnostic and Pagan. This latter group were encouraged to spend a day as a *hijabi* on February the 1st of each year since its inception in 2013, and share their testimonies on WHD. Both groups presented their micro-narratives accompanied by a selfie. Based on the countless postings certain shared patterns emerge in terms of the themes of the posts.

Themes from the non-Muslims who attempted to put on the *hijab* for a day include a political stance as seen where a young lady from China posts her pictures without and with the *hijab* in retaliation against public ignorance. As she says, she is inspired to stand in "Solidarity with our millions Muslim *hijabi* sisters who are discriminated on daily basis." She also posts a Chinese billboard which labels *hijabis* as "uncivilized" and "prehistoric." (See http://worldhijab-day.com/gallery/)

Similar theme of "solidarity" with fellow "sisters" of different faith comes through in the posts by Christian women who donned on the *hijab* for World Hijab Day. As Laura Bohlander who identifies herself as "a devout Christian" from the United Kingdom says in her story about wearing the *hijab*: "We live in a world where being religious has become a sign of stupidity, of a servile attitude or weakness of mind. I believe that [the *hijab*] is a sign of immense strength" (http://worldhijabday.com/hijab-experience-of-a-devout-christian/). An unnamed African American lady, for instance, explains her participation as an act of creating commonality in the face of diversity between people. As she says, "I am a Christian woman and today, I will stand in solidarity with my Hijabi Muslim sisters by wearing a Hijab as well." Her awareness that the *hijab* can be a bridging tool is evident in this statement: "I hope that we can all learn that no matter what your race, faith, creed, religion, nationality, ethnicity, gender, age, sexuality, political party, ability or disability, we are all "fearfully and wonderfully made." The crucial statement of "we are all fearfully and wonderfully made" signals solidarity beyond external appearance (http://worldhijab-day.com/gallery/). Similar acts of solidarity can be seen across the globe when non-Muslim women put on the outer garments upon entering mosques.

In the next example, Kerri-Jo Stewart, a Christian woman from Canada, posts a picture of her 8-year old who joint in the celebration of World Hijab Day by "sporting her favourite scarf." Albeit the experience was not altogether positive, given the "names" "she got called" in school, the impact has been tremendous leaving 8-year old Emma to want "her school" to be involved in next year's World Hijab Day celebration. Emma's experience indicates that irrespective of how she was viewed previously, the minute she wears the scarf she is inadvertently associated with the politics of veiling which Muslim *hijabis* experience.

Many other non-Muslim women who participated in the World Hijab Day experienced similar interrogation by their communities (http://worldhijabday .com/major-life-lesson-eyes-opened-subtleties-racism/). The interreligious learning young Emma and other non-*hijabis* have experienced echoes the true lesson of recognition politics that Taylor (1994, p. 72) speaks of: "Perhaps we don't need to ask whether it's something that others can demand from us as a right. We might simply ask whether this is the way we ought to approach others."

A Mormon lady, had a slightly tense experience with some members of her church as she chose to celebrate the 'World Hijab Day' on February 1st 2015 which happened to be a Sunday by wearing the *hijab* to church. As she narrates, "a few days before WHD, I posted about it in our congregation's Facebook group. I posted a link to the WHD website and said, "this is why I will be wearing a headscarf in church on Sunday." My hope was to prevent causing a disruption, because most of the congregants would not need to ask me about it during the service." The discussion on her congregation FB is equally telling of the enmity the *hijab* is viewed with. As she states, one of the members "strongly disagreed" with her decision and felt that she was jeopardizing her church membership by "making a political statement and protesting our church leaders". However, most of the church members supported her decision citing "scriptures from the Bible" and "historical examples of Catholic and Baptist women covering their heads in church" (http://worldhijabday.com/the-whd-movement-building-bridges/). This dialogue among members of the congregation created opportunities for an awareness raising exercise akin to developing true understanding of the other. As Don Locke (1992, pp. 1–2), the scholar of multiculturalism and diversity studies explains, in any intercultural engagement, only by understanding one's "personal biases, values and interest" can one better understand the other.

Other themes seen in the posting by non-Muslims who participated in the World Hijab Day campaign include a more personal look at being a woman. According to Tia StoneJaa, her experience wearing the *hijab* has left her feeling "liberate[d] not having to constantly worry about [the] hair." Such a realization comes through upon an empathetic act where the *hijabi* is given an "undistorted" (Schaap, 2003, p. 8) view by the other. This act of "walking in the other's shoes" or in this case, scarf, is one of the prerequisites of what Leonard Swidler calls "a mentality of Deep-Dialogue" in which one enters the other's perspectives and "[return] mutually transformed" (Swidler, 2003, p. 83). This sense of "deep dialogue" is evident in other postings by non-Muslim women who participated in the World Hijab Day challenge of wearing the scarf for the day. As Nic, a non-Muslim Australian says, she has a deeper understanding and "appreciation" for the significance of the *hijab* to women who choose to put them on. This deeper awareness can also be seen in the way she articulates the experience of being a *hijabi*: "I have always been supportive of every person's right to choose how to dress, and how to honor their own beliefs, and I feel like my views are now strengthened because of this experience."

Instances of deep-dialogue by these non-Muslim women who chose to take up the World Hijab Day challenge for a day echoes Swidler's (2003, p. 77) argument of the transformative nature of value sharing from within. Talya Leodari, who identifies herself as "Jewish" living in "a very small, very Christian town", illustrates the discomfort the *hijab* appears to make people feel. As she narrates her experience wearing the *hijab* in her small town, "There were some strange looks and people were staring at me—and then looking away quickly when they realized I saw them looking. A few people seemed surprised that I spoke English" (http://worldhijabday.com/jewish-hijab-gave-voice/). However, her own appreciation of the *hijab* is also evident in this statement: "The fact that I was wearing *hijab* gave me the opportunity to talk to my step children about respect, difference, and peace." Other realization that grows out of these empathetic acts of wearing the *hijab* for a day by non-Muslim women includes appreciation for "control [over] who can and can't see you," which as Jennifer Garrett says, "seems very feminist." Unlike the politics associated with veiling discussed earlier which views *hijabi* as subordinated by the religious rules of covering, the realization by Jennifer as shown from her micro-narrative indicates freedom of choice and self-control.

The brief testimonies and self-portraits by the non-Muslim participants of WHD demonstrate the level of empathy and mutual respect towards the veil and the *hijabis* that transcend religious boundaries. Unlike the multitude misrecognition and damaging public representations of the *hijabi* seen in the digital media as discussed earlier, this simple exercise at celebrating a day in which one covers one's body and hair has allowed the non-Muslim participants greater awareness of the world of the *hijabi*, and inadvertently presented a counter narrative for *hijabis* in the social media.

'World Hijab Day' towards Self Positioning

The second category of WHD participants are *hijabis* who share their experiences of wearing the *hijab* by posting selfies and short testimonies of their journey. Although creating a kind of visibility for the *hijabi* which may be read as antithesis to its primary purpose (Begum, 2017), WHD champions self-positioning and self-documentation by the *hijabi*. Consider 30-year-old Desiree from the Netherlands, whose selfie positions her smiling in a *hijab*. Her testimony further adds to her self-positioning when she denounces the claims made by many that *hijab* is a form of "oppression". As she says, "I am a proud, emancipated Muslim and my hijab is part of me." Another *hijabi* from Indonesia, Nika Apriliani, in her testimony makes an obvious yet most times, ignored declaration about being a *hijabi*. The *hijab*, as she rightly points out, does not change the personality of the *hijabi*. "I still joke, laugh, draw, smile, run, play volleyball, bike, do my push-ups during gym class (which I'm terribly bad at, haha!), and I still go outside and breathe the fresh air" (http://worldhijabday.com/oppressed-wouldve-called-police/).

Desree's and Nika Apriliani's point albeit valid needs to be read within the freedom of choice they enjoy to practice their faith. As discussed earlier, in some Muslim contexts, *hijab* is used not as a tool to promote *haya'* but rather as a form of oppression and subjugation of the Muslim women's abilities to play a public role. These *hijabis'* ability to self-position in social media reiterates the significance of WHD where the issue of choice and self-expression of *hijabi* can be given a public platform. As Nika Apriliani states in her testimony: "I know that there are people out there that force and oppress females into wearing the *hijab* (which is something I am completely and strongly against), but sometimes I feel like the "oppressed Muslim girl/woman" is the only image people have when they see Muslim girls wearing the hijab" (http://worldhijab-day.com/oppressed-wouldve-called-police/).

In providing a counter narrative to the oppressive Muslim women image, the WHD testimonies by the *hijabis* are accompanied by selfies or self-portraits that demonstrate a strong physical presence to the cyber world (For examples of selfies by the *hijabis* on WHD see http://worldhijabday.com/random-rants-muslimah/, http://worldhijabday.com/never-felt-beautiful-confident/ http://worldhijabday.com/oppressed-wouldve-called-police/). The theme of freedom of expression and choice are echoed by each of the *hijabis* who used the social media platform to illustrate the availability of unfiltered space that allows Muslim girls and women to continue to carve a space for themselves despite the pressures their respective societies may subject them to.

These self-portraits, notwithstanding on the surface may appear to propagate a "narcissistic or exhibitionistic" (Rettberg, 2014, p. 18) tendency of self-glorification as detractors of selfies label them, are a form of "(forced) embrace" (Warwick in Rettberg 2014, p. 9) "between the face of the person photographed and the camera." The 'selfie embrace' thus can be read as the self-positioning that the *hijabi* chooses to take as a demonstration of public self-representation.

Similar selfie embrace can be seen, by Fatima, who describes her act of exercising *haya'* or modesty as an 'accomplishment.' As she admits, "people have more respect for me because of how I show modesty. I'm so proud of myself because I feel accomplished." In an age where the commodification of the female body continues to be given significance, Fatima's point is crucial. To go against the grain by choosing to cover up in a society that does not value the act, is a tremendous accomplishment as it signifies the woman's strong sense of agency.

Each of the selfie embrace form a kind of "self-documentation", where technology is used to record and reflect (Warfield, 2014) one's public persona. As Jill Walker Rettberg (2014, p. 88) says in *How We Use Selfies, Blogs and Wearable Devices to See and Shape Ourselves*, selfies posted online is the form of self-expression that does not require intermediary: "We no longer need to rely on others to represent us. We represent ourselves." Unlike the re-presentation of the new media discussed earlier, the *hijabis* who participated on WHD demonstrate that they do not rely on the western media to represent their experience. Rather they take ownership of the experience by documenting it on WHD. Consider Qendresa from Kosovo who equates the wearing of the *hijab* to defining her fashion sense. As she aptly says, "Hijab brings a lot of grace and style," allowing each woman to "wear Hijab in [her] own way suitable for [her] own lifestyle."

Using social media as a platform to promote the awareness and experience of wearing the *hijab* through testimonies by fellow *hijabis*, the World Hijab Day Facebook page has created a "filter" to "remove impurities" (Rettberg, 2014, p. 23) of negative perceptions towards the *hijab* circulating in the digital media. In an age of phobia against covering up, where the piece of cloth means more to the politics of the times than as a form of servitude, reclaiming the right to self-document and self-represent appears timely. As seen in another WHD entry, the *hijabi* presents a coy smile in her selfie embrace allows her to filter out the negativity that others hold of *hijabi* in the face of the "freedom" and 'comfort.' As she says, "I wear Hijab because I absolutely appreciate the beauty that lies behind wearing it. I wear it because it gives me the freedom to only expose as much of me as I am comfortable with to the outside world." The unsaid in this testimony is the resistance to equate 'nakedness' to the manifestation of beauty.

Selfie embrace moreover act as a form of self-protection. As Rettberg (2014, p. 29) sums it, "Feeling misrepresented by the camera is one common reason for beginning to take selfies instead of being the subject of other people's photographs." As stated earlier, in an age of heightened distrust of the other based on differences of ethnicity, religion and culture, Muslim women who use the *hijab* have been subjected to scrutiny and media dissection of their choice to cover up. Taking the authority to self-document and self-represent, thus, allows the Muslim women the added agency to exhibit her public persona to her liking as seen from the numerous examples of selfie embrace by *hijabis* on WHD.

In addition, taking Sara Jones' (2014, p. 24) investigation of *The media of testimony*, although for a different context, these postings function as "testimonies" of "ordinary citizens" whose accounts are then imparted to the numerous readers on the social media; the latter then become "secondary witness" to the former's celebration of being a *hijabi*. The *hijabis* thus are reliant on the readers of the WHD: "to act as a further form of secondary witness by ensuring that their testimony finds broader relevance." (Jones, 2014, p. 24). The notion of "witness" incorporates the holistic act of witnessing:

> to have sensory experience of an event—to see, hear or feel something perhaps unintentionally and passively—but witnessing as a verb implies more than this, it 'is also the discursive act of stating one's experience for the benefit of an audience that was not present at the event and yet must make some kind of judgement about it.'

Similar sense of witnessing can be seen in the testimony by 22-year old Omnia Hassan Elshrif from Egypt whose journey as a *hijabi* began at the young age of 11. Although her immediate family were not very supportive of her choice to cover up, her personal inclination of seeing herself as "a queen" in her *hijab*, reiterates self-choice and self-expression. In reading each witness account of the journey into being a *hijabi*, each post on the WHD indicates a choice by the *hijabi* to authenticate their experience and lifestyle choice.

Social media as scholars have defined it connotes sites on the internet that "integrate technology, social interaction and user-generated content." (Siapera, 2012, p. 202; Mandiberg, 2012) One aspect of social interaction that can be used to better understand the content generated by the social media is what Robert Putnam (1995) coined as the two types of social capital, bonding and bridging. The former, i.e. bonding social capital, is the kind of social interaction one does with people one knows well including "close friends and family" (Siapera, 2012, p. 203). The latter, bridging social capital, is what one does with "acquaintances and friends of friends." (ibid.). Scholars studying engagement in the social media, specifically on Facebook, concluded that both bonding and bridging social capital are evident and have increased despite the lack of face-to-face communication (Ellison et al., 2007 in Siapera, 2012). This issue is significant for my current investigation into the representation of the *hijabi* in social media. As I problematized it, the social media can be an important tool to promote greater bridging social capital among *hijabis*. Furthermore, as each post on WHD on average receives between three thousand to over ten thousand likes, the 'social bridging capital' that this Facebook page has created transcends ethnic, cultural and national boundaries, as *hijabis* from all walks of life celebrate their experience of donning the veil. This social bridging capital is akin to a communal agency that supports other Muslim women who have been apprehensive to veil. And this kind of recognition by non-family members and non-friends creates a strong social bridging bond between the one who posted her image and everyone who is following the WHD Facebook site. Consider this post by Hunain on WHD:

> I wanna say Thank you. Because of this page I convinced myself to wear hijab although I wanted to wear for many years but could not ... I'm a weak person. I started hijab from this Monday. People's comments, jokes, taunts made me sad. But when I read posts of this page, I consoled myself & I feel stronger than before.
> HUNAIN (POSTED ON WHD ON 18 MAY 2015)

Such testimonies reiterate the need for social bridging for *hijabis* to both document and celebrate their choice and freedom to veil. Thus, I strongly disagree with Sya Taha (2015, p. np) who claims WHD reifies "the multiple experiences of Muslim women" to a single act, that of "wearing the hijab." As highlighted earlier, *hijabis* in the west are a minority group. Their presence, most times, are felt largely through the public misrecognition in the digital media. Like other minorities, they continue to champion their cause demanding for greater tolerance by the majority while trying to fit within the accepted norms of the secular society. In the virtual world, this demand is made easier as the social media opens up the third space for such normalization to manifest.

Conclusion

At the onset of this discussion, I began by laying out the fundamentals of veiling for Muslim women. The misrepresentation of veiling in many western contexts today is largely rooted in the lack of awareness of the essential purpose of veiling, which is an act of servitude and as a form of *haya'*. The schism between the *hijabi* and the other, the non-Muslim majority, is made acute with the lack of opportunity for interreligious dialogue between Muslim women with *hijab* and mainstream society, in addition to the lack of positive representation of the *hijabi* in the media. This gap is somewhat reduced with the advent of social media platform like World Hijab Day that sets out to promote greater engagement between the *hijabi* and the society at large. In this discussion, I investigated how one individual's attempt to use Facebook as a tool to debunk the politics associated with the *hijab*, has created a stronger social bridging capital both among *hijabis* from different parts of the world, and with non-Muslim Facebook users. On WHD, this on-going interreligious, intercultural dialogue between the *hijabi* and the other, is perpetuated every time a *hijabi* posts her testimony and selfie. As a *hijabi*, WHD also creates an opportunity for intercultural engagement to take place. Even though *hijabis* share in the experience of veiling, each one's journey is unique to her social and cultural environment. Like other aspects of culture, as members of society, *hijabis* continue to 'adapt', 'resist', and 'push' against "the filters that are already embedded in [that] culture" (Rettberg, 2014, pp. 24–25) and position their public image vis-a-vis the culture of the land.

Yet one cultural landscape that all the WHD *hijabis* subscribe to is the social media culture. Embedded in each selfie on WHD is the acceptance of the filtered culture of the Facebook site. This "shared ideas" that the *hijabis* mirror are a type of "filtered culture" which as Rettberg (2014, p. 24) states "affects our choices": "Our cultural filters, the rules and conventions that guide us, filters out possible modes of expression so subtly that we often are not even aware of all the things we do not see." Thus in abiding by the expectations of the WHD, the *hijabis* filter out any major and conflicting differences between them. Accumulatively, these images can be read as a "quantitative self-representation" (ibid. 1) of the current *hijabis* on the social media platform which clearly signals the true range of visibility among them beyond the politics associated with the veil.

References

Akhatar, Rajnaara C. (2011). Muslim women, the Veil and Activism. In Gabriel T. & R. Hannan (Eds.), *Islam and the Veil. Theoretical and Regional Contexts.* (pp. 149–160). London: Continuum International Publishing Group.

Aljazeera. (2017, March 15). Employers allowed to ban the hijab: EU court. Retrieved from http://www.aljazeera.com/news/2017/03/employers-allowed-ban-headscarves -eu-court-170314092627483.html.

Aljazeera America. (2013, September 12). Pastor Terry Jones arrested ahead of planned Quran burning. *Aljazeera America*. Retrieved from http://america.aljazeera.com/ articles/2013/9/12/terry-jones-arrestedjustbeforeplannedquranburning.html.

Amrani, Iman. (2017, March 15). The hijab ruling is a band against Muslim women. *The Guardian*, Retrieved from https://www.theguardian.com/commentisfree/2017/ mar/15/hijab-ruling-muslim-women-religious-identity-european-court-of-justice -resistance.

Asser, Martin. (2006, October 5). Why Muslim women wear the veil. *BBC News*, Retrieved from http://news.bbc.co.uk/2/hi/middle_east/5411320.stm.

Begum, Priya Jasmine. (2017, March 16). Is the hijab being turned into everything it stands against? *The Huffington Post*, Retrieved from http://www.huffingtonpost .co.uk/priya-jasmin-begum/is-the-hijab-being-turned_b_15380682.htm.

Billaud, Julie. (2009). Visible under the veil: Dissimulation, performance and agency in an Islamic public sphere. *Journal of International Women's Studies*, 11(1), 120–135.

Braybrooke, Marcus. (2011). Respect in Plural Society. In Gabriel T. & R. Hannan (Eds.), *Islam and the Veil. Theoretical and Regional Contexts*. (pp. 7–11). London: Continuum International Publishing Group.

Bryden, Joan. (2015). Harper's anti-niqab rhetoric helps terrorist recruiters: philosopher Taylor. *National News Watch*, Retrieved http://www.nationalnewswatch.com/ 2015/03/28/harpers-anti-niqab-rhetoric-helps-terrorist-recruiters-philosopher -taylor/#.WVr9OoiGOUk.

Contractor, Sariya. (2011). Marginalisation or an opportunity for dialogue? In Gabriel T. & R. Hannan (Eds.), *Islam and the Veil. Theoretical and Regional Contexts*. (pp. 129– 141). London: Continuum International Publishing Group.

El-Aabedy, N. (2017, March 16). How does the EU hijab ruling affect Muslim women? *Aljazeera*, Retrieved from http://www.aljazeera.com/indepth/features/2017/03/eu -hijab-ruling-affect-muslim-women-170316073040916.html.

Feldman, Noah. (2015, May 10). The woman in the neon niqab. *Bloomberg View*, Retrieved from http://www.bloombergview.com/articles/2015-05-10/the-woman-in -the-neon-niqab

Gabriel T. & R. Hannan. (2011). Introduction. In Gabriel T. & R. Hannan (Eds.), *Islam and the Veil. Theoretical and Regional Contexts*. (pp. 1–4). London: Continuum International Publishing Group.

Gabriel T. (2011). Reflections on Sartorial Injunctions in Islam. In Gabriel T. & R. Hannan (Eds.), *Islam and the Veil. Theoretical and Regional Contexts*. (pp. 12–19). London: Continuum International Publishing Group.

Hanrahan, M. (2015). Armed bikers plan anti muslim protest outside Arizona mosque. *International Business Times*. Retrieved from http://www.ibtimes.com/ armed-bikers-plan-anti-muslim-protest-outside-arizona-mosque-1943214.

Hume, Stephen. (2015, March 18). Stephen Hume: Woman-hating culture column provokes explosive response. *The Vancouver Sun*, Retrieved from http://www .vancouversun.com/news/Stephen+Hume+Woman+hating+culture+column +provokes+explosive+response/10900508/story.html#Comments

Jones, Sara. (2014). *The media of testimony. Remembering the East German Stasi in the Berlin Republic*. New York: Palgrave Macmillan.

Khola Hasan. (2011). Hijab: A symbol of modesty or seclusion? In Gabriel T. & R. Hannan (Eds.), *Islam and the Veil. Theoretical and Regional Contexts*. (pp. 115–126). London. Continuum International Publishing Group.

Kincheloe, Joe L. & Shirley. R. Steinberg. (1997). *Changing multiculturalism*. Buckingham: Open university Press.

Liptak, Adam. (2015, February 25). In a Case of Religious Dress, Justices Explore the Obligations of Employers. *The New York Times*, Retrieved from http://www.nytimes .com/2015/02/26/us/in-a-case-of-religious-dress-justices-explore-the-obligations -of-employers.html?ref=topics&_r=0.

Lewis, Reina. (2009). Veils and sales. Muslims and the spaces of post-colonial fashion retail. In Richard Phillips (Ed.), Muslims Spaces of Hope Geographies of Possibilities in Britain and the West. New York: Zed Books.

Locke, Don. (1992). *Increasing multicultural awareness. A comprehensive model*. London: Sage Publications.

Methal R. Mohammed. (2009). Cultural Identity in Virtual Reality (VR): A case study of Muslim Women with Hijab in Second Life (SL). *Journal of Virtual Worlds Research* 2(2), 3–10. file:///C:/Users/User/Downloads/Cultural_Identity_in_Virtual_Reality _VR-libre.pdf.

Mahboba Rawi & V. Mickan-Gramazio. (2005). *Mahboba's Promise Sydney*: Bantam.

Mahboba Rawi. (2015). *Mahboba's Promise. An Australian Aid Organiation*, Retrieved from http://mahbobaspromise.org/.

Mandiberg, Michael (Ed.). (2012). *The Social Media Reader*. New York: New York University Press.

Merola, Andrea. (2015). Picture of "High Visibility Burqa." *AVAX News Online*, Retrieved from http://avaxnews.net/fact/Fashion_this_Week_10-05-2015.html.

Muhammad Muhsin Khan (trans.) (1997). *Sahih al-Bukhari*. Vol 1, Book 2, No. 9 Retrieved from https://futureislam.files.wordpress.com/2012/11/sahih-al-bukhari -volume-1-ahadith-0001-875.pdf

Nazma Khan. (2014). World Hijab Day Facebook. http://www.facebook.com/ WorldHijabDay/.

O'Regan, Mary. (2015, April 14). Women need to embrace the empowering veil again. *Catholic Herald*, Retrieved from http://www.catholicherald.co.uk/commentand-blogs/2015/04/14/women-need-to-embrace-the-empowering-veil-again/.

Rettberg, Jill Walker. (2014). *How We Use Selfies, Blogs and Wearable Devices to See and Shape Ourselves.* New York: Palgrave Macmillan.

Raihanah M. M. (2009). Multiculturalism and the politics of Expression" An Appraisal. *European Jounal of Social Sciences,* 7(3),763–70.

Raihanah M. M., Ruzy Suliza Hashim & Noraini Md Yusof. (2012). Muslim Women Memoirists and Spaces of Hope. Advances in Environment, Computational Chemistry and Bioscience—Proceedings of the 3rd International Conference on Arts and Culture (ICAC 12), Retrieved from http://www.wseas.us/e-library/conferences/2012/Montreux/BIOCHEMENV/BIOCHEMENV-00.pdf.

Rummana Hussain. (2015, May 30). Muslim chaplain from NU claims racist remarks on United flight. *Chicago Sun Times,* Retreived from http://chicago.suntimes .com/news-chicago/7/71/648601/muslim-chaplain-northwestern-university-said -discriminated-united-airlines.

Siapera, Eugenia. (2012). *Understanding New Media.* London: Sage.

Sayed Khalil Tabatabai. (2012). *Philosophy of Hijab (Islamic Veil)—An Islamic lecture in English Language* contemporary Islamic issues. Held in Imam Hussain Charitable Foundation, Montreal, Quebec, Canada. Retrieved from https://www.youtube.com/watch?v=r2YLI58K33w.

Schaap, Andrew. (2003). Reconciliation through a struggle for recognition? Working paper 2003/7 Centre for Applied Philosophy and Public Ethics (CAPPE).

Secor, Anna. (2005). Islamism, Democracy and the Political Production of the Headscarf Issue in Turkey. In Falah, Ghazi-Walid & Nagel, Caroline (Eds.), *Geographies of Muslim Women.* (pp. 203–225). London: The Guilford Press.

Shirazi, Faegheh. (2001). *The veil unveiled. The Hijab in Modern culture.* University Press Florida.

Silvestri, Sara. (2012). Comparing burqa debates in Europe: sartorial styles, religious prescriptions and political ideologies. In Ferrari, S. & Pastorelli, S. (Eds.), *Religion in the Public Spaces: A European Perspective.* Farnham: Ashgate.

Smale, Alison. (13 March, 2015). Muslim Teachers May Wear Head Scarves, German Court Rules. *The New York Times,* Retrieved from http://www.nytimes.com/2015/03/14/world/europe/german-court-rules-that-muslim-teachers-may-wear-head-scarves .html?ref=topics&_r=0.

Swidler, Leonard. (2003). *Dialogue in Malaysia and the Global Scenario.* Kuala Lumpur: Center for Civilizational Dialogue, University Malaya.

Sya Taha. (20 April, 2015). The Hijab Obsession: Moving on ... *Aquila Style,* Retrieved from http://www.aquila-style.com/fashionbeauty/shopping/the-hijab-obsession -moving-on/38500/.

Taylor, Charles. (1994). The politics of recognition. In A. Gutmann (Ed.), Multi-culturalism. Examining the politics of recognition. (pp. 25–76). Princeton: Princeton University Press.

The Holy Quran

Woodlock, Racheal. (2009). The Islamicity of different interpretation of Hijab. *Sociology of Islam & Muslim Societies*, 4(2009), 7–9.

Warfield, Kate. (2014, March 26). "Why i love selfies and you should too (Damn It)" Public Lecture at Kwantlen Polytechnic University. Published on YouTube 2 April 2014 https://youtu.be/aOVIJwy3nVo.

Watkins, Russell. (2014). "Malala Yousafzai at Girl Summit 2014" Department for International Development.—https.//www.flickr.com/photos/dfid/14714344864/. Licensed under CC BY 2.0 via Wikimedia Commons—http://commons.wikimedia .org/wiki/File:Malala_Yousafzai_at_Girl_Summit_2014.jpg#/media/File:Malala _Yousafzai_at_Girl_Summit_2014.jpg.

World Hijab Day Blog. Retrieved from http://worldhijabday.com.

Yusuf da Costa. (2002). *The honor of women in Islam*. Washington: Islamic Supreme Council of America.

PART 3

Interrogating Visual Representations

∵

CHAPTER 6

Contemporary Bruneian Cinema in the Context of Sharia Law

D. Bruno Starrs

Introduction

Amid concerns about the disappearance of national and/or cultural specificity due to pernicious, inter-country capitalism and secular globalization, in this chapter I consider Bruneian cinema as the product of an emerging national imaginary, one that fosters a uniquely progressive role for *Muslima* (Muslim women). I do so by focusing upon the example set by Brunei's first feature-length commercial film, the very popular and well-received *Yasmine* (dir. Siti Kamaluddin 2014), which defies most western expectations (many of which are only implied or inferred) about the Islamic country's media representations of Muslim women. Using Benedict Anderson's theory of the sovereign nation as an "imagined political community" (1983, p. 6), I also consider how *Yasmine* ideologically constructs and situates its eponymous character as an authentic gendered subject in the *Melayu Islam Beraja* (MIB)-influenced spaces of both family and nation through the filmic representation of the titular character as the "unfilial" daughter (Chin and Daud, 2014, p. 2), and how the movie therefore provocatively promotes female desire, empowerment and agency. Most important, politically, I speculate as to why such an apparent transgression against the Islamic principles of an evolving Brunei has been not only permitted but financially supported and effectively endorsed by the Sultan of Brunei's ruling theocracy, especially as it moves into its final implementation phase of the extremely controversial Sharia Law. My conclusion is that contrary to wary expectations from the west, the benevolence, tolerance and understanding of the current Sultan's national imaginary either augurs well for the modern Bruneian *Muslima*, regardless of traditional concepts of

* The writing of this chapter has not been funded or supported by any grant or fellowship. Nevertheless, my many thanks must be offered to Professor Madya Dr. Hjh Zohrah Hj Sulaiman (Acting Vice Chancellor, Universiti Teknologi Brunei [UTB]); Muhammad Al-Qusyairi bin Hj Abd Kahar (Lecturer in MIB at UTB); and Dr. Grace V. S. Chin (Lecturer in English Literature, University Brunei Darussalam). All these mentors gave important and valuable advice on the preparation of this paper.

authenticity elsewhere in the Islamic world, or (I suggest very cynically) is nothing more than an elaborate ruse meant to con the western world into believing that women will still have equal rights in Sharia Law ruled Brunei.

Whereas many Asian cinemas have de-territorialized, obsequiously promoting the norms of mainstream Hollywood, the Sultanate of Brunei might, some western commentators apparently expect, aggressively push a foregrounding of strict Islamic ideologies in both its lived society and its state-sanctioned media. With an official national philosophy of *Melayu Islam Beraja* (MIB) (or translated as 'Malay Islamic Monarchy') promoting the traditional (some western chauvinists would unhesitatingly say 'barbaric') norms of Islam and its recent implementation of Sharia Law enforcing such norms, depictions in the public sphere media of western concepts of gender and related human rights equality, particularly in regard to the judicial process, would be discouraged. Such a prospect is alarming to many and there are some Australian politicians, for example, who "will question Brunei over its new criminal law regime—whose punishments include limb amputation for theft and stoning to death for adultery or homosexuality—before deciding whether to proceed with trade negotiations" (Doherty, 2014) whilst in the US the Feminist Majority Foundation described the changes as "anti-female" (Sichel, 2014) as it joined with gay and Jewish groups to boycott the Sultan-owned Beverley Hills Hotel.

As with those Middle Eastern countries where Sharia Law is practiced, such western critics suggest, Bruneian *Muslima* may be forced to cover themselves demurely, abstain from driving, higher education or other means of self-empowerment, and submit to harsh, court-imposed punishments for sexual promiscuity, with the state-sanctioned media duly promoting such moralistic norms as traditional and commendable for authentic Muslims. The idealized screen representation of the Bruneian *Muslima* would be chaste and respectful, unlike many screen portrayals of wanton women in Australia and other western countries (see Starrs, 2006).

At the very least, such western critics might anticipate, Brunei's entertainment media would soon resemble Islamic Turkey's colloquially named "Milli cinema," which "brought Islam back into the movies and showed respect for Islam [and in which a] common theme [...] was to show characters that had adopted western values but who became unhappy and unsatisfied by those values" (Yorulmaz & Blizek, 2014, p. 8). Cinema from Islam-dominated countries such as Turkey, Iran, Afghanistan and even multicultural India, is frequently expected to promote not just adherence to the tenets of Islam, but to validate traditionally patriarchal—and even misogynistic—attitudes to *Muslima* as well. And its covert role is to denigrate the western world's depraved and dissolute mores.

What, then, given the suppositions of the west about Islam and its con-comitant female disempowerment in Brunei, should western commentators make of the award-winning[1] *Yasmine*, a Brunei government-funded film from a first-time female director about a martial arts-obsessed schoolgirl who glee-fully defies her father, rarely wears a veil, doggedly pursues higher education, enthusiastically chases boys and, like many cashed-up, unrestrained, western female teens, drives a racy, eye-catching car? The film's narrative is inarguably one which commends female agency and self-empowerment as the female protagonist plots to win back her boyfriend through involvement as a competi-tor in an inter-collegiate tournament of violent hand to hand combat known as *Silat*. *Yasmine* is quite unlike Yorulmaz and Blizek's "Milli cinema" as the pro-tagonist does not become "unhappy and unsatisfied" (2014, p. 8) through the adoption of western values. Hence, as a response to such an unexpected filmic mediation, in this paper I ponder how this national cultural cinematic arte-fact—understandably lauded by the nation's citizens for its positive depictions of authentic, idiosyncratically Bruneian national icons such as *Kampong Ayer* (the water village), *Ambuyat* (the national culinary delicacy) and, of course, *Silat* (the national martial art)—sits within the theocracy's attempts to main-tain said citizenry's adherence to the religious tenets of Islam, given that many western critics of Sharia Law expect it to herald an inequitable, repressive envi-ronment, albeit an allegedly authentic Islamic lifestyle, for the *Muslima* whom it oversees?

Some Background to Brunei: The Abode of Peace

Before I attempt to answer the questions posed above, the provision of some background information about this tiny, little-known nation (where I was en-gaged as a government employee at the Universiti Teknologi Brunei as Senior Lecturer in Cinema in 2014 and 2015), is in order. The country of Negara Brunei Darussalam, internationally known as the self-described 'Abode of Peace' (a not insignificant sobriquet when notions of the national imaginary are visit-ed, as I will discuss later), is an independent nation of some 433,450 citizens (Countrymeters.info, 2017) and is a geographically bisected state located on the North-western coast of the island of Borneo, a huge equatorial land mass it shares with Malaysia and Indonesia.

---

1   *Yasmine* was awarded "Best Asian Movie" at the Neuchatel International Fantasy Film Festival in 2014 and "AIFFA Award for Best Supporting Actress" (for Nadiah Wahid) in the ASEAN International Film Festival Awards in 2015.

Brunei has, since the 1930s, developed much wealth from the discovery of its extensive oil and natural gas fields. Subsequently it enjoys, after Singapore, the second-highest Human Development Index in South East Asia and is classified as a "developed country" (United Nations, 2009). Petroleum for commuters is amazingly cheap and retails at about half the cost per liter as that for bottled water (Brzeski, 2014). The International Monetary Fund ranked Brunei fifth in the world by Gross Domestic Product (GDP), estimating that Brunei was one of only two countries (Libya being the other) with a public debt at 0% of the national GDP although recent falls in the value of hydrocarbons mean Brunei is currently on track to report a fiscal deficit valued at as much as 16 percent of its GDP (Prusak, 2017).

Significantly, Brunei also boasts the only ruling monarchy in Southeast Asia (other monarchies, such as the Kingdom of Thailand, for example, whilst often immensely popular with the citizenry, leave the actual matters of governance to their ministries). Headed by the Sultan of Brunei (who wears the title of Yang Di-Pertuan Negara), the country's hereditary monarchy has been in continuous power for over 600 years. The present leader, Sultan Haji Hassanal Bolkiah Mu'izzaddin Waddaulah, is the 29th such ruler. Formerly a British protectorate (from 1888 until full independence was granted in 1984), the 1959 Constitution affirms the apparently much-loved Sultan as both head of state and prime minister, and has given him full executive authority including emergency powers since a failed revolt in 1962. These emergency powers have never been revoked and, in effect, now permit the monarch to rule his lands entirely unchallenged.

Shafi'ite Islam is the official religion of Brunei and its precepts are adhered to at all levels of government with the national philosophy of MIB giving credence to the bureaucracy's assiduous devotion. Indeed, the association between Brunei and Islam is one of the oldest in Asia with Seng Piew Loo stating: "the ancestry of MIB purportedly intertwines with the dawn of Islam itself" (2009, p. 153). The monarchy is even said to lay claim to a hereditary link to the prophet, Mohammed, and the significance of this national ethos was affirmed during the reign of Sultan Haji Omar Ali Saifuddien when reference to it was included in the 1967 constitution, and subsequently consolidated upon Brunei's declaration of independence from the British on the 1st of January 1984. On that momentous occasion, Sultan Haji Hassanal Bolkiah declared the country "shall be for ever a sovereign, democratic and independent Malay Muslim Monarchy [founded] upon the teachings of Islam" (Sidhu, 2009, p. 120).

This proclamation has been proudly adhered to ever since, despite the fact that official censuses identify only about 67% of the Brunei population as Muslim, leaving a sizeable minority identifying as non-Muslim, that is, 13% of Bruneians are counted as Buddhist, 10% as Christian, and the remaining

10% as "other" (Bouma et al., 2010, p. 49). Nevertheless, the public celebration of Christmas or Chinese New Year is prohibited (*The Star Online*, 2016) and "All schools are prohibited to teach courses on Christianity. During school time Muslim and non-Muslim female students of government schools are required to wear Muslim attire including a head covering or *hijab*" (Bouma et al., 2010, p. 48). Indeed, teaching any other religious material besides that which promotes Islam is forbidden in schools and indications are that Islamic religious studies will soon be compulsory for all Bruneian school students, Muslim and non-Muslim alike (Harun, 2014).

Although its people share much genetically, socially and culturally with surrounding Malaysia, Brunei is nevertheless quite unique amongst its neighbors thanks to its rare status as an absolute monarchy, with Naimah Talib stating: "the Sultanate of Brunei is often seen as a political anachronism in a region in which democratic institutions of government prevail" (2002, p. 134). The 2004 constitutional amendments even removed the requirement for the Legislative Council to consent before any law is passed, which A. V. M. Horton cynically argues shows "a desire to wrap the kingdom in some of the clothes of a liberal democracy without actually being one" (Horton, 2005, p. 181).

Not unlike democratic Malaysia, however, promoting Islam is a major preoccupation of this non-secular government, with the Ministry of Religious Affairs established in 1986 and consisting of five government departments, those being: Mosque, *Hajj*, Islamic Studies, Islamic Law and Islamic *Da'wah*. The latter office energetically propagates Muslim teachings and includes in its activities the publication of numerous Islamic books and journals, research projects, regional conferences and academic seminars. The center's Publication Control and Censor unit, as the name suggests, enthusiastically censors publications, removing passages that it deems contradict Islamic beliefs. *Radio Televisyen Brunei* (RTB), a government-owned free-to-air TV station, devotes more than 20 hours per week to religious programming, including a short *Qur'anic* recitation to begin and close each day's broadcasting, daily calls to prayer, coverage of the weekly Friday *Khutbahs* (sermons) as well as *Qur'an* reciting competitions and Islamic entertainment shows. There is little happening, culture-wise, that is not monitored by the Ministry of Religious Affairs, and it is a body kept justifiably busy preventing the adulteration of wholesome Islamic life in the Sultanate by the ever-growing influence of non-Islamic, western pop culture.

The real or imagined threat from external, and potentially corrupting, western influences are swiftly (but not necessarily transparently) dealt with by these robust censorship mechanisms, which are bolstered by "the power to arbitrarily shut down media outlets" and to imprison transgressors "for up to three years [...] for portraying the country in a negative light" (Bandial, 2013), hence, Quratal-Ain Bandial alleges, many artists and authors, for whom the guidelines regarding what is unacceptable are never really made clear, "live in constant fear. Fear of overstepping the invisible line in the sand that defines what [they] can or cannot say" (2013). It is important to note that while this controversial newspaper article actually went to hard copy press it was soon removed from *The Brunei Times* online archives. Apparently, the Bruneian government has deemed the mention of state censorship (actual or potential) worthy of, well, state censorship. MIB rules supreme in Brunei, and there is no reason to doubt there is some basis to Bandial's fearful and anxious comments, given the censorship applied to his own writing. Indeed, the world is presently watching with overt anxiety as Brunei slowly unveils its third and final phase of Shariah Law, and many western commentators are wary, with the United Nations calling the laws (which include the amputation of limbs for stealing and death by stoning for homosexuality or adultery): "illegal and inhuman" (Doherty, 2014).

Unfortunately, if only for the veracity of this chapter's reference list, *The Brunei Times* ceased publication as of the 7th of November, 2016 (without explanation apart from a front-page statement blaming unspecified economic factors—perhaps they had crossed that "invisible line"? Ahmed Mansour writes that to survive, Brunei's "news organizations operate in a culture of fear and play it safe by sticking to soft news" [2016]). Several of this article's sources can no longer be accessed, unless the reader finds them in hard copy form. Un-redacted, fortunately, is the comment by the then Singaporean academic, Grace Chin, about Singapore and Malaysia:

> Be it man or woman, the writer located in the plural contexts of Malaysia and Singapore has always been aware of the censorship apparatuses operating within the nation space. S/he has learnt to treat with caution the subjects forbidden in these countries—namely race and religion.
>
> CHIN, 2006, P. 13

Chin might just as well have counted Brunei alongside Singapore and Malaysia—but diverted censors in the country where she was later to find teaching work at the University of Brunei Darussalam—by not doing so. Judicious writing has enabled this academic to retain a lecturing position in English literature at the University of Brunei Darussalam: it may be assumed that Chin practices what she preaches with regard to exercising caution when mentioning race or religion.

The nation of Brunei is, without doubt, aware of her neighbors' lack of autonomy in news reporting, and such practices are perhaps normalized as a result. In addition to Singapore and Malaysia, Brunei is bordered by Indonesia, and Ross Tapsell notes: "self-censorship in Indonesia is encouraged by the powerful ruling elite, whose intention is to limit criticism of its actions" (2012, p. 228). For journalists in Indonesia the "taboo topics" are the allegations of corrupt dealings by the rich owners of the newspapers they write for. Typically avoided is mention of environmental scandals such as the mudflow in Sidoarjo (p. 242), for which certain unscrupulous businessmen allegedly hold responsibility. The difference between Indonesia and Brunei, however, is the identity of that "ruling elite": in Indonesia, it is wealthy businessmen whereas in Brunei it is the Islamic government.

Talib notes, however, that despite the government's dedication to promoting the religion of Islam, the Sultan views the practices of radical Islam as undesirable for his citizens. Nevertheless, Brunei actively seeks to placate those with extremist, puritanical agendas: "Mindful of the *potential threat of Islamic extremism*, the government pays great heed to the religion by building grand mosques, establishing religious schools and colleges, and even sponsoring pilgrims to Mecca" (Talib, 2002, p. 143, my emphasis). Thus, although moderate Islam is highly supported, there has been little interest by the Sultanate in courting the opinions of Islamic fundamentalists and extremists, as many nervous non-Muslims suspect may now happen with the country's 2018 introduction of its so-called third phase of Sharia Law.

And yet the fact remains: despite—or perhaps because of—the existence of a well-funded department dedicated to propagating the cultural aspects of MIB, Brunei has almost no recorded cinematic history, apart from a black and white work produced by the Ministry of Religious Affairs in 1968 entitled *Gema Dari Menara* ("Voice from the Minaret"). Until now no commercial feature film (that is, a screen production of ninety minutes or more duration with international theatrical release and/or festival distribution) has ever been produced by a local filmmaker. But the Sultan has certainly supported cinematic ventures: in 2000 he personally opened the first Bruneian International Film Festival, which was specifically aimed at enhancing diplomatic relations between France and Brunei. Four films were shown from French directors, but not, it must be noted, without censor approval. The event was to be scheduled annually but unfortunately the initiative lost momentum and is apparently now defunct.

The Bruneian National Imaginary

From an understanding of the facts of Brunei as provided by my above notes, we can now turn to a consideration of how Bruneians see themselves. Benedict Anderson's ground breaking work theorizing the generic nation as an "imagined political community" (1983, p. 6) is central to this paper's discussion for it highlights the importance of the link between the national imaginary and the mass media. As Anderson puts it, the nation-state "is imagined because the members of even the smallest nation will never know most of their fellow-members, meet them, or even hear of them, yet in the mind of each lives the image of their communion" (p. 6). Put another way, the idea of one's nation is a mental geography risen from the eidolon of shared cultural experience, meaning, laws and language, through which the powerful sense of "fraternity" (p. 6) is borne, linking the notional co-citizens within limited yet acknowledged territorial boundaries (as are [usually] determined by their political leaders). This shared sense of fraternity is most obviously facilitated by that most ubiquitous of available communication modes, the mass media, including the screen mediums of film, television and the Internet, although Anderson primarily considered the print media. Arjun Appadurai further developed the theoretical underpinnings of Anderson's "print capitalism" (p. 6) and "imagined communities" by describing the complex global media-scapes we inhabit (Appadurai, 1990). The rise of these mass media-scapes has had an immense impact on private and public lives, as well as our social experiences and cultural perceptions in the past half century or so. Cinema, undeniably one of the most important mass media in contemporary society, participates significantly in the quotidian processes of community building, contributing, through a discursive system of signs and representations, to the reinforcement and sustenance of the national imaginary. Andrew Higson notes the parallels between cinema and Anderson's theorizing about the print media when he writes: "films will construct imaginary bonds which work to hold the peoples of a nation together as a community by dramatizing their current fears, anxieties pleasures and aspirations" (2000, p. 26). Communal imagination, as Appadurai argued in 1990, serves not only as "a social practice" (p. 5), but it has further become "central to all forms of agency" (p. 5). As a cultural artefact which involves the expression of Brunei's national imaginary, Kamaluddin's new film *Yasmine*, therefore, provides viewers with a means of critiquing the interrelated political meanings of gender and nation in its representations of the nation's *Muslima*, and most cynics would argue it is unlikely that the persons responsible for approving the film's government funding were unaware of this: for some reason the film was determined to fit sufficiently well with the political goals of the Sultan as to merit the provision of financial support.

Indeed, cinema has long been recognized as an influential tool with which governments and dictators might mold the loyalties of citizens. Alan Williams summarizes: "From the medium's inception, films have defined and reinforced the core values and social structures of countries. They have also helped define—socially and culturally—what is to be considered "outside" the nation and what [...] is to be shunned" (Williams, 2002, back cover). But surprisingly, although established government-funded institutions such as RTB and University Brunei Darussalam have produced educational and nature related videos locally, the nation's government has shown little interest in cultivating the filmic medium in Brunei (apart from the afore mentioned attempt at founding an international film festival in 2000). Even low budget, independent, digital film-making has been virtually non-existent. Tilman Baumgartel writes: "Vietnam, Laos, Cambodia, Myanmar, East Timor and Brunei have for a number of different reasons (state censorship, lack of film culture, extreme poverty) not participated in the recent upsurge of filmmaking" (2012). Why has Brunei failed to ride the wave known as the digital film-making revolution, confirming Jose Lacaba's opinion: "Brunei has no film industry to speak of" (2000)? Could it be, as Baumgartel suggests, "state censorship" is responsible? Undeniably, the state of Brunei is dedicated to MIB and the precepts of Islam and this certainly has a strong influence on the population, possibly forcing Bruneians to distance themselves from allegedly 'decadent' western industries such as film-making, but as has already been mentioned, the country's first feature film was in fact a government-funded, non-commercial work of Islamic propaganda produced by the Ministry of Religious Affairs. Could it be a "lack of a film culture"? Foreign cinema is popular in Brunei and tickets are cheap, and despite its small population, there have been attempts to initiate international film festivals (as previously mentioned), hence this reason is unlikely. It certainly cannot be due to "extreme poverty," for Brunei is an oil-rich, highly developed, "first world" country and many of its middle-class citizens have access to digital film-making technology including high end video cameras and multi-function mobile phones. Indeed, the few disadvantaged Bruneians there are receive generous welfare benefits, whilst waged workers pay no income tax and enjoy one of the highest GDP per capita in Asia, at around US$32,266 (tradingeconomics.com, 2015):[2] the populace certainly inhabits no technological backwater nor cultural desert. The recent indications of an upsurge in interest in film-making, as indicated by the popularity of *Yasmine*, are long overdue, but in my opinion the tardiness in joining this revolution can be attributed to none of the three reasons Baumgartel proposes.

---

2 It must be noted that the average income of Bruneians has steadily been dropping since hitting a high of US$66309 in 1979. With the slump in value of oil and gas, Bruneians standard of living may drop even further in the future.

State Censorship, the Authentic *Muslima* and *Silat*

Or perhaps conservatism regarding the suspiciously western industry of film-making really does exist in Brunei, even if no overt state censoring of cinema occurs. Such would be the expectation of most typically prejudiced western critics of Islamic society, and certainly at least one film, the openly gay-themed *Haram Queen* (dir. Abdul Zainidi, 2014) has been banned, with the Bruneian director of this short documentary film about the nation's underground community of drag queens purportedly receiving death threats (see Isaac, 2014). The proscription has been covert, however: no official decree has been publicly issued. Nevertheless, it is impossible to access this film in Brunei, where homosexuality has long been outlawed. In addition to the outlawing, however, legislative changes taking place may soon see the infliction of severe punishments for such behavior, even if they be acts between consenting adults. Also known as *Syariah* law, Islam's Sharia criminal justice system, *Hudud*, is now being implemented in three stages in Brunei since 2014 and it is the subject of much conjecture from those who fear similarly "harsh and ancient" punishments as are eked out in countries such as Saudi Arabia or Afghanistan where Sharia Law presently prevails (Seal, 2014). In those nations, hand amputations for stealing and death by stoning for homosexuality and adultery are common sentences legally imposed on convicted transgressors. Certainly, the impression abounds in these Middle Eastern countries that the Sharia interpretation of Islam is the world's most authentic judicial system, and that the punishments it inflicts upon the Muslim woman, particularly if and when she embraces the egalitarian, sexually uninhibited mores of the west, are likewise the punitive measures necessary to maintain the authenticity of *Muslima* generally. Sharia Law has, however, been criticized for being a paternalistic system of justice, with women's court testimonials carrying far less weight than men's and rulings that verge on the misogynistic when compared to the gender-equalized judiciary of the west. This phallocentric-ness is true even in the academies of higher learning, with Leila Ahmed bemoaning the influence of "men's Islam": "It is also a particular and bitter irony to me that the very fashionableness of gender studies is serving to disseminate and promote medieval men's Islam as the 'true' and 'authentic' Islam" (2003).

Of course, there have been attempts to counter this notion of the authentic Muslim woman being defined by "men's Islam," with Zahedan writing of the Iranian Islamic Authenticity Movement:

> Ali Shariati (1933–77), a French-educated Iranian sociologist, was instrumental in promoting the concept of authentic Muslim women in Iran [...] women were encouraged to break away from the old notion of gen-

der seclusion and to reject old practices and customs. As modern yet culturally authentic Muslim women, they should seek education and be active in society, working side-by-side with men (2007, pp. 75–98).

Significantly, the producers of *Yasmine* refrain from making any reference to Sharia Law nor to allegedly authentic Muslim womanhood, let alone depicting a normalized Islamic society in which women are prevented from self-advancement or independence and forced to wear a veil. The main character, Yasmine (Liyana Yus) only wears a veil once, and that scene can be interpreted as little more than a contrivance for humor, as the gormless teenager is mocked for wearing a bright red veil to her new school when the dress code actually stipulates a dull gray. Indeed, the film does nothing to positively idealize the religious headwear for its only consistently veiled female character is the overweight, greedy Nadia (Nadiah Wahid) who undoubtedly functions as another source of comic relief. But Yasmine's awkwardness regarding her school time wearing the veil is short-lived in the film's narrative, and the significance of such Muslim attire to notions of the authentic Bruneian *Muslima* remain unexplored: the storyline soon boosts Yasmine's social standing as she sets out to win the local school tournament in the country's national martial art, *Silat*. Enjoying near folkloric status, this sport has various forms across the Malaysian, Indonesian and Philippines archipelagos, with most involving not only unarmed combat but the use of bladed weaponry as well. Its champions and practitioners are highly revered, with Gabriel Facal stating that "in Brunei, *Silat* is still regarded as part of the national culture" (2014, p. 1). But this unequivocally violent activity is not very MIB at all, as Facal promptly elaborates:

> [...] in the proclamation of independence on 1st January 1984, the Sultanate added the term Darussalam ('land of peace') to the name of Brunei, and as a way of promoting cultural homogenization, Islam was then designed to maintain peace in the state [...] Thus silat needed to adapt to the national orientations [and] silat has been more and more abandoned by the royal family (p. 3).

Indeed, within a national imaginary arguably promoted by the Sultan, one that emphasizes peace and non-violent harmony, combative blood sports are decidedly out of place. Therefore, *Silat* may have only a limited future in MIB-aligned Brunei, according to Facal, due to its traditional preoccupation with bloodthirsty violence: "Nowadays, mastery of these [*Silat*] weapons by the practitioners is threatened because of laws regarding the holding of weapons" (Facal, 2014, p. 8). Perhaps potentially fatal martial arts, no matter how traditional their association with Islam (for many practitioners putatively see it as an activity exclusively for Muslims) do not and cannot sit well within a national policy of promoting Brunei as the 'Abode of Peace.' Certainly, royal attitudes toward the sport have waxed and waned over the centuries with O'ong Maryono noting that initially in Indonesia, considered to be the birthplace of *Silat* by many of the sport's gurus, "the art of pen-cak silat self-defence was exclusively for members of the royal family to prepare themselves as defenders of the empire" (2000). On the other hand, encouragement of *Silat* might be a tool to foment greater national allegiance. In 1970s Indonesia, in the wake of a communist coup of 1965 and Suharto's rise to power, troublesome youth "presented a particular problem for the new regime [... hence] Silat in particular, was viewed as a means of installing military type discipline and loyalty to the state amongst the general public" (Wilson, 2002, p. 22). Without any obvious unrest amongst the youth in present day Brunei, however, this possibly attractive aspect of the martial art is largely irrelevant. Nevertheless, it must be noted that the glamor of violence is a trope that has long sustained Hollywood's cinematic output, one that marks much of the film as western-influenced and which in itself might make *Yasmine* prone to government censorship.

But where exactly does the film position itself ideologically with regard to the potentially deadly martial art of *Silat*? First and foremost, it must be conceded that the training Yasmine and her college team mates undertake is unarmed and there is no mention of bladed weaponry. On the other hand, the potentially deadly nature of the sport is fundamental to the narrative conflict: towards the film's climax it is revealed that the reason her father withholds permission for his daughter to train in *Silat* is that he was himself a former champion, but one who resorted to an unbecoming technique he calls the punch of death, which put his former opponent (now, co-incidentally, Yasmine's off-campus trainer and mentor) into a wheelchair for life. Yasmine is tempted to use this seemingly unethical technique to win her championship bout but demurs to better sportsmanship, winning anyway. Nevertheless, the film is unequivocal: *Silat* is a violent, potentially deadly activity. But the allegation its non-peaceful nature is inherently non-MIB is never implied, let alone actually stated. Similarly unstated is the relationship between *Silat* and Islam, although a running joke concerns the college's inept *Silat* instructor, a fan-waving effete who constantly alludes to the power of Chi, a notion more usually associated with Taoism or Chinese martial arts than with Islam. Like much of the potentially controversial subject material in this film, the writers have steered away from making firm statements either way about *Silat*, MIB or Islam: they rub up against "the invisible line in the sand that defines what [they] can or cannot say" (Bandial, 2013) but do not brazenly overstep it. The film's subtextual message is that the unethically violent *Silat* Yasmine's own father participated in is a thing of Brunei's brutal past and that Yasmine's weapon-less version of *Silat* and her subsequent win fit more with the present Sultan's agenda for a contemporary, peaceful Brunei.

Could it be that the censors from the Publication Control and Censor unit, those Islamic doyen of the Sultan who are charged with upholding *Da'wah*, actually looked the other way when the seemingly western-influenced *Yasmine*, with its dubious depictions of debauched western cultural ideals, was screened for them in the preview? The film not only features the favorable depiction of a girl engaged in violent sport, but hints at extra-marital contact and blatantly foregrounds an overarching theme of female empowerment. Normally, Siti Halim writes: "programs that are shown on RTB, especially those produced locally, must adhere to the teachings of Islam. For example, female and male characters must never touch each other unless they are related through marriage" (2010, pp. 43–44), but the character Yasmine comes perilously close to overstepping that line with her boyfriend. Furthermore, Yasmine blatantly defies her father, who forbids her to train in *Silat*, despite social pressure upon young Bruneians to conform to *Awar galat*. Patrick Low and Sik-Liong Ang clarify the meaning of this phrase as follows:

> This Malay proverb which is uniquely Bruneian when directly translated means, 'humble and respectful.' The saying specifically applies to the younger generation [...] All the positive relationship (sic) to attain peace and harmony in a society should start with the practice of filial piety or respect at home (2011, p. 297).

An example of non-conformation to *Awar galat* is the unfilial child, or *Anak derhaka,* which is a common trope for Bruneian creative works, typically showcasing "a formulaic trajectory that [leads] to a conclusive ending: either the disloyal or unfilial child is punished by familial and/or divine will, or s/he submits to the parents' wishes and family order is restored" and reflects what has been described as a national anxiety "to maintain local identity and cultural values amid the chaos of external, global pressures and events" (Chin & Daud, 2014, abstract and p. 2). In contrast, the rebellious Yasmine displays very little *Awar galat*, and this filial disrespect, combined with her non-Muslim dress, intense boy chasing and fast car driving, which ultimately see her apparently achieve her carnal desires, might have rung alarm bells for the *Da'wah* Control and Censor unit, if they were preoccupied with promoting traditional notions of the authentic Bruneian Muslima. But, if it did, those alarums were either silenced or ignored. This silence is somewhat perplexing, since, as Grace Chin and Kathrina Daud state: "With the family unit acting as a micro-entity of the state, all challenges to parental authority are significantly refigured as transgressions against the state, since unfilial children are ultimately disloyal to the very values espoused by MIB" (2014, p. 5).

Perhaps the explanation for the unexpectedly lax Islamic censorship regarding *Yasmine* lies with an understanding of MIB as a "unifying ideology which would bolster [the Sultan's] power, blunt the appeal of those calling for a stricter observance of Islam, and develop a *sense of purpose in the young*" (Saunders, 1994, pp. 187–188, my emphasis). For the Sultan's political advisers, it appears, cinema need not necessarily pander to the extremism which fundamentalist Islam would fain enforce upon the citizenry, nor should it necessarily diminish the goals and ideals of the younger generations. Why might the Sultan, who as one of the richest men in the world undeniably luxuriates in unchallenged, absolute power, be even remotely cautious about Islamic fundamentalism, emphasizing in a recent address to the United Nations that he "rejects extremism" (Yap, 2014, p. 1)? Talib hints that such reticence is in his best interests:

> [...] modernisation undercuts the king's power and authority, requiring monarchs to share power with important new groups such as the expanding middle class. [...] To alleviate the 'king's dilemma,' the Sultan absorbed new well-educated elites in his government so as to reduce discontent among emerging new social groups. By allying himself with these new elites, the Sultan was also able to reduce his dependence on the royal and traditional elite (2013, pp. 2–3).

Despite being one of the richest men in the world, the Sultan quite likely wants to appear non-elitist, a man of the people, and he knows that Bruneians are not illiterate, impoverished villagers, as is commonly (although incorrectly) believed about the Middle East populace. Accordingly, Talib might have suggested, the Sultan prefers to keep an unpreventably Internet-connected population, well-informed by the fashions of western society, happily modern in their tastes and interests.

Additionally, the frequency of Hollywood films appearing in Bruneian cinemas means many cultural artefacts of non-Muslim ideals prevail. Gary Shore's blockbuster, *Dracula Untold* (2014), for example, recently enjoyed full houses with no less than thirteen daily screenings at one suburban Bandar Seri Begawan Cineplex, despite its overtly pro-Christian narrative foregrounding the Catholic crucifix in a typical gesture of Catholic propaganda arguably promoting proselytization, as did Bram Stoker's classic 1896 novel *Dracula* (see Starrs, 2004). Furthermore, and most provocatively, the villain in *Dracula Untold* is identified and frequently referred to as a Sultan. Although the film's evil Sultan is Turkish, not Bruneian, and there is not any verbal mention of the religion's name, viewers were shown a Hollywood codified interpretation of Islam as the evil Other. Even religious-themed cinema, it seems, can survive the censors under the (Bruneian) Sultan's benevolent rule.

The recent indications of an upsurge in interest in Bruneian film-making are long overdue, but the belated participation in this revolution can be attributed to no reason Baumgartel proposes. Rather, I suspect the advance stems from efforts by a paternalistic but benevolent, personalized monarch to modernize, rather than historicize, Islam in Brunei generally and MIB, including Sharia Law, specifically. Talib hints at the potential for the Sultan to personalize his rule: "the monarchical system of government has proven to be a rather congenial regime in the Islamic world. While monarchies are essentially traditional polities, they are by no means incapable of accommodating new demands brought about by socio-economic change" (2002, p. 136), and I suspect this is not news to the Sultan. He recognizes the "new demands" of the 21st Century and his mission appears to be one of modernizing Bruneian Islam, not historicizing it.

Conclusion: Quotidian Life under Sharia Law in 2017 Brunei

Hollywood has long demonized the Muslim in its films (see Shaheen, 2001; Ramji, 2005; and Semmerling, 2006, for example), so it is hardly surprising if some western commentators expect that, with the implementation of Sharia Law, Bruneian society would devolve into a strictly punitive, evil and misogynistic Islamic state, featuring *Hudud*-based law enforcement characterized by "draconian" (Seal, 2014) punishments such as hand amputations for stealing and death by stoning for adultery or homosexuality, or the harassment of women for being un-veiled in public, undertaking higher education or simply driving motor vehicles—and that the nation's cinema would reflect this. The reality is that, according to my own firsthand experience of life before and after the implementation of phases one and two of Sharia Law, the Sultanate has experienced absolutely no perceptible changes in quotidian life so far. Despite being shrilly described as "the Sultan's brutal legislation" (Robb, 2014), no violent, bloody sentences have been handed down and everyday society appears totally unchanged. *Muslim Village* writes:

> Nevertheless, not unlike the cinemas in Malaysia, those in Brunei do not require male and female patrons to sit separately, and the lights are not left on during screenings. [...] In the streets and malls of Brunei, it is not

impossible to see some cross-dressers, attesting to the fact that the law (not more than B$1,000/RM3,000 fine or three-month imprisonment or both for cross-dressing in public) is not strictly enforced. [...] From what can be seen, theft and robbery cases are still dealt with the 'old way' and amputation is not yet enforced against such offenders (2016).

The historic first conviction under Sharia Law in Brunei was of a Muslim Indonesian caught smoking tobacco during the fasting hours of Ramadan (Zailani, 2014). He was sentenced to six month's imprisonment but given the option of paying a $2500 fine (understandably, he chose the latter). This conviction went almost entirely uncommented upon in the western media, an unlikely result had it been a case involving a female transgressor against the traditionally misogynistic conventions of Sharia Law. Against alarmist western expectations, perhaps, young Bruneian women still go out in public, unescorted by their husbands or family, unveiled and dressed in revealing western fashions, driving cars, pursuing careers and higher education and leading lives no different from those led by women in western, secular, democratic societies— or no different than the life led by the lead character in *Yasmine*. In fact, the nation recently re-committed to "promoting and protecting women's rights on the country in line with the [United Nations] Convention on the Elimination of Discrimination Against Women" (Kamit, 2014, p. A8) and many women continue to hold offices of high power and authority in the governmental, medical, pedagogical and judicial systems. As an example of the nation's commitment to fighting discrimination against women, Royal Brunei Airlines recently flew a Boeing 787 Dreamliner with an all-female crew to the relatively misogynistic country of Saudi Arabia—where women are not allowed to even drive cars— thus demonstrating the extent to which the two Sharia Law-run Muslim nations differ (Taylor, 2016).

Nor has there been any evidence of an increased governmental clamp down on other cultural influences from the west or even upon fictional representations of secular western society transplanted onto Bruneian soil, such as in *Yasmine*. All indications are that Bandial's comments that artists "live in constant fear" (2013) are greatly exaggerated, and Siti Kamaluddin has never mentioned any lack of confidence or anxiety let alone fear while directing the western-styled *Yasmine*. Indeed, were it not for the cameo-like representations of iconic Bruneian landmarks and tropes, a viewer could believe the movie was set almost anywhere: there are not even any of the ubiquitous royal portraits of the Sultan and his wife, Her Majesty Raja Isteri Pengiran Anak Hajah Saleha, in the film's *mise-en-scene*.

Typically, the invested authority of the ruling powers in a sovereign state is reflected in the conjunction of society, state-censored media and the judiciary, but some commentators believe this to be waning globally. Wendy Brown, for example, argues that "states do not dominate or order" but instead "react" (2010, p. 67). This may well be the case in Brunei with the Sultan *reacting* to western cultural influences rather than attempting to fully dominate them, even as it commences implementation of its final phase three of Sharia Law, with life in Brunei still remaining very much westernized. Time will tell, however, if the forthcoming implementation of phase three of Sharia Law will also do little to change the everyday lives of ordinary, law-abiding citizens in Brunei, but the apparent reality is that the Sultan is more interested in a peaceful, modern interpretation of Sharia Law and MIB than a Middle Eastern style of punitive sovereignty. His national imaginary for Brunei and the emerging (hopefully burgeoning) Bruneian film industry,[3] I suspect, permits and even foregrounds those cultural artefacts which demonstrate the successful and harmonious integration of an absolute monarchy, MIB, Sharia Law and the western values of gender equality, as contrasted, for example, by nearby Indonesia where "the Indonesian national imaginary has revolved around the phallocentric rhetoric and representation of women as secondary citizens" (Chin, 2012, p. 142). Brunei simultaneously resists and embraces globalization: The Sultanate is forging a unique identity as a Southeast Asian Islamic Monarchy run according to Sharia Law that nevertheless respects its citizen's modern, western ideals. It covertly rejects the archaic, extremist premise of an allegedly 'authentic' *Muslima*, her face and her ambition kept covered and repressed, her societal role marginalized and her identity devalued. Instead, she is able to live a self-actualized life under MIB, and the indicators are that for all Bruneians, male and female, the Sultanate will remain the 'Abode of Peace' for the reigns of many more Sultans to come. Either that or I cynically propose that we in the west are being bottle-fed a version of a repressive Bruneian life for *Muslima* which will, in the future, be anything but the truth. Certainly, this prospect, as unwelcome as it may be, is not unpredicted by other commentators. Jeremy Ludi alleges that "Despite the world's third highest social media penetration rate (86%), users [in Brunei] are regularly threatened with indefinite imprisonment without trial under the Internal Security Act" (2017) and this level of social control, combined with

---

3   Brunei's royal family is apparently not averse to involving itself in the western industry of film with Patrick Brzeski noting *"The Sultan's son, Prince Azim, with Naomi Campbell, has moved into film producing, recently debuting a Hilary Swank project in Cannes"* (2014).

censorship of news reporting as per the ill-fated *Brunei Times*, prompts writers such as Mansoor to bemoan:

> The future does not augur well for Brunei unless it is willing to adapt to the times. In the internet age with the public appetite for information growing, it is increasingly difficult to curb speech and police thoughts. Only time will tell in which direction Brunei will lean—toward greater transparency or greater censorship. For now, all signs point to the latter (2016).

Given the illuminating example set by Siti Kamaluddin's *Yasmine*, I prefer to think positively with regard to Brunei's future, and feel that the fears expressed by commentators such as Bandial, Ludi and Mansoor are unfounded. Rather, I believe the Sultan is committed to a less-repressive, more modernized and gender-equalized nation operating under a relatively relaxed and westernized version of Sharia Law and that the future therefore bodes well for the fortunate inhabitants of the Abode of Peace.

References

Ahmed, L. (2003, October). Dossier 25. A border passage. *Women Reclaiming & Redefining Culture.* Retrieved from the Women Living Under Muslim Laws website: http://wrrc.wluml.org/node/465.

Anderson, B. (1983). *Imagined communities: Reflections on the origin and spread of nationalism.* London: Verso.

Appadurai, A. (1990). Disjuncture and difference in the global cultural economy. *Public Culture, 2*(2), 1–24.

Bandial, Q. (2013, May 4). The case for press freedom. *The Brunei Times,* Retrieved from The Brunei Times website: http://www.bt.com.bn/2013/05/04/case-press-freedom (accessed 8 September 2013, taken down on 7 November 2016).

Baumgartel, T. (2012). *Independent cinema in Southeast Asia.* Singapore: National University of Singapore Press.

Bouma, G., Ling, R. & Pratt, D. (2010). *Religious diversity in Southeast Asia and the Pacific.* Berlin: Springer.

Brown, W. (2010). *Walled states, waning sovereignty.* Brooklyn, NY: Zone Books.

Brzeski, P. (2014, November 6). 48 hours in Brunei: *Hollywood Reporter* infiltrates the underground gay scene. *Hollywood Reporter,* Retrieved from the Hollywood Reporter website: http://www.hollywoodreporter.com/news/48-hours -brunei-hollywood-reporter-710691

Chin, G. V. S. (2006). Expressions of self-censorship: Ambivalence and difference in Malaysian and Singaporean Chinese women's prose writings in English. *South-east Asia: A Multidisciplinary Journal, 6*(1), 13–34.

Chin, G. V. S. (2012). Imagined subjects: Polygamy, gender and nation in Nia Dinata's *Love for Share. Journal of International Women's Studies, 13*(3), 137–152.

Chin, G. V. S. & Daud, K. (2014). Negotiating difference: The trope of *anak derhaka* and ideological endings in Bruneian writings. *The Journal of Commonwealth Literature.* Retrieved from the Sage Journals website: http://jcl.sagepub.com/content/early/2014/07/20/0021989414543909.abstract.

Countrymeters.info. (2017). Brunei Darussalam population clock. Retrieved from the Country Meters website: http://www.countrymeters.info/en/Brunei_Darussalam/.

Doherty, B. (2014, June 29). Australia to question Brunei over stoning laws before trade talks. *Sydney Morning Herald.* Retrieved from the Sydney Morning Herald website: http://www.smh.com.au/federal-politics/political-news/australia-to-question-brunei-over-stoning-laws-before-trade-talks-20140629-zsq1h.html#ixzz3Ii483Uzl.

Dracula Untold. Shore, G. (dir.) 2014.

Facal, G. (2014). Silat martial ritual initiation in Brunei Darussalam. *Southeast Asia: A Multidisciplinary Journal, 14*, 1–13.

Gema Dari Menara (Voice from the Minaret), Ministry of Religious Affairs, 1968.

Halim, S. N. K. H. A. (2010). *Making public service broadcasting attractive in Brunei*, Honours thesis, School of Media and Technology, Royal Melbourne Institute of Technology, Australia.

Harun, A. M. K. (2014, October 21). Compulsory Islamic studies for harmonious community. *The Brunei Times.* Retrieved from The Brunei Times website: http://www.bt.com.bn/news-national/2014/10/21/compulsory-islamic-studies-harmonious-community (accessed 8 September 2013, taken down on 7 November 2016).

Higson, A. (2000). The limiting imagination of national cinema. In M. Hjort & S. Mackenzie (Eds.), *Cinema and Nation.* (pp. 63–74). NY and London: Routledge.

Horton, A. V. M. (2005). Window-dressing an Islamizing Sultanate. *Asian Survey, 45*(1), 180–185.

Huntington, S. P. (1968). *Political order in changing societies.* New Haven and London: Yale University Press.

Isaac, T. (2014, September 30). *Haram Queen* (Review)—Brunei's first ever LGBT-themed short film. *Big Gay Picture Show.* Retrieved from the Big Gay Picture Show website: http://www.biggaypictureshow.com/bgps/2014/09/haram-queen-short-film-review-bruneis-first-ever-lgbt-themed-film/.

Kamit, R. (2014, November 2). Rights of women protected in Brunei. *The Brunei Times.* Retrieved from The Brunei Times website: http://www.bt.com.bn/news-national/2014/11/02/rights-of-women-protected (accessed 8 September 2013, taken down on 7 November 2016).

Lacaba, J. F. (2000). *The films of ASEAN*. Manila: ASEAN Committee on Culture and Information.

Loo, S. P. (2009). Ethnicity and educational policies in Malaysia and Brunei Darussalam. *SA-eDUC Journal, 6*(2), 146–157.

Low, P. K. C. & Ang, S. (2011). Confucius, Confucian values and their applications on marketing—the Bruneian perspective. *Journal of Research in International Business Management, 1*(9), 293–303.

Ludi, J. (2017, February 4). Under the radar: Did Trump's victory seal Brunei's fate? *Global Risks Insight*. Retrieved from the Global Risks Insight website: http://global riskinsights.com/2017/02/did-trump-victory-seal-brunei-fate/.

Mansoor, A. (2016, December 23). Brunei on edge amid oil slump: Nervous authorities throttle media discussion. *Nikkei Asian Review*. Retrieved from the Nikkei Asian Review website: http://asia.nikkei.com/Viewpoints/Ahmed-Mansoor/Brunei-on-edge-amid-oil-slump.

Maryono, O. (2000). Pencak Silat as humanistic discipline. *Rapid Journal, 5*(2), 35–37.

Muslim Village. (2016, October 5). Brunei: Life normal after Sharia "hudud" take effect. *Muslimvillage.com*. Retrieved from the Muslim Village website: https://muslim village.com/2016/10/05/120447/brunei-life-normal-after-sharia-hudud/.

Prusak, M. (2017, February 17). Brunei's economy running on empty. *The Diplomat*. Retrieved from The Diplomat website: http://thediplomat.com/2016/02/bruneis -economy-running-on-empty/.

Ramji, R. (2005). From *Navy Seals* to *The Siege*: Getting to know the Muslim terrorist, Hollywood style. *Journal of Religion and Film, 9*(2), article 6. Retrieved from the University of Nebraska Omaha website: http://digitalcommons.unomaha.edu/jrf/vol9/iss2/6.

Robb, D. (2014, September 7). Beverley shillbillies: Hollywood hypocrites shun hotels while hawking wares to rights abusers. *Deadline Hollywood*. Retrieved from the Deadline Hollywood website: http://deadline.com/2014/09/beverly-hills-hotel -boycott-hollywood-829350/.

Saunders, G. (1994). *A history of Brunei*. Kuala Lumpur: University of Oxford Press.

Seal, M. (2014, July 22). The Beverley Hills Hotel celebrity boycott: Who is it really hurting? *Vanity Fair*. Retrieved from the Vanity Fair website: http://www.vanityfair.com/vf-hollywood/beverly-hill-hotel-celebrity-boycott-sultan-of-brunei.

Semmerling, T. J. (2006). *Evil Arabs in American popular film: Orientalist fear*. Austin: University of Texas Press.

Shaheen, J. G. (2001). *Reel bad Arabs: How Hollywood vilifies a people*. Northampton, Ma: Olive Branch Press.

Sichel, J. (2014, May 8). Sultan's new Sharia Laws prompt Jewish groups to shun Beverly Hills Hotel. *Jewish Journal*. Retrieved from the Jewish Journal website: http://www

.jewishjournal.com/los_angeles/article/sultans_new_sharia_laws_prompt_jewish
_groups_to_shun_beverly_hills_hotel.

Sidhu, J. S. (2009). *Historical dictionary of Brunei Darussalam*. Washington: Scarecrow
Press.

Starrs, D. B. (2004). Keeping the faith: Catholicism in *Dracula* and its adaptations.
Journal of Dracula Studies, 6. Retrieved from the Journal of Dracula Studies website:
http://dractravel.com/drc/.

Starrs, D. B. (2006). The maternal monster in *Suburban Mayhem*. *Metro Magazine, 151*,
22–24.

Talib, N. S. (2002). A resilient Monarchy: The Sultanate of Brunei and regime legitimacy
in an era of democratic nation-states. *New Zealand Journal of Asian Studies, 4*(2),
134–147.

Talib, N. S. (2013). Brunei Darussalam: Royal absolution and the modern state. *Kyoto
Review of Southeast Asia, 13*, 1–8.

Tapsell, R. (2012). Old tricks in a new era: Self-censorship in Indonesian journalism.
Asian Studies Review, 36(2), 227–246.

Taylor, A. (2016, March 16). All-female crew lands plane in Saudi Arabia, a country
where they're forbidden to drive. *Sydney Morning Herald*, Retrieved from the Sydney
Morning Herald website: http://www.smh.com.au/world/allfemale-crew-lands
-plane-in-saudi-arabia-a-country-where-theyre-forbidden-to-drive-20160315
-gnjwzq.html.

The Star Online. (2016, October 2). The deep impact of the law on non-Muslims. *The
Star Online*, Retrieved from The Star Online website: http://www.thestar.com.my/
news/nation/2016/10/02/the-deep-impact-of-the-law-on-nonmuslims-many-feel
-heavy-burden-of-hudud-law/.

Tradingeconomics. (2017). *Brunei GDP Per Capita*. Retrieved from the Trading
Economics website: http://www.tradingeconomics.com/brunei/gdp-per-capita.

United Nations. (2009). *Human Development Reports*. Retrieved from the United
Nations Development Programs website: http://hdr.undp.org/en/data.

Williams, A. (2002). *Film and nationalism*. New Brunswick, New Jersey: Rutgers
University Press.

Wilson, I. D. (2002). *The politics of inner power: The practice of Pencak Silat in West Java*.
Dissertation, School of Asian Studies, Murdoch University, Australia.

Yap, A. (2014, September 26). HM: Brunei united with world in fighting terror. *The
Brunei Times*. Retrieved from The Brunei Times website: http://www.bt.com.bn/
frontpage-news-national/2014/09/26/hm-brunei-united-world-fighting-terror
(accessed 8 September 2013, taken down on 7 November 2016).

Yorulmaz, B. & Blizek, W. R. (2014). Islam in Turkish cinema. *Journal of Religion and
Film, 18* (2), 1–18.

Zahedi, A. (2007). Contested meaning of the veil and political ideologies of Iranian regimes. *Journal of Middle East Women's Studies, 3*(3), 75–98.

Zailani, N. (2014, July 23). Indonesian convicted under Syariah law. *The Brunei Times*, Retrieved from The Brunei Times website: http://www.bt.com.bn/news-national/2014/07/23/indonesian-convicted-under-syariah-law (accessed 8 September 2013, taken down on 7 November 2016).

CHAPTER 7

Visual Discourses of (Un)veiling: Revisiting Women of Allah

Esmaeil Zeiny

Introduction

Islam and Muslims have always been attracting major attention in the West and continue to be the limelight of many political controversies. In this, Muslim women seem to have become one of the main focuses of debate for the past two centuries. Many in the West believe that veiled Muslim women are victims of religious bias and always oppressed and silent. At the outset of this chapter, it is important to note that it is incontrovertible that some conservative interpretations of Islamic religious scripts are misogynist and in favor of patriarchy but as it has already been noted by many scholars, a great number of Muslims are staunch supporter of women's right and there are countless numbers of articulate veiled women in the Muslim world. However, in Western discourses on Muslims, historically, women have been narrowly constructed as weak, inferior and victims of religious and patriarchal rules. This engineered and institutional mode of Muslim women's representation seems to have accelerated since 9/11; Muslim women are represented as gendered slave in dire need of "saving" by the West. For instance, the war in Afghanistan in the aftermath of 9/11 was partly based on a feminist cause as President Bush campaigned frequently to gather support for saving Afghan women from the brutalities of patriarchy and religion. This is indicative of the fact that Muslim women are used as the war propaganda against Islam. Muslim women's rights are used as an alibi to legitimize their colonial presence in the shape of neo-conservatism. Race, gender and religion are discourses that have scripted the terms of involvement in the 'war on terror.' The Western systematic representation of Islamic extremism and backward, oppressed and politically immature Muslim women is the revitalization of Orientalist tropes to create Islamophobia. Triggered by 9/11, the colonial motifs of Muslim women have regained alarming currency in the Western discourses as they have been soaked in images of veiled Muslim women and stories of their victimhood in an Islamic society.

Soon after 9/11, visual discourses about Muslim women appeared and flooded not only the media but also the art and literary markets. Based on Western ideology of Muslim women, these images are so powerful that they easily affect and change the public's perceptions about Muslim women. This stereotypical visual representation of women which relates to a wider geopolitical discourse has served to bolster the images of Muslim society as the cultural, political, and moral "other" of the West. The Western cultural and visual media do not portray voiceless images of Muslim veiled women in vacuousness, rather these Islamophobic misogynist portrayals suggest how the West positions Muslim women which feed dehumanization and appropriation in popular culture of the West. As a continuing legacy of colonialism and as a modern version of Orientalism, neo-conservatism has found that the efficient way to make Westerners believe that Muslim women are being victimized in their societies is through the narratives of Muslim women themselves. Since then many diasporic Muslim women have been creating discourses that reiterate and consolidate the stereotypical images of Muslim women. However, there are works that tend to challenge these clichés such as Shirin Neshat's *Women of Allah* (1993–97). As an Iranian artist in exile, Shirin Neshat's black and white photography of *Women of Allah*, which deals directly with the visual representation of Muslim women, is also often misunderstood as reinforcing the misogynist stereotypes but the postcolonial critics' reading of her photography makes Westerners re-examine their pre-packaged assumptions about Muslim women. Drawing upon Hamid Naficy's the exile culture of "here and there," Neshat is a culturally hybrid artist who simultaneously shatters and challenges the Islamophobic misogynist stereotypes while questioning the patriarchal and confining rules upon women in Iran.

Although produced in the 1990s, one cannot deny the immediacy and relevancy of this series of photographs to our present world. That this series of photographs is still on exhibitions around the world such as the 2016 She Who Tells a Story: Women Photographers from Iran and the Arab World at National Museum of Women in the Arts in Washington, justifies its relevancy two decades after its production. Her *Women of Allah* series will never get old and is always relevant and current with the continuing anti-Muslim sentiment and hate crimes in the West. The immediacy and relevancy of these photographs emanate from our anxieties and uncertainties of the present day rather than the conditions of its original production. Recent years and days have witnessed ugly episodes of racist Islamophobic attack against Muslims in the West. The latest major episode of anti-Muslim violence occurred on 26th May, 2017 in Portland, Oregon on a train when an American man started yelling and screaming obscenities and anti-Muslim slurs at two Muslim teenage girls, one of whom was wearing *hijab*. He stabbed two people to death and seriously injured a third one who had come forward to calm him down and prevent him to harm the two girls (ABC). Another instance is the December 2016 hate crime attack in London where a Muslim woman has been dragged along the sidewalk by her *hijab* (The Independent). Neshat's *Women of Allah* possesses a pedagogical and dialogical function that can phase out the centuries-old stereotypes of Muslim women and simultaneously questions the Iranian government's confining rules on women such as the mandatory dress code. Contrary to what the title of this chapter conjures up, this article is not only a review of Neshat's *Women of Allah*. While underscoring the series' dialogical and pedagogical functions, I reveal murals and posters of Muslim women and argue that they have been Neshat's specific source of inspiration. Produced in Iran, these images promote *hijab* and the role of Iranian *hijabi* women in war which also possess both dialogical and pedagogical function.

Islamophobia and the Veil

'Whether cradling her baby, carrying an assault rifle, or walking ten feet behind her oppressor husband, the stereotypical images of a usually fully veiled Muslim woman are burned deep into Western consciousness' (Yvonne Haddad et al., 2006, p. 40).

Islamophobia is not a recent phenomenon as the world has witnessed annals of religious and racial intolerance under a different terminology. The intolerance in the US, for instance, began prior to her encounter with the Muslim world. From the conquest of the Americas and the subjugation of the indigenous to the slave trades and treating of the Japanese diaspora during the Second World War, the United States of America has a record of infringing the human rights and freedoms of the racialised groups (Bakali, 2016). Islamophobia is a novel term for an old fear which has portrayed Islam as a menace to the West and has emerged in genocides, wars and crusades over the centuries. This fear and mistrust towards the Muslim 'Other' have roots in Europe and North America. As Weller notes, "Islamophobia is undeniably rooted in the historical inheritance of a conflictual relationship that has developed over many centuries involving the overlap of religion, politics and warfare" (2001, p. 8). It became an international spotlight after the events of 9/11. There has been a remarkable increase in hostility and abhorrence towards Muslims since 9/11 (Allen & Nielson, 2002). Many countries in the West have, indeed, reinforced increased anxieties towards their Muslim residents and Islam in light of terrorist attacks. This rapid increase in violence and hatred developed into discrimination and racism which serves as the basic ideology of Islamophobia (Fiore, 2010). According to Allen (2010), Islamophobia, as an ideology, bears

similarity with racism and other related phenomena that "sustains and per-
petuates negatively evaluated meaning about Muslims and Islam in the contemporary setting in similar way to that which it has historically ... inform[ed]
and construct[ed] thinking about Muslims and Islam as Other" (p. 190). This
description brings to light the historical roots of Islamophobia and elucidates
that it is a phenomenon which has been impacted over the centuries by many
different strains of thoughts and ideologies that considered Muslims and their
societies as the 'Other.'

This ideological formation has been produced by a culture that deploys a
fixed set of beliefs, analysis, and representation which informs the policies of
the governments, and creates a particular set of political and media discourses
along with social beliefs and practices. As Lean (2012) mentions, "anti-Muslim
sentiment [is] not just a feeling among certain segments of the population.
It [is] state-sponsored praxis that aim[s] ... to reinstate the heyday of white
Christian ..." (p. 171). The anti-Muslim prejudice has been disseminated and
normalized in the Western context through the supports of the governments.
Thus, Islamophobia is "discrimination, dehumanization, and misrepresenta-
tions of Muslims, those of Muslim heritage, and a systematic miseducation
about Islam itself" (Kincheloe, Steinberg & Stonebanks, 2010, p. x). What has
contributed to the propagation of Islamophobia has been the negative depiction of Muslims in media. Whether it is a news report or a film about Islam,
"the picture drawn is a unanimous one. 'Islam' means the end of civilization
as 'we' know it. Islam is anti-human, antidemocratic, anti-Semitic and anti-
rational" (Said, 1980, p. 5). The Western media have achieved creating a common understanding amongst Westerners that misogyny and oppression of
women is the shared feature of the Muslim world. Resulting from these images,
Islamophobia is a common phenomenon in many parts of the Western world.
In the United States, it is the renunciation of establishing an Islamic Cultural
Center near Ground Zero, and in Europe, it is the banning of veils or *hijab* in
schools and public places. What Said (1994, p. 282) describes as a "legacy of
connections" between the colonial past and the imperial present can best be
epitomized by the images of veiled women in the Western discourses.

Thus it can be argued that the depiction of veiled women being victimized
under patriarchy and Islamic despotism in Western discourses is an instance
of continued Orientalist discourse and typology under the current guise of
Islamophobia (Bordeaux, 2007). The portrayals of the veil and the oppression of Muslim women have been one of the most frequent stereotypes in the
media and popular culture of the West to publicize Islamophobia. Since the
nineteenth century, the veil has symbolized Muslim women's inferiority for

the West and it still is a powerful symbol used to reinforce the so-called binary of the progressive West and the digressive East. Western visual discourses are fraught with images of veiled women as static, unchanging, inferior, backward and illiterate. Emanated from the perpetual bombardment of these negative depictions of Muslim women is the stereotype that became a "system of ideas ... unchanged as teachable wisdom ... a created body of theory and practice in which, for many generations, there has been a considerable material investment" (Said, 1978, p. 7). In the post 9/11 climate of Islamophobia, Muslim women are portrayed with no variations; whether it be in Saudi Arabia, Iran or Malaysia, Muslim women are depicted as exotic and oppressed "other" in most of the Western visual discourses. One may never repudiate the fact that women have been experiencing discrimination and oppression in some Islamic societies; as noted by Moghissi (1999, p. 2) "From Afghanistan to Algeria to Sudan, Pakistan and ... [Saudi Arabia]—indeed, everywhere in the Islamic societies women are systematically brutalised and caught in a deadly crossfire between the secular and fundamentalist forces." However, violence against women is not an Islamic phenomenon, rather it is present almost everywhere in the world. In her study of 230 media photos, Wilkins (1997) argues that the occidental media has been loaded with Orientalized stereotypes of Muslim women as an insignia of "collectivistic" conventional society which could be as the opposite of Western individualism.

The image of Muslim women is produced from colonial discourses in order to generate a colonial subject which is a social production hinged on 'difference.' This depiction has been utilized to differentiate and devalue the Muslim women as "other" from the Westerners. Therefore, the "veiled female body is central in the construction of discourses on the difference of the Muslim as 'other' with the non-Muslim 'self'" (Chakraborti& Zempi, 2012, p. 269). Veiling has been one of the tools that mark the difference between the East and the West. There are several reasons why a Muslim woman wears the veil but in the light of Islamophobia, many Western scholars perpetuate to diminish this issue to a symbol of Muslim women's oppression. Islamic societies in these discourses are depicted as a single community following a single ideology of women's oppression. Such presentation of these images insinuates the notion that Muslim women are homogenized regardless of their background. Whether they embrace the ideology of veiling or not, there are many active Muslim women who have been trying to enhance their socio-economic position in the Islamic societies but whose work usually go unnoticed for many Western scholars. Therefore, Islamophobia reintroduces and reaffirms a global racial structure through which dissimilarities are preserved and extended. It is the reintroduction and reaffirmation of ideologies of Orientalism because veiled women have been the symbol of difference for the Westerners from the early days of Orientalism. Kahf (1999, p. 8) notes:

> When the Orient was Orientalized (to paraphrase Edward Said), when a vast and complex body of knowledge about the Islamic Other developed simultaneously with Western subjugation of that world, the image of the Muslim woman most familiar in the West today emerged.

These images formed derogative stereotypes about Islam which caused an Islamophobic attitude in the minds of many Westerners. Stereotypical representation is never used to show an accurate depiction of colonial subjects, but rather to simply ensure their inferiority. These stereotypes are "current episodes in a series of subjugations" (Foucault cited in Bouchard, 1977, p. 148). These images are the production of racist and misogynistic constructs of women of non-Western culture. Islamophobia spreads the idea that veil is inherently oppressive and its removal equals freedom of Muslim women. Most scholars in the West ignore the fact that there are many Muslim women who choose to wear the veil as for them, the veil is a "source of respect, virtue, and pride;" it is a symbol of "passage from childhood to adulthood" (Milani, 1992, p. 35). For a considerable number of Muslim women the veil is deemed as a 'second skin' as it is passed down from past generations. It is also a sign of resistance when worn at times of revolution to resist the Westernization of culture. Veiling should not be considered as intrinsically a sign of oppression unless it is forced. The obsession of Islamophobia to unveil Muslim women can be associated with elements of coercion. Both forced veiling and unveiling make women's body into a ground of contention where ideals of resistance and Westernization are acted upon. Akin to forced veiling, unveiling in the light of Islamophobia has a dramatic impact upon Muslim women. For instance, the Unveiling Act of 1936 in Iran as an agenda to Westernize the country had serious ramifications. Hoodfar (1993, p. 261) writes:

> For many women it was such an embarrassing situation that they just stayed home. Many independent women became dependent on men, while those who did not have a male present in the household suffered most because they had to beg favors from their neighbors ... Women became even more dependent on men since they now had to ask for man's collaboration in order to perform activities they had previously performed independently. This gave men a degree of control over women

they had never before possessed. It also reinforced the idea that households without adult men were odd and abnormal.

The Islamophobic discourses are so dominant and ubiquitous that leave no place for apparent realities, such as the earlier-noted fact that many Muslim women wear the veil of their own volition and they feel liberated, not suppressed. The prevalence of these sorts of discourse is so overwhelming that the public in the West developed an antipathy towards veiled women. This level of antipathy which still exists in the West transmogrified the veiled women residing in the West into an object of hatred and discrimination. The lofty discourse of saving women from the male chauvinism and Islamic patriarchy has given its place to misogyny towards veiled Muslim women. The impact of Islamophobia is the erasure of multiple meanings of veil where only a single meaning stands out which is a symbol of gender inequality and oppression. These clichés about the veil as an insignia of oppression coupled with the assumption of Muslim women's subservience make veiled women ideal subjects against whom anti-Muslim hostilities are enacted. Therefore, as a negative behavior towards Islam and Muslims, Islamophobia includes "hostility, violence, rejection, exclusion and domination" (Dekker & Van Noll, 2009, p. 3). The systematic representations of the veiled women in visual discourses of the West metamorphose the Western public perception of a woman living in Islamic societies. A review of Nehshat's *Women of Allah* and the critics' take on her work will confirm the dialogical and pedagogical function of her work, and affirms its potentiality to reconcile and bridge the two cultures of East and West.

Women of Allah (1993–97) & the West

'All cultures are located in place and time. Exile culture is located at the intersection and in the interstices of other cultures. Physically placed outside its original homeland, it is mentally and emotionally both here and there, and as a result, it is both local and global.' Hamid Naficy (1993, p. 2).

Over the past two decades, the Iranian diaspora communities have grown considerably. This growth is not just an increase in numbers because the majority of Iranians residing abroad settled in their "homes in exile" over thirty years ago; rather it is the growth of the community as a community and as a segment of the society that has been attracting attention during the past twenty years. This community awareness within the Iranian diaspora communities has led to the production of a myriad of discourses that have brought the Iranian diaspora experience to the realm of popular culture. Iranians in exile have been creating a work engaged with what have become the most propitious topics of the day for Western readers: immigration, exile, Islamic fundamentalism and women's right. One of the most striking features of this emerging work is its obsession with reversing the distorted images of Iranian Muslim women as they are much misunderstood outside of Iran. While the Western media is somewhat more sophisticated in their depiction of Iran than they were three decades ago, Said's critique of media coverage of Iran in that era still holds true today. Iran is still "no more than a poorly defined and badly misunderstood abstraction" (Said, 1981, 83). The 1979 Iranian Revolution, the mandatory dress code of women and the disputed 2009 presidential election trigger dismal images of agonized people, especially black *chador*-cladded women under a highly theocratic political system with a deep-seated antagonism towards the West. Many of these sentiments might be true but it is by no means a proper understanding of Iran and Iranian Muslim women.

Undoubtedly, Iranian diaspora communities can debunk these stereotypical images and create a better sentiment through their creative work. Although many in doing so reinforce the stereotypes and therefore exacerbate the image of Iranian Muslim women, there are diasporic works that can challenge the centuries-old Muslim women stereotypes. The modern Iranian diaspora is the by-product of various trends of emigrations, expedited by the incident of 1979 Iranian Revolution, the subsequent Iran-Iraq war and the resulting recent severe transmutations of the Iranian society. Shirin Neshat, an Iranian artist residing in America, left the country before the 1979 Iranian Revolution but cites a return trip to Iran as a seminal moment in her creative production. Born in Qazvin, Iran in 1957, Shirin Neshat was raised in a 'well-to-do family.' As a physician, her father was a staunch supporter of the Shah and his Westernization policies. In an interview with Suzie Mackenzie (2000, p. 1), Neshat states that her father "fantasized about the west, romanticized the west, and slowly rejected all of his own values; both my parents did. What happened, I think, was that their identity slowly dissolved, they exchanged it for comfort. It served their class." Like many supporters of the Shah who engaged in sending their children abroad for higher education, Shirin Neshat's father sent both his sons and daughters to pursue their studies in England and the United States of America.

At the age of 17, Shirin Neshat was sent to America to continue her education. In 1982, she has received her Master's degree in fine arts at the University of California, Berkeley. She was still in America when the Iranian Revolution of 1979 happened and did not return to her homeland until 1990. Her first visit back was both a painful and an exhilarating experience. It was painful because the sociopolitical situations had changed post-1979 Revolution. She explains that "the difference between what I had remembered from Iranian culture and what I was witnessing was enormous. The change was both frightening and exciting. I had never been in a country that was so ideologically based" (Bertucci, 1997, p. 84). However, this first trip back to Iran after twelve years of absence became the inspiration that fuels her artwork; she returned to the United States loaded with ideas for her work. As returning to Iran gives her the status of eyewitness to the issues she is representing, she employs meta-narrative in her work quite effectively. Meta narrative is "telling a story about something that happened to one's self in the first person [and] establishes a special kind of relationship with one's audience" (Babcock, 1984, p. 64). Therefore, encapsulated within the metaphors of Nehsat's *chador* are the meta-narrative of gender, culture, religion and exile. Since she enjoys the status of being insider/outsider in creating her work, the work discussed in this chapter is positioned in the liminal space of "here and there," Iran and the West as Naficy observes in regard to exile culture.

Upon returning to America, she has started to incorporate her experiences into her creative work and worked on her first series of photograph *Women of Allah* (1993–97). Resulting from the trip back to Iran and the exposure to the daily stereotypes of Muslim women in the West, Iranian women became the theme and subject matter of her artwork. These photographs show a woman, usually the artist herself, in long black *chador* whose hands, feet and face are oftentimes decorated with Persian scripts. In some of these photographs, the woman bears a gun. Much of the Western art criticism of Neshat's work exhibits that she is reaffirming the dichotomies of East/West, Tradition/Modernity, and Oppression/Freedom which are the hallmark of Orientalist myth. In discussing Neshat's *Women of Allah* (1993–97), Western art critics argue that her work is highlighting the repression and seclusion of Muslim women. People in the West who have been fed stereotypical media images of Muslim women think of the veiled women in Neshat's work as poor and voiceless women (Baily Jones, 2007). At first glance, Neshat's artwork carries stereotypes of sexualized, voiceless and exoticized femininity. A great number of Western art critics regard her work as a bolstering of all they already know about Muslim women.

The Western assumption that Iranian Muslim woman is a unitary subject conveys the idea that these women cannot be a driving force for any action rather they are considered as an object controlled by the state. This Western perception of a voicelessness, passivity and similarity of all Muslim women, especially Iranian women, was influenced by Hollywood clichés and stereotypes about Muslims, and it was exacerbated by memoirs such as Betty Mahmoodi's *Not without My Daughter* (1987) and Azar Nafisi's *Reading Lolita in Tehran* (2003). As soon as one sees an image of Muslim woman in the West, one "fills in all the blanks regarding the subject's ideology, background and intent" (Walker Parker, 2005, p. 52). This filling in comes from the mainstream Western media which has been portraying Muslim women in need of liberation. What today's Western 'liberators' have in common with the 19th century colonialism is the exploitation of Western feminist idiom to legitimize their violence. On a speech made by the then First Lady Laura Bush, Lughod (2003, p. 78) writes:

> Laura Bush's radio address on November 17 revealed the political work such mobilization accomplished ... There was a blurring of the very separate causes in Afghanistan of women's continuing malnutrition, poverty, and ill health and their more recent exclusion under the Taliban from employment, schooling, and the joys of wearing nail polish. On the other hand, her speech reinforced chiasmic divides, primarily between the "civilized people throughout the world" whose hearts break for the women and children of Afghanistan and the terrorist-and-the-Taliban, the cultural monsters who want to, as she put it, "impose their world on the rest of us." Most revealingly, the speech enlisted women to justify American bombing and intervention in Afghanistan and the "War on Terrorism" to which it was coupled. As Laura Bush said, "Because of our recent military gains in much of Afghanistan, women are no longer imprisoned in their homes. They can listen to music and teach their daughters without fear of punishment. The fight against terrorism is also a fight for the rights and dignity of women."

Obviously, Neshat's *Women of Allah* series depict images of Iranian women clad in *chador* rather than Afghan women with their face covered with *burkas*. However, many people in the West, under the influence of Islamophobia, paint all Muslim women with the same passive brush of oppression as if veil is inherently a sign of oppression. To most Western observer of Neshat's artwork, the veil is a sign of "unadulterated women's oppression—a symbolic wall dividing Iran from the rest of modern society" (Camhi, 2000, p. 150). Many Westerners believe that veiling is "an obstacle that bars [women] from social interaction and individual expression" (Cichoski. 2004, p. 4). Art critic, Reid (1996, p. 105) states that Neshat's *Women of Allah* series are indeed "contradictions—seductive feminine beauty and religious circumspection, Western conceptual art practice and traditional Islamic craft, not to mention 'submissive' Islamic women with large guns—(that) provide an irresistible intellectual and visual frisson." It is apparent that the notion of submission of veiled women is prevalent in the West. Dabashi (2005, p. 47) opines that the presupposition that Muslim women, be it Iranians or Arabs or Indians, have sat home and been "secluded to 'feminine private' quarters, while the public domain is left to men, is an Oriental lunacy ..." He critiques Western art critics and argues that these critics interpret Shirin Neshat's work through the distorted Eurocentric lenses:

> Through the intermediary of a body of interpretive essays and articles, the reception of Shirin Neshat's work is today almost inseparable from the body of work itself—to the point where the body of work itself is no longer distinguishable from the way that it has been received, the interpretive apparatus that has been generated around it. (2005, p. 33)

Being exposed to Western media representation of Muslim women and knowing of the Iranian women's situation in Iran, Neshat builds her artwork upon this history. She is familiar with the Western culture and media on the one hand and one the other hand she is an Iranian who is well-aware of the fact that veiling has different layers of meaning for Iranian women. The fact that her photography is mostly self-portrayed wearing the veil and *chador* bears an important message. As an American-Iranian who does not practice *hijab* in the day-to-day life in the West, putting on *chador* for the purpose of her photography indicates practicing Iranian tradition. She demonstrates implicitly that it is quite an easy task to "'create' various identities and work on people's perception of them" (Machowski, 2009, p. 3). In fact, what seems to be an image of oppressed and silent woman is "rather an artistic expression of a fundamental democratic right to choose your identity" (Machowski, 2009, p. 1). By donning the *chador* on herself, she is accentuating the fact that veiling should not be always frowned upon rather it should be respected in the context of voluntary veiling, as no one has forced Neshat to wear the *chador*. She is demonstrating to the Western general audience that there are women in Iran who wear *chador* but are present and articulate like herself. Neshat is one of the many Muslim women in the West who has been trying to prove that voluntary veiling is empowering. Within this collection in the essay entitled 'World Hijab Day': Positioning the *Hijabi* in Cyberspace, Raihanah also points out how Muslims and non-Muslim women are donning *hijab* and putting up their photos in social media to raise awareness on voluntary veiling, promote presence, and tackle the misrepresentation of Muslim women.

Neshat's frequent depiction of the veil in her photography also helps her process the drastic change that took place in Iran in her absence. She was keen to figure out how the 1979 Revolution transformed people's lives, especially women. She admits that *Women of Allah* series "has evolved around my personal interest in coming to terms with the 'new' Iran to understand ideas, behind Islamic fundamentalism, and to reconnect with my lost past" (Bertucci, 1997, pp. 84–87). While challenging the Western stereotypes of silent Muslim women, her photography questions and criticizes the patriarchal and confining Islamic rules upon Iranian women as well. For instance, her *Untitled* (1996) which depicts a hand graced with Persian calligraphy resting on a woman's parted lips whose face is cropped indicates the silencing of women in the Islamic Republic. Curator Fereshteh Daftari (2006) agrees that the image of two fingers placed on the lips suggests the disagreement from within by silencing herself. By cropping her face, Neshat is implying that the Iranian governments have been trying to repress women's voice or identity. However, the text over the hand functions as a voice which implies that Iranian women have a voice despite the coercion to be silent. Neshat has been reviled for pandering to Western viewers by confirming this assumption about Muslim women but her photography bears a complexity of social and religious identity for Iran that many Western viewers fail to understand. Most of Neshat's Western audience sees her photographs as either ratification of terrorism or a feminist accusation of Iranian culture (Devine, 2011). On the surface, Neshat's photography seems to comprehensively match the Iranian legitimate constrictions concerning the public exhibition of women's body in contemporary Iran. It is true that Neshat is criticizing the forced dress code through her *Women of Allah* series but this should not be taken as the totalizing and holistic reading of her work.

Part of this sort of misreading can be attributed to the fact that diasporic images generate several meanings and associations. According to Mirzoeff (2000, p. 7) diasporic images, from a certain starting point, can "create multiple visual and intellectual associations both within and beyond the intent of the producer of that image." What Mirzoeff (2000, p. 7) calls "intervisuality" is apparently the problem in this kind of reading. He believes that the "diasporic visual image is necessarily intertextual" which makes the audience "to bring extratextual information to bear on what is seen within the frame" to fully understand the meaning of it. However, it should be noted that "in the visual image, intertextuality is not simply a matter of interlocking texts but of interacting and interdependent modes of visuality that I shall call intervisuality." The intervisuality here is the perception and the meaning of the veil that a Western viewer picks from the Western media representation of Muslim women. The ambiguity of the images is also adding to the misreading of Neshat's images. By "seeming to strictly conform to Islamic-Iranian codes of public conduct, Neshat denies the viewer an immediate and simplistic reading of equating freedom with unveiling" (Dadi, 2008, p. 130). Rather than reading Neshat's photographs as simply endorsing orientalist portrayals of harem interior and veiled women or as just documentary recounting the real condition of Iranian Muslim women, one should enhance his/her knowledge of veiling and women in the context of Iran as they have complex meanings. Neshat makes her own body the subject and object of her work. She writes on the photographs of her own face, hands, and feet. She uses her body in the photograph as a canvas to write. As a Muslim woman's body is a site of contention, she is utilizing her body as a metaphor; the body of a woman is the most odd 'thing,' for "it is never quite reducible to being merely a thing; nor does it ever quite manage to rise above the status of thing.... Bodies are not inert; they function interactively and productively" (Grosz, 1994, p. xi).

The bodies in Neshat's *Women of Allah* series are usually tattooed with Persian calligraphy. The Western audience of Neshat's photography takes up this Persian inscription as Islamic pronouncements delineating women's behavior in an Islamic country (Jacqueline Larson, 1997). The sight of a *chador* cladded woman surrounded in the seemingly Islamic texts conjures up the stereotypical representation of veiled and oppressed Muslim women for Westerners. The non-Muslim viewers assume that the texts are derived from the Quran. The Persian calligraphy within the photographs is suggestive of a more verbal expression through writing. Through the inclusion of Persian calligraphy over the images, Neshat "creates a pure, sensual, visual presence, and a material ornament that indicates meaning but hides it from most Western audiences who will, in most cases, be unable to read or understand it" (Zabel, 2001, p. 22). It is precisely "the emptiness of meaning that makes room for stereotypes" (Zabel, 2001, p. 22). Although the veiled woman of the photographs looks silent, there is a revolutionary potential in the written words that empowers her. The Persian calligraphy in the photographs of the series of *Women of Allah* is the poetry of the radical Iranian women poets who wrote of resistance and agency.

The two poets are Forough Farraokhzad (1935–1967) and Tahereh Saffarzadeh (1936–2008). Farrokhzad was famous for her sensuality and eroticism in her feminist poems and Saffarzadeh was known for her religious fervor and respect for martyrdom. Utilizing the poems by the two poets is symptomatic of the plurality of voices of women in Iran. As Farrokhzad wrote about taboo subjects such as love, women's emotion and sexual desire in a patriarchal society, her verses are used in Neshat's photography to demonstrate the existence of Iranian women who are unhappy with the state's discrimination against women and resist the stringent patriarchal rules. Therefore, they have a voice in articulating their uneasiness with the restrictive Islamic rules. In an interview with Sheybani (1999, p. 208), Neshat admits "No other women before [Farrokhzad] had ever dared to speak so freely on the subjects of female emotional and sexual desires." While shattering the stereotypes that Muslim/ Iranian women have no voice, the poetry is also indicative of Neshat's questioning the Iranian regime on women's right such as the mandatory *hijab*. Since Farrokhzad's poetry is fraught with a melancholic tone expressing dissatisfaction with the state, her texts overlaid Neshat's images of veiled woman may also suggest that those women who wear *hijab* are not necessarily pious and religious but rather Iranian women must wear *hijab* irrespective of their belief which is what Neshat is protesting against.

Saffarzadeh's poetry, on the other hand, is used to exhibit the revolutionary and religious sentiment of Iranian women. She was known as a true fundamentalist who was a staunch supporter of Khomeini and his ideologies, and in the meantime she was insistent on preserving women's right. Her poetry ratifies the universal character of Islam and demonstrates the active presence of Iranian women in the society. Her texts over the photos of Neshat suggest the presence of militant Muslim women who supported Ayatollah Khomeini in defending the country against the Shah and the foreign intervention. The verses, which make the Western viewer uncomfortable reading the images, are "the literal and symbolic voice of women whose sexuality and individualism have been obliterated by the chador or the veil" (Sheybani, 1999, p. 207). The poetry overlaid different parts of the women's body functions as a voice against the stereotypically negative portrayals of Muslim women. Cichoki (2004) has also explained this sentiment by arguing that "the radically self-revelatory feminist poetry of Farrokhzad and the prerevolutionary neotraditinalist poetry of Saffarzadeh," help Shirin Neshat to address "issues that are dear to ... women who sat at two opposite positions within the spectrum of women's experiences. The poetry provides these women with a voice ... and its divergent content deny any totalizing claim on the experience of Muslim women." By employing the two poets' texts in her photography, Neshat is shattering the stereotype of Muslim women being a unitary subject. She shows how veiled Iranian women embody different roles and she is highlighting the presence of articulate and puissant women who are not submissive as well. In an interview with Lila Azam Zanganeh, Neshat states:

> Westerners have this sense that Iranian women are submissive victims. But they're not victims, and they're certainly not submissive.... through their resistance and strength, Iranian women have had a voice in Iranian society, and they continue to have a voice, perhaps more so today than ever before.... Because women are under so much pressure, they end up being more innovative about dealing with crises and devising ways out. They become more subversive (2006, p. 47).

Through Persian calligraphy, Neshat is also subverting the stereotypical and neo-orientalist images of Muslim women in her photography. Either intentionally or unintentionally, she is highlighting the fundamental lack of knowledge of Iranian cultural tradition on the part of Western viewership. Her photographs become subversive only if one reads the texts inscribed over the photos otherwise they replicate the stereotypes. Thereby, the ability to read the Persian poems inscribed on the photos could alter the expected readings of the work. Another element which evokes Islamic terrorism in Neshat's photography is the existence of guns. Black *chador*-cladded woman sometimes carries a rifle in the photographs. Many Western viewers take the images of Muslim women with rifle in their hands as an artistic depiction of terrorism (Machowski, 2009). The first glance at the images will give the impression of militancy and Islamic extremism. Cichocki admits that "When I first saw Neshat's photographs at the 1995 Transculture exhibition in Venice, I immediately thought that I recognized the represented person: I knew I was looking at an Islamic terrorist" (2004, p. 11). However, Neshat uses guns to suggest women's activism and also resistance against intervention. It is a symbol of defending the country. The woman in the image stands for the Iranian women involved in the 1979 Revolution and Iran-Iraq war. By portraying this image, Neshat denies that Iranian women are reduced to oppressed women who have no control on their being. Iranian women have been constantly active in the country's political culture from the 1906 Constitution Revolution through the 1979 Revolution to the 2009 Green Movement of the protested presidential election. They proved that they are not silent and passive subjects of a patriarchal society.

As one of the woman-with-the-gun photos, *Speechless* (1996) contains a woman's portrait, cut off along the nose scripted with calligraphy. Next to her cheek right at the height of her ear emerges a gun from under her *chador*. Although the gun is indicative of violence, the perfect positioning of it at the place of an earring cannot be overlooked as a coincidence. Neshat states that the "gun placed beside the woman's cheek is at once a warning and an object of beauty. Both are divided in terms of their purpose- their combined statement is deliberately puzzling" (Goodman, 1998, p. 53). Therefore, she uses the gun to convey that "what can be threatening can also be very beautiful" (Neshat in an interview with Enright& Walsh, 2009, p. 26). The veil is also portrayed with the same subtlety; it can be a symbol of oppression and also stands for independence and freedom. The juxtaposition of Persian calligraphy, guns and veil is the communicative capacity of *the Women of Allah* photos (McDonald, 2004). The combination of these three elements might bring up the notion of Islamic terrorism for the Western viewers but the presence of these elements in the photography of Shirin Neshat is indicative of the existence of different facets of Iranian women. Like Persian calligraphy, the images of the gun in her photographs confer agency and resistance to Muslim women. What is highlighted in her work is her hybrid identity which offers a potent amalgamation of personal, cultural and cross-cultural elements. Her photography exhibits the experience of coexisting in different spheres. Hence, she is always keen to patch up the so-called differences between the West and East in her work.

The complexity of these elements makes it difficult for the Western viewers to understand the images. However, what makes her photography complex and ambiguous is her own contradictions and struggles in coming to term with the Iran she no longer recognizes after the Iranian Revolution. The work that she creates is not only the production of her constant exposure to the stereotypes but also it is the result of her rupture upon return to Iran which revolves around female resistance, action and agency despite the fact that the women in her work are veiled. Not only does she struggle to challenge the Western notion of Muslim women, but also she tries to display her disapproval of forced veiling delicately. There is a sense of duality in her work. What she creates "is always in critical dialogue with both Iran and the West" (Navab, 2008, p. 51). Moreover, Neshat's series speaks to the need for a transcultural dialogue that contains the voice and expression of Muslim women. It is also in dialogue with the viewers because art creates dialogues and is dialogical in nature. Her *Women of Allah* engages the viewers into its web of meanings and recognizes the viewers as active subjects in a process of vitality and reciprocity with the work. The figures in *Women of Allah* communicate with the viewers through their postures, scripts and the return gaze. Neshat uses this return gaze also to free the female body from the 'male gaze' and break free from centuries of subservience stereotype to male or Western desire. The frontal postures, gazing back, *chador*, and the Persian calligraphy are collectively the means of making conversation with the viewers. Extending Mikhail Bakhtin's *dialogic* on the role of words in verbal discourses to Neshat's photography, *Women of Allah* can be taken as dialogical works. Bakhtin (1981) argues "every word is directed toward an answer and cannot escape the profound influence of the answering word it anticipates" (p. 280). In a similar vein, Neshat's *Women of Allah* awaits responses by the viewers and expects them to get rid of their presuppositions about Iranian women.

It is Neshat's hybrid identity of Iranian-American that makes her "capable of seeing each through the assumptions of the other" (Wallach, 2001, p. 137). Her in-between place cements her authority in breaking the stereotypical binaries of East/West and Freedom/Oppression as well. In reference to the existence of duality in her work, Neshat (2002, p. 51) explains that she is not approving or promoting any sense of oppression of all the dark side of Iranian culture, but rather "giving it a fair chance to speak of its very complex situation. And in that way, I think my work has all these elements of duality in it." It is this ambivalent position which lets her be "not quite the Same, not quite the Other ..." (Trinh T. Minh-ha, 1995, p. 5). She knows well that photography is an effective medium to subvert the existing media imagery of Muslim women. She takes the Orientalist stereotypes and inverts them, thereby challenging the Western observers' perception of Muslim women. Her opinions are "informed concomitantly by the role of gender in the political and social structure of her birth culture and by the American media's representative images of that culture" (Devine, 2011, p. 59). She sabotages the media stereotypes that use the images to portray a passive and repressed woman with no or little education; the "dissident woman who sees "fundamentalism" as a passage to non-Western identity and domination; and, finally, the fanatical terrorist" (Devine, 2011, pp. 59–60). Although Neshat was caught saying "I'm not an activist, but an artist," she puts a lot of effort in her photography to empower women while understanding the imposed patriarchal rules in Iran. She states:

> I'm an artist so I'm not an activist. I don't have an agenda. I am creating work simply to entice a dialogue and that's all. I do intend to show the stereotype head on and then break it down. There's the stereotype about the women—they're all victims and submissive—and they're not. Slowly, I subvert that image by showing in the most subtle and candid way how strong these women are.
>
> HORSBURGH, 2000, PP. 44–45

Her photography makes Westerners aware of "the constructed, artificial nature" (Zabel, 2001, p. 17.) of images of veiled women in the West. Following Naficy's argument on artists in exile, Neshat is moving in between the different social collectives and artistic approaches where she can question and criticize the accepted values and practices at both her homeland and her adopted country. Her images of veiled women question and rely upon the implications of veil in Iran and the West as she resists the stereotypes and protests against the imposed stringent and restrictive rules upon women. She is well-aware of the fact that veiling is not inherently an insignia of oppression. There are women who embrace the practice and there are others who still think of the Veiling Act of 1983 as an oppressive means to subjugate and segregate women. Unfortunately, this scope of perspectives within Iran is little noticed in the West. Her photography does not fall in the 'poornographic' thematic images loop where images of veiled women invoke "cry for us because our fates are so bad" (Azimi, 2006, p. 105). While not denying them, she is, indeed, against these poor, repressed and worth-your-sympathy stereotypes and tries to show other facets of veiled women. The next section explores Shirin Neshat's source of inspiration in Iran for her *Women of Allah* series of photography.

Women of Allah and the Post-Revolutionary Iran

Neshat cites a return trip to Iran in early 1990s as a significant moment for her creative production of the *Women of Allah* series of photography but never mentions the specific source of her inspiration. This series of photography which contains a set of four components such as the veil, the gun, the gaze and the text bears uncanny resemblance with the murals and posters of the 1980s and early 90s Iran. Given that Iran has then just weathered the 1979 Revolution and the Iran-Iraq war (1980–88), one would expect to see images of Ayatollah Khomeini as the father of the Revolution, the heroic battle scenes of the war, traditional Islamic imagery, portraits of the war martyrs, and Ayatollah Khamenei. Moreover, there were images of Iranian religious women (or women of Allah) veiled and *chador*-cladded women carrying guns everywhere in the country. These images which would appear on the walls and posters across the country entered a public discourse and "represent a genre of public portraiture that stresses both the Islamic Republic Shi'i-Persian identity and governance and the duty of all Muslims, both at home and abroad, to sacrifice themselves to a greater cause by fighting and dying in war" (Gruber, 2013, p. 3). Touching upon issues of tradition, religion, identity and belonging, the murals and posters have graced and given meaning to the state's ideologies. They became the canvas for the post-revolutionary Iranian government to promote its messages and instill their ideologies. These political murals and posters in public spaces were also set to mobilize or inspire people (Rolston, 1991).

One of the most conspicuous symbols of cultural change in Iran has been the mandatory dress code in public for all women. Unlike Mohammad Reza Shah's era, women were no longer free to opt either to veil or not to veil. Irrespective of the differences in religion, ethnicity and class, veiling became a must. While for many veiling was empowering and like 'second skin' to them, many opposed the forced Veiling Act of 1983 and had found it difficult to comply. However, the government believed that the practice of veiling was a "facilitator for a professional workspace, where women could do their job with no fear of sexual harassment" (Zeiny, 2013, p. 70). It was upon the advent of the 1983 Veiling Act that Ayatollah Khomeini stated: "what we don't want and what Islam doesn't want, is to make a woman as an object, a puppet in the hands of men" (quoted in Ramazani, 1980, p. 30). Consequently in the years

FIGURE 7.1
A mural of 1980s & 90s in Iran. Hijab: A shell for a pearl. From author's collection of murals on hijab.

FIGURE 7.2 *A mural of 80s & 90s. "The graceful and the pure is an angle of the angles. A woman in Hijab is like a pearl inside a shell." From author's collection of murals on hijab.*

FIGURE 7.3 *A poster mounted on a wall. "A woman in Hijab is like a pearl in a shell."*
From author's collection of murals on hijab.

following the establishment of the Islamic Republic, one of the most common murals was the image of *chador*-cladded women to promote *hijab* and modesty. Paintings of veiled women gazing down or looking straight with the 'pearl in shell' theme were abundant across the country (figures 7.1, 7.2, 7.3). The 'pearl in shell' not only symbolizes the outer cover and veiling of the body but also, according to Karimi (2013, p. 45), it alludes to a "woman's virginity and a protective enclosure ..." Therefore, while the outer veiling and modesty is the obvious message of these paintings, the latent message could be taking care of the virginity until marriage.

All these large and gigantic images were reproduced to foster dialogue about *hijab* on a greater scale. They were meant to encourage women to wear *chador* as the government was of the idea that *chador* is a sign of resistance and a better means to *hijab*. Although both veiled and unveiled women had an active role in toppling the Shah and the 1979 Revolution, unveiled women now had no choice but to don *hijab*; the ideal *hijab* was, of course, wearing the *chador*. For these *chador*-cladded women images to be available to the mobilized masses, these paintings had to be enormous. A country where its paintings were mostly of the miniature scale (Grabar, 2000) now produced huge murals and posters. The large-scale murals and posters were, indeed, propaganda paintings in "support of radical change" (Chehabi & Christia, 2008, p. 2). These paintings and posters became more organized and instructed in the spirit of war. According to Varzi, "it was the war that ultimately defined the Islamic republic as an image machine" (2006, p. 26). Halfway through the war, the Office of Propaganda in the Artistic and Cultural Bureau of the Qom Seminary distributed a set of detailed instructions and guidelines for muralists and painters of the public art. These instructions highlighted the important role of murals and posters as a propaganda medium:

> Under all circumstances the effectiveness of the revolutionary mural must be kept clearly in mind. Vague, indirect and superfluous paintings should be avoided at all cost. 'What is significant is to consider what a passer-by (sic) can take away in his memory and mind.' The artist must study religious texts as seriously as he examines the techniques of other artists. Murals with a theme or a scene are preferable to portraits with no specific message. Revolutionary posters should not be merely copied. Every artist must let go of his unique imagination and create something unique. The location of the murals must be selected carefully so that a passerby can clearly see the complete picture. But the ultimate objective should be brevity of message, deliberate and emphatic brush strokes,

clear cut shapes and brilliant colors. Every mural should be framed by solid colors, selected from one of the dominant colors of the picture.

CHELKOWSKI & DABASHI, 1991, P. 291

Women's active role was once again recognized as the Iranian government asked them to defend the country at the outset of the Islamic Republic and later to participate in the war. This message appeared in visual forms such as photography and paintings. '*A Young Girl Carrying Rifle*' (1979) is one such visual representation that shows a young girl in *chador* holding a rifle with a flower inserted into its muzzle (figure 7.4). The caption which quotes Ayatollah Taleqani reads: "Our army does not belong only to our brothers in the armed forces. Men and women, young and old in our country are the members of the Islamic army, and guardian of Islam." This sort of images tended to emphasize the contribution of every Iranian both men and women, and young and old in defending the country. The war front was no longer a domain of men, and women were welcome to fight in the war. Now it was time to produce images of religious and warrior women. The earlier images would have depictions of women along with men defending the country. A painting that best illustrates this is Khusrawjirdi's 1981 '*Mullah, Mother, and Soldiers*' (figure 7.5). This painting shows a clergy man, a soldier, and a woman defending the country. The woman carries an infant in one arm and has a red tulip in another. The infant represents the role of women as a mother and the tulip suggests her willingness to sacrifice herself for the country. Another painting that shows the participation of women in the war is Palangi's 1980 '*A Woman Holding a Rifle*' (figure 7.6). Having spent three years on the front, Palangi witnessed many women taking weapons and joining soldiers to defend their hometown. This painting is black and white sketches of a woman he had seen carrying a rifle and heading towards the front to fight. Farangis Heidarpour is one of these women whose mural was painted in her hometown, Kermanshah, to commemorate her bravery during the Iran-Iraq war (figure 7.7). Known as a woman with an ax; Farangis' statue was also erected in Kermanshah. She was 18 years old when she confronted two Iraqi soldiers in her hometown on her way back home from the funeral of 8 members of her family. She had killed one soldier with the ax and arrested the other one.

These murals, paintings and photography are just few examples of many visual representations that were deployed by the government to stimulate the public and encourage military enlistment in support of the war. The muralists and painters made sure that their paintings enjoy the presence of some strong visual cues of the Shi'a faith and belief (Chehabi & Christia, 2008). The Shrine of Imam Hossein in Karbala, geometric shapes and designs, calligraphy, curvilinear patterns, and red flowers such as rose and tulip combined with some particular signs and symbols such as the hand whose five fingers symbolize Prophet Mohammad, Imam Ali and his wife Fatimah, Imam Hassan and Imam Hossein are the most common visual components in these visual discourses. These are the specific sources of Neshat's inspiration for her *Women of Allah* (1993–97). This work is arguably heavily influenced by these 1980s and 90s murals, paintings and photography in Iran in terms of containing the same

FIGURE 7.4
Young Girl Carrying Rifle, 1979. Middle Eastern Posters Collection. Box 3, Poster 60 Special Collections Research Center, The University of Chicago Library.

FIGURE 7.5
Mullah, Mother, and Soldiers, 1981. Husayn Khusrawjirdi, Middle Eastern Posters Collection. Box 3, Poster 72, Special Collections Research Center, The University of Chicago Library.

FIGURE 7.6
*A Woman Holding a Rifle, ca. 1980. Nasser
Palangi, Middle Eastern Posters Collection. Box 3,
Poster 65, Special Collections Research Center,
The University of Chicago Library.*

FIGURE 7.7   *A woman with an ax. Farangis Heidarpour's mural in Kermanshah. From author's
collection of murals on hijab.*

elements of veil, gun, red flowers, hands, and calligraphy. Neshat is brilliantly borrowing these elements from these works to strike and question the Iranian state's control of the Iranian women's body while correcting the orientalist assumptions. Neshat's *Women of Allah* and the 1980s and 90s women of Allah in murals, paintings and posters also merit comparison for a number of other significant reasons: both have continued their presence in the public discourses. Although Iran has now shifted towards a different theme in murals, posters and paintings for public spaces through its Beautification Organization,[1] the veiled women (or women of Allah) have a strong presence in the murals and posters. Plus, both of them possess pedagogical and dialogical functions too. After all, even when visual culture is consumed to be entertained, it functions on both pedagogical and dialogical level.

Conclusion

While reviewing Neshat's *Women of Allah* (1993–97) to emphasize its dialogical and pedagogical function, this chapter explores its relationship with the Iranian murals and posters of the 1980s and 90s, and concludes that she is dramatically influenced and inspired by the 1980s and 90s murals, paintings and posters in Iran for creating her first series of photography. The presence of the *chador*, gun, hand, gaze, bloodstain and calligraphy in her work is symptomatic of Neshat's close relationship with the Iranian post-revolutionary murals, paintings and photography produced in the 1980s and early 90s. It is exactly this borrowing and incorporating of these elements that help her confront and challenge the stereotypes of passive and voiceless Iranian Muslim women in the West and question the rights of women in Iran. Produced by the object of orientalist art and the Islamic patriarhcy, i.e. women, Neshat's series is a visual expression that creates a visual form of dialogue for questioning the stereotypical codes in both her homeland and hostland; Neshat is indeed, in a very unique way, challenging the visual imperialism of both Iran and the West. If the political discourses take the real and distort it in tandem with the political agendas of enemy-making, in particular Islamophobia, or twist it in alignment with the ideology of the state such as the discriminatory laws against women in Iran, the artistic can do the reverse, unearth and promote the real into the

---

1 For a detailed discussion on the evolution of post-1979 Revolution murals in Iran, see Christiane Gruber, "The Message is on the Wall: Muran art in Post-Revolutionary Iran," *Persica*, 22, pp. 15–46.

beautiful. Its dialogical and pedagogical functions assist the Western viewers to let go of their preconceived notions about Muslim women and better understand the complexity of her photography. Many of her images are endowed with a sense of empowerment which subverts the Western notion of gender roles and power in Iran and other Muslim societies in a broader perspective. By combining the elements of veil, gun and Persian calligraphy, she overrides the stereotypes to exhibit that Muslim women have power and agency. This understanding will hopefully diminish the hate crimes against Muslims and Muslim women in the West. Through the Persian calligraphy scripted over the photographs, the women speak despite the compulsion to remain silent. Neshat's insider/outsider position helps her in better framing the issues for her Western audiences. Knowing the Western culture and media and being an Iranian gives her the privilege to both shatter the stereotypes and question the Islamic restrictive rules on women.

References

Allen, Christopher., & Nielsen, Jorgen. (2002). Summary Report on Islamophobia in the EU after 11 September 2001. Retrieved from http://fra.europa.eu/sites/default/files/fra_uploads/199-Synthesis-report_en.pdf.

Allen, Christ. (2010). *Islamophobia*. Surrey: Ashgate Publishing.

Azimi, Negar. (2006). Don't Cry For Me, America. In Lila Azam Zanganeh, (Ed.) *My Sister, Guard Your Veil; My Brother, Guard Your Eyes.* (pp. 104–111). Boston: Beacon Press.

Babcock, Barbara A. (1984). The Story in the Story: Metanarration in Folk Narrative. In Richard Bauman (Ed.), *Verbal Art As Performance.* (pp. 61–76). Waveland Pr Inc.

Bakali, Naved. (2016). *Islamophobia*. Sense Publishers: The Netherlands.

Bakhtin, Mikhail. (1981). *The Dialogic Imagination: Four Essays*. Translated by Caryl Emerson and Michael Holquist. Austin: University of Texas.

Bailey Jones, Rachel. (2007). (Re)Envisioning Self and Other: Subverting Visual Orientalism throughout the Creation of Postcolonial Pedagogy. Dissertation, The University of North Carolina at Greensboro.

Bertucci, Lina. (1997). Shirin Neshat: Eastern Values. *Flash Art*, 30 (197), 84–87.

Bouchard, Donald. (1977). *Language, Counter-Memory, Practice: Selected Essays and Interviews by Michel Foucault.* Ithaca, Cornell University Press.

Bordeaux, Elizabeth H. (2007). Un-Veiling Islamophobia in the post-9/11 era: Orientalism in the veil debate in France and the United States, December 2003 to June 2004. Master thesis, University of North Carolina at Chapel Hill.

Camhi, Leslie. (2000). Lifting the Veil. *Art News* 99 (2), 148–51.

Chakraborti, Neil & Zempi, Irene. (2012). The veil under attack: gendered dimensions of Islamophobic victimization. *International review of victimology* 18 (3), 269–284.

Chehabi, H. E. & Christia, F. (2008). The Art of State Persuasion. *Persica*, 22 (0), 1–13.

Chelkowski, Peter & Dabashi, Hamid. (1999). *Staging a Revolution: The Art of Persuasion in the Islamic Republic of Iran*. New York.

Cichocki, N. (2004). Veils, Poems, Guns, And Martyrs: Four Themes of Muslim Women's Experiences in S. Neshat's Photographic Work. *Third Space* 4 (1), 47–65.

Dabashi, H. (2005). Shirin Neshat: Transcending the boundaries of an imaginative geography. In Octavio Zaya (Ed.), *The last word* (pp. 31–85). Edizioni Charta Srl.

Dadi, Iftikhar. (2008). Shirin Neshat's photographs as postcolonial allegories. *Signs* 34 (1), 125–150.

Daftari, Fereshteh. (2006). *Without Boundary: Seventeen Ways of Looking*. The Museum of Art: New York.

Devine, Erin C. (2011). From translation to transgression: The feminism(s) of Shirin Neshat. Dissertation, Indiana University.

Dekker, Henk and Van der Noll, Jolanda. (2009). Islamophobia and its origins. A study among Dutch youth. Paper presented at the annual meeting of the ISPP 32nd annual scientific meeting. Trinity College, Dublin, Ireland.

Enright, R. & Walsh, M. (2009). Every frame a photograph: Shirin Neshat in conversation. *Border Cross Magazine*, Retrieved from http://bordercrossingsmag.com/article/every-frame-a-photograph-shirin-neshat-in-conversation.

Fiore, Nicole. (2010). Reading Muslim women: The cultural significance of Muslim women's memoirs. Master thesis, McGill University.

Goodman, J. (1998). Poetic Justice. *World Art* 16, 48–53.

Grabar, Oleg. (2000). *Mostly Miniatures: An introduction to Persian Paintings*. Princeton.

Grosz, Elizabeth. (1994). *Volatile Bodies: Toward a Corporeal Feminism*. Bloomington: Indiana University Press.

Gruber, Christian. (2013). Images of the Prophet Muahammad in and out of Modernity: The Curious Case of a 2008 Mural in Tehran. In idem & H. Haugbolle (Eds.) *Visual culture in the modern Middle East: Rhetoric of the image*. (pp. 2–31). Bloomington: Indiana University Press.

Haddad, Yvonne Yazbeck; Jane I. Smith; and Kathleen M. Moore. (2006). *Muslim women in America: The challenge of Islamic identity today*. Oxford: Oxford University Press.

Hoodfar, Homa. (1993). The Veil in Their Minds and On Our Heads: the Persistence of Colonial Images of Muslim Women. *Resources for Feminist Research*, 22 (3/4), 5–18.

Horsburgh, Susan. (2000, August 14). No Place Like Home. *TIME Europe*, Retrieved from: http://www.time.com/time/europe/webonly/mideast/2000/08/neshat/html.

Kahf, Mohja. (1999). *Western Representations of the Muslim Woman: From Termagant to Odalisque*. Austin: University of Texas Press.

Karimi, Pamlea. (2013). Secular Domesticities, Shiite Modernities: Khomeini's illustrated Tawziah al-Masail. In Gruber, C. & Haugbolle, S. (Eds.) *Visual Culture in the Modern Middle East.* (pp. 32–56). Indiana University Press.

Kincheloe, J. L., Steinberg, S. & Stonebanks, C. (2010). *Teaching Against Islamophobia.* New York, NY: Peter Lang.

Larson, Jacqueline. (1997). *Shirin Neshat: Women of Allah.* Vancouver: Artspeak Gallery.

Lean, Nathan. (2012). *The Islamophobia industry: How the right manufactures fear of Muslims.* London: Pluto Press.

Lughod, Lila Abu. (2003). Saving Muslim Women or Standing with Them?: On Images, Ethics, and War in our Times. *Insanyaat* 1 (1).

Machowski, Matthew. (2009). Women of Allah: Veils, Words and Guns: Gender and the Media Coverage of Islam. *MidEastJournal,* 22 Nov.

Mackenzie, Suzie. (2000, July 22). An unveiling. *The Guardian,* Retrieved from https://www.theguardian.com/lifeandstyle/2000/jul/22/weekend.suziemackenzie.

Mahmoody, B. with Hoffer, W. (1987). *Not without My Daughter.* New York: St Martin's Press.

McDonald, Scott. (2004). Between Two Worlds: An Interview with Shirin Neshat. *Feminist Studies* 30, (3), 621–659.

Milani, Farzaneh. (1992). *Veils and Words: The Emerging Voice of Iranian Women Writers.* Syracuse: Syracuse University Press.

Minh-ha, Trinh. (1995). No Master Territories. In Bill Ashcroft, Gareth Griffiths, and Helen Tiffin (Eds.), The *Post-Colonial Studies Reader.* (pp. 215–18). New York: Routledge.

Mirzoeff, Nicholas. (2000). Introduction: The Multiple Viewpoint: Diasporic Visual Cultures. In Nicholas Mirzoeff (Ed.), *Diaspora and Visual Culture: Representing Africans and Jews.* New York: Routledge.

Moghissi, Haideh. (1999). *Feminism and Islamic Fundamentalism: The Limits of Postmodern Analysis.* London and New York: Zed Books.

Naficy, Hamid. (1993). *The making of Exile Cultures: Iranian Television in Los Angeles.* University of Minnesota Press, Minneapolis.

Nafisi, Azar. (2003). *Reading Lolita in Tehran.* New York: Random House, Inc.

Navab, Aphrodite. (2008). Unsaying Life Stories: The Self-Representational Art of Shirin Neshat and Ghazel. *The Journal of Aesthetic Education,* 41, 39–66.

Neshat, Shirin & Ebrahimian, Babak. (2002.) Passage to Iran. *PAJ A Journal of Performance and Art,* 24, 51–53.

Osborne, Samuel. (2016, December 12). Forest Hill stabbing: Attacker shouted 'I want to kill a Muslim' while chasing passengers. *The Independent,* Retrieved from http://www.independent.co.uk/news/uk/crime/forest-hill-stabbing-kill-muslims-attacker-suspect-station-london-train-a7470016.html.

Ramazani, Nesta. (1980). Behind the Veil: Status of Women in Revolutionary Iran. *Journal of South Asian and Middle Eastern Studies*, 2, 27–36.

Reid, Calvin. (1996). Shirin Neshat. *Art in America*, 84, 105.

Rolston, Bill. (2004). Visions or nightmares? Murals and imagining the future in North Ireland. In Brian Cliff and Eibhear Walshe (Eds.), *Representing the Troubles: Texts and Images, 1970–2000*. Dublin: Four Courts Press.

Said, Edward. (1978). *Orientalism*. New York: Vintage Books.

Said, Edward. (1980, April 3). Islam through the Western eye. *The Nation*, Retrieved from https://www.thenation.com/article/islam-through-western-eyes/.

Said, Edward. (1981). *Covering Islam: How the Media and the Experts Determine How We See the Rest of the World*. New York: Pantheon Books.

Said, Edward. (1994). *Culture and Imperialism*. New York: Vintage Books.

Sheybani, Shadi. (1999). Women Of Allah: A Conversation with Shirin Neshat. *Michigan Quarterly Review*, Spring, 204–224.

Varzi, Roxanne. (2006). *Warring Souls: Youth, Media, and Martyrdom in Post-Revolution Iran*. Durham: Duke University Press.

Walker Parker, Sharon, L. (2005). Embodies exile: Contemporary Iranian women artists and the politics of place. Dissertation, The University of Arizona.

Wallach, Amei. (2001). Shirin Neshat: Islamic Counterpoints. *Art In America*, October, 136–189.

Weller, P., Feldman, A. & Purdam, K. (2001). *Religious discrimination in England and Wales*. London: Home Office Research Study.

Wilkins, Karin Gwinn. (1997). Middle Eastern women in western eyes: A study of u.s. press photographs of Middle Eastern women. In Yahya Kamilpour (Ed.), *The U.S. Media and the Middle East: Image and perception*. (pp. 50–61). Westport: Greenwood.

Windsor, Morgan. (2017, May 28). Portland fatal stabbings point to rise in hate speech, civil rights advocates say. *ABC News*, Retrieved from http://abcnews.go.com/US/portland-fatal-stabbings-point-rise-hate-speech-civil/story?id=47680789.

Zabel, Igor. (2001). Women in Black, *Art Journal*, 60 (4), 16–25.

Zanganeh, Lila Azam. (2006). *My Sister, Guard Your Veil; My Brother, Guard Your Eyes*. Boston: Beacon Press.

Zeiny, Esmaeil; Yusof, Noraini & Mahmoodi, Khalil. (2013). Bearers of culture: images of veiling in Marjane Satrapi's Persepolis. *3L; Language, Linguistics and Literature, The Southeast Asian Journal of English Language Studies*. 19(2) 65–74.

CHAPTER 8

Visibility and Veiling: Iranian Art on the Global Scene*

Hoda Afshar

Aboriginal Art—It's a White Thing
RICHARD BELL (2002)

∴

In this essay, I bring together several lines of inquiry that have informed my own research and artistic practice in recent years, both of which have focussed on, and sought in part to respond to, issues affecting artists of non-Western background such as myself who are engaged in making visual works that reflect, in some way, their local cultural experiences or history. In particular, I am interested in the situation of those artists living and working (whether occasionally or permanently) outside Iran, and how their practice has been shaped by different discourses—especially those operating within and through the field of cultural production and consumption.

Below, as well as examining some of these issues in relation to some other artists' works—artists who share a similar cultural and artistic background to myself—I shall also communicate my own interest in this area as one such artist who is affected by them. Thus, although this essay contains a considerable degree of personal reflection, I have taken this approach in part in order to demonstrate how an artist of Iranian background working outside Iran has sought to respond to the sort of concerns that I raise here through the medium of her research-based practice.

---

* This paper includes material drawn from my Ph.D. dissertation (not yet submitted). An earlier version was presented at the Ballarat International Foto Biennale Symposium (2013): "Contesting Identities, Narratives and the Self," Ballarat, Australia. I would like to thank the reviewers of the present publication for their welcome feedback and comments, and also Timothy Johannessen, who also provided invaluable insights about its central arguments.

Broadly then, my research and practice are both motivated by a personal and theoretical interest in issues to do with (cross) cultural production and translation, the politics of representation and the aesthetics of "speaking across borders." But more narrowly, the reflections that I present here are intended to distil the central concerns that informed a body of work I completed in 2014: a series of manipulated photographs titled *Under Western Eyes*. In this series, I was seeking to respond visually to a critical question about why, in my diagnosis, many of the most widely circulated and commercially successful works of Iranian visual artists from the preceding decade-or-so tended to share a certain uniformity, both as regards their subject matter and visual style.

For example, examining the works of some of the most well-known visual artists from Iran such as Shirin Neshat, Shadi Ghadirian, Shirin Ali-Abadi, Shahram Entekhabi and Houra Yaghoubi, as well as Iranian artists based in Australia such as Nasim Nasr, what was striking about them to me—despite this diagnosis in no way applying to all of their produced works, nor to each of them in the same way[1]—was their often singular focus on just a few overarching themes: female identity; the struggle of Iranian women; their being caught between two opposing currents—tradition and modernity. Not only this, their works all tend(ed) to encode or communicate their subject-matter in a highly similar, and almost formulaic visual language involving visual juxtaposition, or the clash of heterogenous elements and contexts—an almost post-modern language of "mélange"—and tying together their visuality and subject-matter, a single recurring image: the veil.

Now, it is important to note at the outset that it is not the *mere* presence of these visual motifs or thematic concerns in these works that concerned me then or now. Each of them describes a certain reality in Iran, and there is no reason why an Iranian artist, whether living inside or outside Iran, should not find reason to communicate these themes through the medium of her practice. Regarding the constant appearance of the veil in such works, for example, this is perhaps easily explained by its constant presence in Iranians' lives. But what is notable is its particular foregrounding and visibility—and its visualization—in these works: the curious way that it frames its subject and at the same time becomes its subject. Its excessive visibility.

So my question—and one that has certainly been raised before—was and is about why this particular image, the veiled Iranian woman, has come

---

1 Example works include: Shirin Neshat, *Unveiling* (1993) and *Women of Allah* (1993–1997); Shadi Ghadirian, *Qajar* (1998) and *Like Every Day* (2000–2001); Shirin Ali-Abadi, *Miss Hybrid* (2008); Shahram Entekhabi, *Islamic Vogue* (2001–2005); Houra Yaghoubi, *Who is My Generation* (2005).

to represent in such a prominent way the face (pun intended) of Iranian art and women in the global art scene. For despite its omnipresence in their lives, the veil is still perhaps only the most visible expression of Iranian women's struggles.

Notable too is the somewhat different reactions that such works have tended to provoke inside and outside Iran respectively; for while it is certainly not the case that even the most successful of those artists mentioned above have been uncritically praised in the West, still, their works have generally received far more negative critical attention in Iran. Thus, in response to both Western, but especially Iranian critics, artists such as Shirin Neshat have often had to defend themselves against charges of "stereotyping" Iranian women and highlighting their misery; of "fetishizing" the veil, and so on. In the art scene that I grew up in Iran, the appearance of a new work that seemed to depict the veiled female Iranian subject in this way would very often elicit the same response: "It smells like the dollar," many would say. The criticism being not that an artist might choose to make work about this subject as such, nor even endeavor to achieve the same success as, say, Neshat, but rather that the particular visual formula used to communicate it had become so formulaic, or typical. Fairly or not, it was and is often held to involve (or result in) a certain stereotyped, or flat representation of its subject.

Stepping back, as Hamid Keshmirshekan (2010) has examined in detail, from the 1990s onwards in Iran there has been a general trend against art-making that is perceived as relying on a stereotyped view of Iranian identity, or shaped in any strong way by "the expectation and evaluation" of "others" (Keshmirshekan, 2010, p. 491)—works that are perceived to be based on a "subjective exotic view" of what is Iranian and contemporary, or made to meet the foreign demand for culturally "authentic" works (p. 498). But it is a trend that, for some, still exists. In an incendiary article published in e-flux, for instance, Barbad Golshiri (2009) writes: "I have distinguished a few dominant orientations in Tehran's Art scene of today ... Among these, the art market has chosen a certain trend: aestheticization of stereotypes." But as both Keshmirshekan and Golshiri are careful to observe, this perceived "trend"—or turning it around, the critique of this perceived trend—has much to do with the contact between Iranian art(ists) and the global contemporary art scene, which is itself shaped by hegemonic structures. Thus, for these critics, and others too such as Foad Torshizi (2012), the immediate question is not necessarily whether "self-exoticism" functions in an artist's works, but rather why it is that globally, the most successful or widely exhibited artworks of Iranian artists appear to many Iranian critics to be chosen "on a selective and representative basis," which is to say, "provided that they reveal appropriate signs of cultural difference"

(Keshmirshekan, 2010, p. 502). In other words—and granting that these works do share more than a superficial resemblance—these critics' (and my) question concerns, in part at least, why it is that outside Iran especially, the works that have come to be seen as representative of Iranian art appear to deal with so few themes, and in so similar a fashion, as described earlier. For again, if an Iranian artist is criticized by her peers for "stereotyping," this does not necessarily mean that she has consciously employed stereotypes; rather, it often reflects a view that her work, its visuality, lends itself to being read in terms of such stereotypes—of being suited to (if not consciously made for) a particular "outsider" gaze. Similarly, the dilemma for many critics and artists alike is not that a work is saleable as such, but rather that its saleableness/visibility is perhaps determined by its employment of a visual regime that serves to locate the artist and her artwork in a certain way, both in relation to and in the eyes of the (Western) viewer—and so too confirming a stereotyped view of what Iranian art is, and therefore what it is to be "Iranian."

Now of course, the commercial success of certain (ostensibly) similar works outside Iran may reflect nothing more than a passing trend and the dynamics of the international art scene, which tends both to demand, and therefore to produce, periods of predictability and conformity. Similarly, the international success of certain artists may have—and certainly does have—much to do with their locality: their working outside Iran, or in closer contact with European and North American galleries and so on, and thus closer to the "global center." However, there are almost certainly deeper reasons for this too—reasons that have to do not only with the aggressive commodification of certain artists and their work, but also the "politics of location" and of "reception," which work together to construct what Foad Torshizi (following Hamid Dabashi) has referred to as an "imaginative geography" in which the works of Iranian artists are transformed "into tokens of their ethnic alterity and the falsely manufactured pastness attached to the name of their country" (Torshizi, 2012, p. 557). I say "not only," but in fact the two are closely related; for the marketability of many works of non-Western artists, it can be argued, has everything to do with the alterity industry operating in and through the global art scene, whose agents do not simply discover, but are actively involved in constructing the aforementioned "imaginative geography" while mining it (or its inhabitants) for new and culturally different works to enrich the market.

This, then, raises a crucial question about the way in which (neo)colonial and other discourses are not only involved in shaping, but are precisely sustained through what Tirdad Zolghadr (2006) once humorously referred to as the avenues of "ethnic marketing." Today, that is, while the non-Western subject is authorized to speak—to re-present herself, rather than being represented as in earlier colonial discourses—still, "the 'representational' role of non-Western artists," as Khaled Ramadan (quoted in Kesmirshekan, 2015, p. 119) notes, continues to be bound up with the strategy of "cultural difference," which, he adds, "is now being institutionally legitimized through the construction of the 'postcolonial other' that is allowed to express itself only as long as it speaks of its own Otherness" (p. 119). From a slightly different perspective, Keshmirshekan (2010) has also noted how the problem of the marginality, or "invisibility" of non-Western artists is bound up with "a rather perverse turn of thought that reconceptualizes cultural marginality" (p. 502). Continuing, he writes:

> This thought presumes cultural marginality no longer as a problem of "invisibility" but one of an excessive "visibility" in terms of a reading of cultural difference that is too readily marketable. This also relates to the tendency in colonial thought to associate what is visually verifiable with "truth," where superficial characteristics reflect the inner truth of being. (p. 503)

In the following sections, then, I shall briefly describe some of the ideological and discursive structures—forces operating behind and through the global contemporary art scene—that have (arguably) contributed to the visibility of certain works of Iranian artists, shaping in different ways *what* is seen and *how* it is seen, or how such putatively marginal works come to acquire value and meaning, and serve different interests in different contexts.

Veiled Commodities

In his work *The Post-Colonial Exotic: Marketing the margins*, Graham Huggan (2001) has provided one of the most insightful analyses describing the profound way in which (what he refers to as) "postcolonial cultural production" is profoundly shaped by its contact with the global market. He notes, in the first place, the manner in which postcolonial literature specifically, although the formula applies just as well to other forms of artistic production that share similar concerns, is caught between two "regimes of value"—what he refers to as "postcolonialism" and "postcoloniality," respectively (p. 5). The former, as he describes, "relates to an ensemble of loosely connected oppositional practices, underpinned both by a highly eclectic methodology of 'cultural embattlement' ... and by an aesthetic of largely textualised, partly localised resistance" (p. 6). Postcoloniality, on the other hand, which Huggans identifies as a function of postmodernity, describes a regime of value pertaining to symbolic and material exchange "in which even the language of resistance may be manipulated and consumed" (p. 6). As "a value-regulating mechanism within the global late-capitalist system of commodity exchange," Huggans notes the way in which, within its sphere:

> [v]alue is constructed through global market operations involving the exchange of cultural commodities and, particularly, culturally 'othered' goods. Postcoloniality's regime of value is implicitly assimilative and market-driven: it regulates the value-equivalence of putatively marginal products in the global marketplace. (p. 6)

Noting that postcolonialism's own "politics of value" is quite obviously opposed to such global processes of commodification, Huggan observes the way in which "these two apparently conflicting regimes of value" are nevertheless, or have become, mutually entangled (p. 6). Moreover, his entire critique is aimed at showing what happens when putatively marginal discourses and products, valued as loci of "resistance to socially imposed standards and coercive norms" (p. 20), "arrive" at the center: although they continue to be valued there—and not in spite of, but precisely because of their opposition to its own logic of value—they become, as it were, accommodated to it: denuded of any genuine difference that may challenge the center.

Now, what is most important for my purposes in Huggan's analysis is the mechanism through which this occurs: commodity fetishism, which—quite revealingly—he argues "links up with earlier forms of exoticist representation, arguably becoming the postmodern version of exoticist mystique" (p. 18); and while it is impossible to provide a much deeper analysis of either commodity fetishism or exoticism here, what I do want to highlight (something that Huggan does not explicitly discuss) is the way in which what we might refer to as the "semiotic structure" of the fetishized commodity reflects not only the form that culturally "othered" goods assume when they reach the market—and here specifically, the sort of visual artworks of Iranian artists that I shall discuss below; in addition, this structure is also often mirrored in their own visual language. That is, assuming the classic Marxian formulation of commodity fetishism, which, as Huggan summarizes, "describes the veiling of the material circumstances under which commodities are produced and consumed," and, through a process "mystification ... the illusion of the severance of the finished work from its process of production" (p. 18), what is striking is the way in which many of these works ironically—which is to say, knowingly—point to their very status as (exotic, fetishized) commodities through their own visuality. Recalling Frederic Jameson's (1991, p. x) well-known characterization of postmodernism as "the consumption of sheer commodification as a process," many of these works might be read as submitting to this process—as embracing their own "simulacral" reality; and I suggest, this is perhaps one of the reasons for their appeal and success; they act as a mirror, or one side of a semiotic circuit, reflecting the desires of a viewer that seeks authenticity without, perhaps, fully believing in it.

A clear example of this employed in many of these works is their embracing what Huggan calls (following Appadurai) an "aesthetics of diversion" (p. 16). Noting that under the aegis of postmodern "exoticism" the allure and the value of the exotic everyday object is "attendant upon its diversion," or the "placing [of such] objects and things in unlikely contexts" (p. 16)—a phenomenon that describes not only the appeal of World art and music, but equally current hipster fashion trends—what is striking, again, is the way that many works of visual artists encode this way of seeing in their works, embracing the politics of diversion and display in the very way they combine their very visual signs, not only anticipating, but already suggesting their own essentially disconnected reality.

That is, it is not simply that as cultural commodities these artworks (because they contain specific cultural signifiers) appear detached from their original cultural context; often, such works point within themselves, through their visuality, to their own decontextualized reality. Thus, clashing cultural signifiers or culturally-specific elements are often combined in a way that suggests—quite conspicuously—their incompatibility: a veil-clad woman peers out of her "anachronistic" covering wearing the superficial signs of the modern Western fashion-loving woman—high-heel shoes, make up, the plaster aftermath of a nose job—or brandishing recognizable tokens of their modernity: a coke can or a mobile phone. In this way, a collision of heterogenous but clearly recognizable elements, each of them highly typified, combine in different works to communicate different meanings, but many of them broadly sharing a similar theme to do with a singular subject, "the contemporary Iranian women"—her being caught between tradition and modernity, or somewhere beneath the real and symbolic weight of the veil.

Thus, in one of her most well-known series, *Like Every Day* (2000–2001), Shadi Ghadirian humorously depicts Iranian women using home utensils shrouded in colourful patterned fabric (clearly recalling the image of the *chador*), "ironically exaggerating misogynist typecasts" related to their assigned roles as domestic "slaves" in order to challenge their negative stereotyping (Saatchi Gallery, n.d.). Similarly, in her *Ghajar* series (1998–1999), Ghadirian recreates Ghajar-era portraits of Iranian women—each of them "jarringly interrupted by the presence of contemporary products—a phone, boom-box,

hoover," in order "to describe a contemporary Iranian female experience of existing as if outside of time" while "pointing to a culture clash of tradition and
progress." Each of the women, too, is defiant; they "stare out from the photos
with an unnerving directness, detached from their environment, and confi-
dent within themselves" (Saatchi Gallery, n.d).

Similarly, in her series *Miss Hybrid* (2008), Shirin Ali-Abadi presents us with
typified images of young Iranian women displaying the current fashion trends
in order to capture "the aesthetic nuances that shape, reshape and reinvent
the identity of the new Iranian girl." She shows how these women, "under
the auspice of the Islamic veil," transform themselves by means of cosmetic
surgery and other acts of self-beautification—all of which "can be regarded
as a healthy exercise in cultural rebellion and global integration" (Landscape
Stories, 2014).

Thus, as a recurring image in contemporary Iranian art, this figure—the
female Iranian subject—has come to serve, quite literally, as an ideological
battleground. And this is right, for in Iran today, as in previous generations,
women have often found themselves caught in the center between different
competing forces. None of this can be questioned, nor the fact that an Iranian
(female) artist might seek to explore these issues through the medium of their
practice. Furthermore, each of these works that I have just mentioned—and
others that might be grouped alongside them—diverge in important ways
both as regards their specific concerns and modes of visualising their subjects,
and nothing that I have said is meant to preclude, or stand for, a deeper and
more engaged reading of them. But again, the specific question that I am ask-
ing is not about these issues as such, but rather why it is that outside Iran, a
particular style of art-making—and one focused on a fairly narrow range of
thematic concerns—has been embraced so one-sidedly, and thus (arguably)
come to be seen as representative of Iranian art. In other words, I am in the
first place interested in why the market has tended to prefer those works that
encode their subject in a particular way, employing a commodified language in
the fairly precise sense that I discussed a moment ago: the use of recognizable,
or readily decodable signs of cultural difference which nevertheless appear, as
it were, floating, detached from their referents.

Now, one reason for this might be easy to find: it is simply indicative of a
trend or style of art-making that is (or was) more widely used and recognized,
in part perhaps because it reflects our postmodern condition, or concerns having to do with the "crisis" of meaning and representation—questions about
the unitary subject and the questioning of master narratives, and so on. In
this light, it is crucial to observe here, as many other critics have, that post-
colonialism and postmodernism do both share many of the same formal and

thematic concerns. In her classic article "'Circling the Downspout of Empire': post-colonialism and postmodernism," for example, Hutcheon (1989) notes that both are—albeit in different ways—obviously concerned with issues to do with marginality, or marginalization, challenging claims to different forms of universality and so on, and often place questions about "textual gaps in the foreground," even though "their sites of production differ" (p. 73). Furthermore, both embrace "discursive strategies like irony and allegory," in which the former specifically is employed as a "trope of doubleness"—a "split discourse which has the potential to subvert from within" (p. 73). About this "mode of address," Hutcheon notes the way in which irony becomes

> a popular rhetorical strategy for working within existing discourses and contesting them at the same time. Its inherent semantic and structural doubleness also makes it a most convenient trope for the paradoxical dualities of both post-modern complicitous critique and post-colonial doubled identity and history. (p. 75)

Although Hutcheon is here specifically discussing the field of postcolonial literary production, and therefore those discourses that have been shaped by and sought in part to contend with the colonial imposition of an imperial culture, it is arguable that Iranian visual artists are engaged in a similar project of negotiating their "dual history," and seeking ways to "subvert" a dominant culture from within. That includes, for many Iranian artists, not only the weight of local (Islamist) forces that came to the fore in the post-Revolutionary period, but also the cultural and political hegemony of the West, or the forces that continue to construct Iran as an "other." Again, it might be said that it is their shared concern with "doubleness" (of identity, history and so on) that unites the postcolonial and contemporary Iranian experience on the one hand, and the latter to postmodernism as a form of (cultural) critique and art-making, and as a style of thought—their "twofold vision." Similarly, both are engaged in ways of disrupting—of revolting against—attempts to enforce cultural sameness through the revalorization of marginality or difference. But notably too, and as Hutcheon (1989, p. 75) notes, this struggle—the attempt on both sides to counter a dominant pattern—is nevertheless one that occurs *within* the dominant paradigm; and it for this reason that irony or parody and other "split discourses" become especially relevant as vehicles not only for the expression of this condition—of marginality—but also as tools of subversion. Thus, Hutcheon crucially points to the fact that, as forms of critique, they are each in some way (albeit in different ways) complicit in the very cultural dominants that they seek to challenge—just as Hellen Tiffin (1988) had earlier noted the way in which post-colonial literature is inevitably "informed by the imperial vision" (p. 172). Furthermore, while Hutcheon and others have been careful to note that postcolonial criticism differs from many expressions of postmodernism in this sense at least, that it has a more distinct political agenda—or as Huggan (2001, p. 6) observes, in that it "does not, or at least does not aim to, share [postmodernism's] somewhat irresponsible lack of commitment, its self-regarding obsession with play"—what she perhaps fails to draw out is that regardless of the political or other intention that stands behind it, the very language of postcolonial artistic production unfortunately makes it indistinguishable from the latter (postmodernism) much of the time—that is, from an audience perspective.

Thus—and returning to my main focus—it might be argued that the sort self-reflexivity and (often) ironic forms of expression through which many Iranian artists have sought to explore and to critique questions about their contested identity, the perceived imposition of cultural norms and so on, are caught up in this very sort of dilemma. That is, a legitimate criticism of many of their works is that they might be seen as indirectly—and it must be said, often unintentionally—reinforcing the very structures that they oppose. Thus, speaking about the select use of the veil in particular in the works of Shadi Ghadirian, Shirin Ali Abadi and other Iranian artists, Barbad Golshiri (2009) contends that they "perpetuate the dominant image in a very direct way ..."; that is, they "take advantage of doxa and hegemony and submit to it in the name of subversion." More concretely, though somewhat simplistically, Golshiri notes the curious way in which the visual statements in these works are often, in a sense, indistinguishable from the ideological statements they are seeking to subvert. Thus, Ghadirian's *Ghajar* series "embraces 'our anachronistic life' as common wisdom does: Westoxication"—a visual statement that is intended ironically here, but reflecting a view that is, nevertheless, shared by the ministry of culture in Iran. Similarly, Golshiri writes that

> [the] way Neshat treats the chador is the way the culture factory of the Islamic Republic beautifies its restrictions; they too aestheticize the veil in their murals, posters, and slogans. For them, a woman in a veil is like a pearl in its shell.

Whether or not Golshiri is right that these artists are guilty of "aestheticizing stereotypes," the more fundamental question concerns the way in which such artworks, employing similar visual strategies to those described in order to communicate locally or culturally specific knowledge, are all-too-easily read by non-local audiences. More broadly, the question concerns whether such

visual strategies employing "split discourses" are indeed capable of challenging dominant narratives "from within," supposing that this is at least one of
their aims.

Here, then, we arrive once more at Huggan's competing "regimes of value,"
discussed earlier. Again, Huggan points to the way in which the language of
resistance is so easily manipulated and consumed once it encounters the
value-regulating mechanisms underlying systems of "commodity exchange";
and regarding the circulation of works of Iranian artists outside Iran specifically, what the preceding brief discussion was intended to show was that it is
not merely the reception of marginal or culturally-"othered" goods within the
global art scene that is relevant here, but their very visual language or way of
encoding certain information, and indeed, that it is in part this very language
that explains their excessive visibility.

In connection with this point, it is worth highlighting too that it is not only
the (narrowly understood) political or oppositional content of such works that
tends to be compromised by this assimilative tendency of the market, but the
very strategy of highlighting or communicating cultural difference. Here, recalling Huggan's (2001) crucial observation that commodity fetishism "links
up with earlier forms of exoticist representation" (p. 18), it could be argued
that the visibility or success of certain works of Iranian artists outside Iran
has also to be explained by their being so suited to being "re-read" or valued
within the structures of certain exoticist modes of production. Noting that exoticism is "in one sense, a control mechanism of cultural translation which
relays the other inexorably back again to the same" (p. 14), Huggan describes
how "the exotic functions dialectically as a symbolic system, domesticating the
foreign, the culturally different and the extraordinary" (p. 14)—an attempt to
"to ensure the availability of the margins for the mainstream" whilst "keeping
it out of harmful reach" (p. 23) through assigning new but predictable meanings to the unfamiliar, or a way of enriching the market without threatening
its abiding logic. Thus, Huggan writes, exoticism "in this context, might be described as a kind of semiotic circuit that oscillates between the opposite poles
of strangeness and familiarity," such that "[w]ithin this circuit, the strange and
the familiar, as well as the relation between them, may be receded to serve different, even contradictory, political needs and ends" (p. 13).

It must be emphasized, then, that the frequent labelling of certain works
of Iranian artists as "exotic" or "stereotyping" (a charge often thrown about by
other Iranian critics or artists) is, perhaps, unfair; for as the preceding points
suggest, what is considered typical or exotic describes in the first place a system or mode of perception, and only secondarily—and quite vaguely—the
object that might exude this sense to a particular viewer or class of viewers.

Moreover, it is in some sense inevitable that an artwork incorporating locally or culturally specific elements will be, to different degrees, read or viewed in this way (which is to say, if not mis-read, then at least approached in a way that is perhaps destined to result in an impoverished or merely surface reading). To take a rather obvious example: an Iranian artist may choose to incorporate some form of Persian writing in one of her artworks, both as a vehicle of concrete expression and in light of the centuries-long practice in Iran (as in other Islamicate societies) of using calligraphy in different graphic media. But since Persian writing is indecipherable, if not unrecognizable, to most Western viewers, it may appear strangely familiar to them—which is precisely to say, exotic—and even stereotypical, but not legible as such. Were it actually legible to them, it would perhaps appear as exotic as their own English writing.

This points to a genuine dilemma for Iranian artists, then—as indeed for any marginal artist engaged in communicating local or culturally specific knowledge to non-local audiences. For there is nothing at all wrong with either seeking or employing strategies to encode such knowledge in a way that is more likely to be familiar to non-local audiences; and yet to do so risks not only inviting the criticism of other local critics or artists, but also the real possibility that these strategies will only serve to reinforce, in different ways, either the dominant narratives that they might be used to oppose, but also the underlying mechanisms through which cultural difference and oppositional discourses are frequently assimilated to the logic of the market.

A Mirror and Screen

In this section, I shall discuss how some of these concerns are related to the reception of many of those artworks in which images of veiled female subjects appear prominently, and how this overlaps with issues about the politics of representation or the contested status of the identity of women of Islamic background, including how they are perceived in the West. For as many critics have observed, in recent decades, images of veiled women have been constantly reappearing in contemporary art exhibitions that are aimed at promoting, or showcasing (what is often vaguely referred to as) "contemporary art from the Middle East." Indeed, the veil has arguably come to serve—particularly in the West—as a recurrent, and rather fixed signifier of female Islamic, or even Iranian or Middle Eastern identity.

Now, a typical criticism directed at the use, or a particular way of imaging the veil (or the veiled female subject) in visual artworks is that it tends to show Islamic women as a singular, monolithic group—as an identical and homogenous group of "victims." As a visual signifier, and a marker of cultural identity, it is argued, the veil envelops its subjects in too severe a manner, eclipsing the local and personal identities of those who embrace it (or those whom it embraces). Of course, a common counter-criticism is that it is Islamic veiling as a practice that is really responsible for erasing women's identities; and thus an artist who chooses to depict the veil in this way has simply succeeded in communicating its reality.

Be this as it may, what I am more concerned to show in this section is the way in which such visual representations may feed into and support dominant attitudes about non-Western women and their locality, positioning them in relatively fixed ways and as a semi-real category at best. Once again, in the context that I am discussing, the question about what an artist may have intended to communicate in presenting its subject in this way is secondary; the more important point is rather how these visual codes interact with the ideological framing of these subjects. For as just indicated, in the West the veil has arguably come to occupy the paradoxical, but not inconsistent position of a sort of super sign; a sign that is characterized by its carrying both an excess and paucity of meaning. That is, it tends to say too much and too little at the same time, and often evokes different and contradictory perceptions for different subjects, and even for the same subjects at the same time: fear or horror; anger or sympathy; community, or solidarity; and different registers of desire.

Much of this, of course, has to do with the fact that the veil itself has served, in highly different ways and contexts, as real and symbolic site in different struggles among women from the Middle East. Thus, as Fadwa El Guindi (quoted in Cichocki, 2008) writes:

> Few items of clothing have been as disputed and as charged with political meaning as the veil worn by Muslim women. It is a complex symbol: female emancipation can be denoted by either wearing it or removing it; the veil can acquire both secular and religious meaning in that it either denotes resistance to colonization, or ties with the Islamic tradition.

But equally too, it has come more and more to acquire different (though again, increasingly polarized) meanings for different (Western) viewers— perceptions that reflect changing attitudes towards, and the repositioning of, Muslims and other groups in the Middle East, both in response to changing world events, as well as broader political and discursive concerns. Here, then, my aim is to examine not in close detail, but quite generally the way in which the very presence of this recurring image in the works of Iranian (and other) artists may serve to simply reinforce or reflect back different viewer interests or preconceptions regarding their subjects, regardless of—which is to say, often contradicting—the intention of the artist. More specifically, my aim is to connect such "reflected" readings (which may be more or less benign) and a certain way of visually encoding the veil—its excessive visibility.

By way of example, we might consider Shahram Entekhabi's series *Islamic Vogue* (2001–2005), which aims to "openly [confront] the question of visibility and Islamic alienation," as well as European perceptions about the veil (which has become a topic of security debate, and which is often seen "as a symbol of the subjugation of women in the name of religion") while also pointing out its close ties to Muslim identity, and thus, for Muslim women in Europe, its focal importance in their experiences of (often forced) cultural assimilation (Entekhabi, n.d.). In this series, Entekhabi uses paint and permanent marker to draw "chadors" on a number of Vogue Magazine images of women to confront us with these issues, while also questioning the manner in which such media images, reflecting Western tastes, dictate our ideas of beauty and fashion (Entekhabi, n.d.).

Thus, what Entekhabi's work shares in common with some of those discussed earlier is not only a surface level of visual play or juxtaposition that is designed, in some way, to disrupt our expectations, but also an overlapping concern with issues to do with the self-perception and contested identity of a relatively fixed category of subjects: "contemporary Iranian women," "Islamic women," and so on. Furthermore, what it also shares in common with them is its concern with the different gazes directed at these groups: how a certain "we" or "they" perceive ourselves/themselves, or how an "Other" perceives them/us, and using a sort of knowing humor to critique these perceptions. But as described earlier, this effect is achieved in one way only through provisionally submitting to, or admitting the very stereotyped image that it seeks to parody or invert. Again, this is just irony of course, and the formula for most joke-telling whose humor depends on disrupting our expectations apropos some well-known racial or other stereotype. But what is notable, in the first place, is the fact that the intended effects of such visual strategies are so unstable, despite operating within a relatively closed circuit of meaning. Thus, for example, Entekhabi's images can in one way be read as a straightforward commentary on the stupid irrationality of veiling as much as the irrational fear it provokes. And yes, this is the point, of course. But only for those who get the joke. Thus, at the ideological extremes where irony is lacking, both the culture warriors and Islamists will likely nod in agreement, though for entirely different reasons. So once more, this is not to discourage such visual strategies, but simply to say that as an informational strategy, it is perhaps only likely to achieve its (intended) effect among those who already know.

Now of course, only the dullest readers are likely to miss the intended message in this work; but from another point of view, it could be argued that this very strategy dulls the senses in another way, or compromises any possible oppositional message it might contain, precisely because its language is so suited to commodification as earlier described. Thus, because the work never really rises above the plane of "established" meaning, it might be argued that the possible effects it might achieve are somewhat compromised by a sense of playful knowingness that dilutes its message.

Furthermore, a similar result may occur when visual or informational strategies such as this are employed not in the context of making a super-commentary on the different "outsider" attitudes or gazes directed towards the veiled subject, but in expressing an artist's own personal experience of the limiting and oppressive effects of living beneath, or in the midst of, the veil. More specifically, by presenting the veiled female subject in a highly typified way that foregrounds certain attributes associated with an individual's own perception and experiences, it may result in—and again, whether this is intended or not—an artwork's being read as just such a commentary, and one carrying more weight because of its personal/experiential dimension. But here too, this commentary—consciously or not—may simply feed into and support certain pre-existing assumptions held by different viewers, thus reproducing systems of knowledge that discursively position different subjects in different (binarily opposed) ways. That is, when such an artwork itself employs fairly straightforward oppositions (again, involving juxtaposition and playing on audience knowledge/expectation and so on) and super-saturated symbols that are used to identify different categories, they may invite intended or unintended politicized commentary. And again, while such politicized readings of a work of art (their merely confirming viewer biases, and so on) are always prone to emerge no matter how an artist treats their subject, my argument again is that a strategy which involves using highly typical representations of their subjects and binary oppositions to play on audience knowledge and expectation, then the danger is often not that they will be misread, but rather that, precisely because an ironic sense is always parasitic on, because it presupposes, a grasp of something's literal meaning, that it will never really escape this closed circuit of "truth." Rather than departing from the substantial sense of what we already know, what is more likely to be perceived as novel in the work of art employing stereotypes is largely the effect of their collision. Thus, despite seemingly inverting, or confronting our expectations and so on, what they often produce—not incidentally, but as a result of their internal logic—is simply shock, not knowledge. But veiled by a sense of irony.

Something similar to this may also result when an artist relies not on stereotypes as such, but rather a heavy use of symbolic metaphors to describe either a personal or general experience, though because as signs they may have multiple concrete referents, they are likely to be read not only metaphorically, but literally—or vaguely both at the same time. Here, the danger is that the boundary between the sign (in its multiple functions) and the referent may be lost sight of, or that the former may carry an excess of meaning, so that the particularity of its referents is crushed under the weight of metaphor.

A particularly strong example of this is arguably found in the Australian-based Iranian artist Nasim Nasr's work *Women in Shadow* (2011), which incorporates similar elements to those found in her previous work such as *Unveiling the Veil* (2010), *Erasure* (2010), and *Rebirth* (2009). As part of *Women in Shadow*, Nasr staged a "fashion" show featuring catwalk models clad in black *chadors* and sporting heavy black, gothic-looking eye makeup. Wearing otherwise plain, though coldly haunting faces, the models slowly and ominously walked up and down the catwalk, occasionally posing between the two facing groups of audience members, split by gender; the only other "incongruous" element about their attire being their high-heel shoes, just visible below their *chadors*, which serve as the only visual link between these models and their glamourous/commercial setting—everything else appearing out of place, precisely because of our expectations.

Exploring issues to do with cultural identity, the "chador," "erasure," "the gaze" and "shadow," while also communicating her contrasting experiences as a young women living in Iran and Australia, Nasr notes that through her practice in general—and specifically in the context of this series—she "seeks to represent not only the socio-cultural invisibility of women in Iran but also their disempowerment, that fades them into shadow" (Nasr, 2014). Commenting on the title of this work, she writes "By 'shadow' I mean suppression, left in darkness, not having a recognized history, and being silenced without visibility" (Nasr, 2011). Thus, while Nasr is careful to note that this work is ostensibly, or in one way, about her own experience, the viewer is naturally inclined—and encouraged—to read this work, whether directly or indirectly, as a strong critique of the practice of veiling, and a portrait of the plight of Iranian women more generally; and once more, because of the fairly straightforward coding of its subject, utilising binary oppositions and so on, it lends itself to being read just in this way—as a clear political and social commentary with a fairly recognizable cast of heroes and villains, and monsters.

This reading is fully corroborated, too, by Professor Catherine Speck (2011), who contributed a piece for the exhibition program. She observes:

The Iranian Revolution of 1979 ushered in an Islamic State, and its associated fundamentalist codes immediately impacted upon women, intel-
lectuals, artists and free thinking citizens. Women were ordered to wear
the *chador* when out of doors, and inside the home in front of strangers.
Nasr's performative art speaks on behalf of women currently living in
Iran who have to observe this fundamentalist dress code, and to Iranian
émigrés who carry the cultural memory of being disenfranchised. (p. 9)

Speck here provides the reader/viewer with a discursive reminder supporting Nasr's visual suggestion that the *chador*, specifically, is an all-embracing
and suffocating reality in Iran, suggesting erroneously—or without qualifica-
tion—that (all?) "women currently living Iran" are still "ordered to wear the
chador when out of doors" (p. 9), when in fact the fundamentalist dress code
that applies is, while still being fundamentalist, not in fact the *chador*. But it
makes a more striking image, and the uninformed reader is not likely to notice,
even though someone who is forced to wear one certainly would. Furthermore,
Speck has her cast of heroes and villains play their familiar roles. After commenting on the way in which this dress code "fundamentally disempowers
women," leading to their "loss of freedom, loss of identity and loss of corporeal
presence," she observes:

Women in Iran, as in other oppressive regimes, have negotiated ways
around these codes and, in finding some sense of dignity, have turned
their gaze onto their own bodies and what lies beneath their overbear-
ing covering. Sexy underwear, high-heel shoes, well made-up eyes that
peer out from the chador and designer jeans are all a part of the 'secret
wardrobe.' (p. 9)

Nevermind that this "secret wardrobe" is, curiously, described in terms well
suited to another kind of objectifying male gaze; this statement corroborates
in words another reading of Nasr's work that lies just beneath the surface: by
becoming "like" the ideal fashion-loving Western woman, the uniformly oppressed Muslim woman (who is identical to all other Muslim women) shall
escape her victim status.
   Furthermore, what is striking is that the visual metaphor that is used to
carry this meaning/message—or one side of the binary opposition that it sets
up: the black *chador*—is caught between its purely symbolic and concrete des-
ignation. The *chador* (especially the black *chador*), that is, is just one of the
concrete expressions that veiling takes in Iranian society; but it is a powerful visual metaphor that, for many, captures the oppressive reality of veiling,

period. Here, in *Women in Shadow*, it would not have suited Nasr's aims to portray her veiled subjects in the way that, say, Ali-Abadi does in *Miss Hybrid*, where the *hijab* appears out of place, to be sure, but more quirky than suffocating. And this is right, because it is how Nasr experienced it. But again, since that experience is being communicated here, at least in part, metaphorically, albeit through the medium of a concrete and historically/locally specific (and recognizable) image, it is notable that this artwork is only able to communicate its meaning through a kind of symbolic violence that mirrors, in a way, the same violence it opposes: its erasing difference. That is, the black *chador* is used here to locate, and to communicate semi-metaphorically a personal and shared experience, and one that is associated with the experience of veiling as such (and not only wearing the *chador*, since it is not in fact a universal reality in Iran) through one person's eyes. But since this metaphor corresponds, albeit in an exaggerated, sensationalized way, to a limited, but concrete historical reality, it is likely—and not accidentally—to be read as a pointed commentary. As a concrete symbol, it serves to locate a particular group; then as a metaphor, it violently embraces (by forcing them into it) an entire category of women; and finally, it demonizes them.

Now, this will happen to different degrees, of course, among different audiences—those possessing different levels or varieties of knowledge and experience in relation to such works' subject matter. And whether or not they are read as targeted commentaries, or as records of personal experience (which different viewers will recognize/identify with in different ways), it does raise a question about the intended or unintended effects that may be produced by such works among different audiences, and in different contexts. For example, an Iranian woman who has experienced living under Iran's restrictive laws may identify strongly with the personal experience communicated in *Women in Shadow* (and for her it may even serve as a form of therapy), while for an audience member who has not, it will at best simulate part of that experience, and perhaps serve more as a commentary. But in this case, we may ask whether the particular formula used to simulate this experience—and if it is read in this way, the knowledge that it ostensibly provides—might not have other unintended effects.

Obviously, one danger in communicating in this way is that, lacking the same knowledge as the Iranian viewer, this "simulation" may be taken for reality, and thus too simplistically. Again, it may be argued that the reality just is as simplistic as the simulation; but that is not only to gloss over the complex social and historical realities that surround the veil in its myriad expressions, given that it has occupied different positions at different times (before and after the Revolution); at the same time, since the picture that it paints of the predicament of Iranian women today is presented in purely Manichean terms, this simulation (involving the viewer in a particularly strong way, and therefore providing a kind of intimate knowledge) might contribute to a false sense of having "mastered" its subject. In slightly different terms, such ways of representing the veiled female subject might simply reinforce their ideological framing as victims, and so on. Thus, as Hamid Dabashi (2015) has recently written about Shirin Neshat's works:

> In a time when cliché conceptualisation of "Muslim women" or fetishised conceptions of "veiling" is integral to a globalized "war on terror," all predicated on the ludicrous notion that Muslim women need saving from Muslim men, especially by white men in military uniform (to paraphrase Gayatri Spivak's apt phrase), works such as Shirin Neshat's become easy prey to abusive encounters.

Furthermore, it could be argued that such representations both reflect, and thus serve to reproduce, an image of Muslim women as "other" in the precise sense of the term referring to the formation of subjectivity, and so precisely in the way that such representations functioned within the context of colonial discourses. That is, granting that it is through the construction of an other (like a mirror image of the self) that the subject discovers itself as a separate subject, thereby gaining self-awareness and mastery, it might be argued that these images function in the context of their wider circulation in the West (which of course we can no longer assume as a fixed category) in much the same way that they have always functioned within colonial discourses—but with a spin. For while the latter-day construction of the female Muslim as uniformly "oppressed," and so on, still has everything to do with the ideological mechanisms through which various Western powers (as just suggested) justify their military excursions into the Middle East, it has to be noted too that—again, just as in earlier colonial discourses—such discourses operate on a much more intimate level as well. That is, recalling the very precise sense in which, as Edward Said (2003) notes, Western representations of the "Orient" (which is always described in negative terms that discursively construct the West as superior) have historically been vital in helping the West not only to "control" the latter, but also in defining, and thereby gaining "knowledge" about itself, by providing "its contrasting image, idea, personality and experience" (p. 2), it might be argued that for many Western individuals—and perhaps Western women especially—these images today serve a similar function. In their reflected surface, that is—or beneath the veil—the "ideal" Western viewer discovers herself: modern, fashion loving, sexually free, in control of her own body, she becomes the norm or referent in relation to the struggles of these Muslim women—the ideal that they should strive to become. In this way she comes to occupy a superior but (perhaps) sympathetic position towards the "oppressed" othered female subject; and so too then, in the act of viewing or choosing to promote the sort of works that codify this relationship, the Western agent might not only be emboldened by granting the artist (or its subject) a sort of real or imagined freedom through her own act of will; for her, this sublimated act of viewing may also result in a sort of veiling of the circumstances surrounding her own lack of freedom, and so on.

Standing back, a less contentious, but still crucial point, perhaps, is one that the transnational feminist Chandara Monhanty (1988) raised in her famous article, "Under Western Eyes." Questioning the tacitly hierarchical language that is often found in Western feminist literature, and which often presents all third world women as an identical group of victims, she notes the way in which Western feminism might be seen as enacting another kind of discursive colonization that simply affirms the superiority of the Western female subject. Thus Mohanty asks: "What happens when this assumption of 'women as an oppressed group' is situated in the context of Western feminist writing about third world women?" Her answer: "Western feminists alone become the true 'subjects' of this counter-history. Third world women, on the other hand, never rise above the debilitating generality of their 'object' status" (1988, p. 351).

Reflection

Today of course, no more nor less so than in previous centuries, it is impossible to treat these categories ("the West" versus "the rest," and so on) as fixed categories, just as it is to assign different subjects as belonging to them essentially. Moreover, none of the preceding observations are in any way meant to implicate any particular individuals associated with the field of cultural production that I have been discussing—whether they be producers or consumers of the sort of works that I have been drawing attention to—just as I have noted that the sort of analysis I have been pursuing here has been far more concerned with the field in which the latter circulate and acquire different meanings and value than the works themselves, as such. What I should stress as well, however, is that the initial motivation to examine the sort of concerns that I have been discussing have more to do with my own personal experience as a practicing artist—as an Iranian woman who has found herself living and working abroad, and thus communicating with new audiences—than any detached theoretical interest. For quite aside from my recognition, early on, that such questions might be asked about the sort of works that have tended to be viewed as representative of Iran and Iranian art(ists), the more decisive moment for me came when I did begin making and exhibiting work outside Iran; for after that time, I quickly came to discover that there is a sort of expectation that, as an Iranian artist, I should—or might find strong reasons to—make work that highlighted my background and cultural experience in a particular way. That is, I was not only explicitly encouraged to produce work that made these facts about my "biography" visible (which is to say, using typical elements and so on), but even when I consciously avoided doing so, the very fact that I am Iranian meant that my work was very often read in terms of the sort of familiar themes I have been discussing (which is to say, those themes were somewhat forcibly read onto them).

Now this is fine, and I do not expect that an audience so geographically and culturally remote from my native culture should be able to read these works in any other way (though I might still hope that they might be—and of course, they very often are). But again, a more decisive moment came when I began discussing these issues in different forums, and in particular, gently raising the question about whether the constant reappearance of certain stereotyped images of Iranian/Muslim women in different art galleries and so on might not have something to do with a certain expectation. (Pointing to the anonymous collective the Guerrilla Girls, who produced a poster with the slogan of "Do women have to be naked to get into the Met. Museum?" (1989), critiquing the fact that the museums all over the world are filled with paintings of naked women, I would joke, "Do women of Islamic background have to be depicted as veiled to get into the world's museums and galleries?") What struck me then was just how often I would hear the same (though differently worded) and wonderfully ironic retort: something to the effect that I should not question these things because as a woman of Muslim background, I am "privileged" to be here and making art work in the West ... free!

It was partially in light of these experiences, and also in response to the sort of concerns that I examined in the earlier section (on marginal exoticism) that I decided to make a work employing irony to such an extreme degree that its message would not, I hoped, be lost: a series of manipulated images of "veiled" Muslim women depicted in a clearly Andy Warhol-esque fashion in order to reflect their status as pure commodities, and nothing more. Simulacra without referents.

Predictably, some of my Iranian peers chastened me for this—that is, for once again making "Iranian" art fashioned specifically for a Western gaze. But of course it was not ever intended for an Iranian audience; and to say that this series was made for this "gaze" is not quite right either, for it was meant to be nothing more than a mirror reflecting back that gaze. Still, it might be criti-cized (among other things) for adding yet one more layer of accrued mean-ing that has stubbornly clung itself to the veil, not least the very criticism that I myself presented above, in relation to the unstable meaning of such ironic statements. Again, while this is true, I have been careful to articulate (both visually, and in my accompanying statements) that this work has nothing at all to do with "Muslim women"—not even the "misconceptions" that surround them.

Another (self-)criticism of this work, though, and one that is similar to the critique that I mentioned just now and earlier has to do with "the critique of the spectacle," discussed by Jacques Rancière. In his penetrating work *The Emancipated Spectator* (2009), Rancière questions the ability of political art that assumes a straight transit between modes of artistic production and their supposed or intended political and social effects. In particular, he is critical of art that seeks to reveal the reality (of domination, exploitation and so on) lying behind "appearances" through strategies such as montage and (Brechtian) distanciation. There is no reason, Rancière thinks, that such strategies will be understood (presupposing, as they do, the sort of uncomplicated connection between means and effect as just described), nor that the rupturing of sense, or particular awareness the that they produce (such as an awareness of the om-nipotence of the commodity) (Spencer, 2010) will not in fact weaken political efficacy, given that such effects are all bounded by suspicion. My series *Under Western Eyes*, employing as it does a similar strategy, falls squarely within this sort of critique.

Now, and to conclude, I have included these (self-) criticisms and reflections not in order to answer, but simply to point to a larger question about how an artist of "marginal" cultural background such as myself, engaged in producing art that is aiming to communicate both local and global concerns to a non-local audience, should go about this, given that she is destined to find herself pulled in opposing directions, or caught between different competing forces or inter-ests at different times. As a site of cultural translation, that is, the non-Western artist who is engaged in making work that is destined to be read by a Western audience, she must not only contend with the immediate problems of finding ways to speak in a global language about the local, nor yet simply the fact that this global language is still in some ways parochially "owned" by the West, in the sense that Iranian and other artists are still often faced with the dilemma of having "to choose between 'derivative' production (never considered as good as the European model) or [displaying] ... one's otherness" (Keshmirshekan, 2010, p. 499); in addition, and as I have argued in this essay, she also faces the problem that the language that she may find herself speaking is, in a very real sense, an imperial one.

References

Bell, R. (2002). Bell's Theorem: ABORIGINAL ART—It's a White Thing!, Retrieved from www.kooriweb.org/bell/theorum.html.

Cichocki, N. (2004). Veils, Poems, Guns, and Martyrs: Four Themes of Muslim Women's Experiences in Shirin Neshat's Photographic Work. *Thirdspace: A Journal for Emerging Feminist Scholars*, 4. Retrieved from http://journals.sfu.ca/thirdspace/index.php/journal/article/viewArticle/cichocki/161.

Dabashi, H. (2015, April 13). Being at home in exile: Shirin Neshat at work. *Al Jazeera*. Retrieved from http://www.aljazeera.com/.

Entekhabi, S. (nd). *Islamic Vogue*. Retrieved from Shahram Entekhabi website: http://www.entekhabi.org/htm/Islamic_Vouge.html.

Golshiri, B. (2009). For They Know What They Do Know. *e-flux Journal*, September. Retrieved from http://www.e-flux.com/journal/08/61377/for-they-know-what-they-do-know/

Huggan, G. (2001). *The postcolonial exotic: marketing the margins.* New York: Routledge.

Hutcheon, L. (2004). 'Circling the Downspout of Empire': Post-Colonialism and Postmodernism. *Unhomely States: Theorizing English-Canadian Postcolonialism*, 71–93.

Jameson, F. (1991). *Postmodernism, or, The cultural logic of late capitalism.* Durham: Duke University Press.

Keshmirshekan, H. (2010). The Question of Identity vis-à-vis Exoticism in Contemporary Iranian Art. *Iranian Studies*, 43(4), 489–512.

Keshmirshekan, H. (Ed.). (2015). *Contemporary art from the Middle East: regional interactions with global art discourses.* London: I.B. Tauris.

Landscape Stories. (2014). *Shirin Aliabadi: Miss Hybrid.* Retrieved from Landscape Stories website: http://www.landscapestories.net/issue-16/ls_16-007-shirin-aliabadi?lang=en.

Mohanty, C. T. (1988). Under Western eyes: Feminist scholarship and colonial discourses. *Feminist review*, (30), 61–88.

Nasr, N. (n.d.). *Women in Shadow*. Retrieved from Nasim Nasr website: http://www.nasimnasr.com/new-page-1/.

Nasr, N. (2011). *Women in Shadow Nasim Nasr* [exhibition catalogue]. Australian Experimental Art Foundation, Adelaide.

Rancière, J. (2009). *The Emancipated Spectator* (G. Elliott, Trans). London and New York: Verso.

Saatchi Gallery (n.d). *Shadi Ghadirian*. Retrieved from Saatchi Gallery website: http://www.saatchigallery.com/artists/shadi_ghadirian_resources.htm.

Speck, C. (2011). Women in Shadow. In *Women in Shadow Nasim Nasr* [exhibition catalogue]. Australian Experimental Art Foundation, Adelaide.

Spencer, J. (2010). [Review of the book *The Emancipated Spectator*, by J. Rancière]. Retrieved from http://marxandphilosophy.org.uk/reviewofbooks/reviews/2010/188.

Tirdad Z. (Ed.) (2006). *Ethnic Marketing*. Tehran: Toseh.

Tiffin, H. (1988). Post-Colonialism, Post-Modernism and the Rehabilitation of Post-Colonial History. *The Journal of Commonwealth Literature*, 23(1), 169–181.

Torshizi, F. (2012). The Unveiled Apple: Ethnicity, Gender, and the Limits of Inter-discursive Interpretation of Iranian Contemporary Art. *Iranian Studies* 45(4), 549–569.

CHAPTER 9

From Woman to Tehran: The Shifting Representations of the Islamic Republic of Iran on Book Covers by Iranian Writers in English

Sanaz Fotouhi

Introduction

It is so that when you walk into a bookstore in a Western country today, the Middle East section is immediately identifiable because of the similarity, almost uniformity, of the images on these books. Row after row of books, with the Muslim women as the object of attention and desire on the covers, half veiled, half unveiled, with piercing eyes, from across the loosely demarcated region of the Middle East, invite curious readers into their worlds. This depiction of Middle Eastern book covers, instigated dramatically after the events of 9/11 and America's 'war on terror' which brought with it an interest, half resting on the West's uncertain position in relation and understanding of the Middle East, half drawing on exotic fantasies of the unknown lives of Middle Eastern women in their seemingly limited and patriarchal societies, framed the way narratives about the Middle East were received. Hidden amongst these piercing eyes or shrouded figures that invite readers in understanding their mysterious lives, all the way from Saudi Arabia, Iraq, Morocco, Jordan, and many other places, have also been narratives from Iran. While stories emerging from Iran could easily be lost amongst all the other books by and about the Middle East due to similarity of their cover, a closer look reveals that there has been a shift in the covers of the books about Iran, a shift which is directly related to the West's understanding and political relationship with Iran and the kinds of stories that interests readers. A shift which takes the gaze off the women and rests it instead on the cityscape.

In this chapter, I trace the changing nature of selected covers of books by Iranian writers in English, situating them against the shifting political and social nature of the Islamic Republic of Iran, and its relationship with the West. Given that books have many different prints and digital formats in our time, and given that the scope of this paper cannot compare or encompass all different types of covers, this study is limited to printed books of either hard cover or paperback. This study comes to life from my observation of over 280 covers of

© KONINKLIJKE BRILL NV, LEIDEN, 2018 | DOI 10.1163/9789004357013_011

printed books published between the late 1980s and mid-2010s by Iranian writers in English. I frame my argument on the study of these printed books around Dougals Slaymaker's hypothesis that there are usually 'two key sites of otherness: the Other of foreign cities, and the Other of woman,' (2007, p. 109) where he believes these two elements often frame how we set out to understand the Other and our relationship with it. Using this as the framework, I first examine how the Orientalist historically tainted Western imagination of the Middle East and Muslim countries, coupled with the Islamic Revolution of 1979, the hostage crisis and the events of 9/11, positioned the image of the veiled Iranian woman as a site of Otherness, and how this consequently affected the kinds of typical narratives and corresponding images that were being seen on book covers to represent Iran. Then, I examine how the shifting nature of social media, which has in recent years opened up a new understanding of the current situation in Iran, and the Middle East in general, framed specifically through the 2009 controversial Iranian elections, produced an interest in new kinds of narratives that are emerging from the region. Drawing on the significance of social media, and the new kinds of images that it has started to bring to the attention of viewers in the West from inside Iran and the Middle East, I examine the shift from the Iranian woman to the city as the site of Otherness, highlighting how the city of Tehran has gradually replaced the veiled woman's image on the covers. While the examination of the actual content of these books and their relationship to the way they are covered makes for an interesting study, since space does not permit for this detailed analysis, the focus of this study is purely on the covers of these books, hinting at their content only when necessary.

A note needs to be made here about the use of 'the publisher.' Throughout this chapter, I refer to those responsible for the final presentation of the book covers as 'the publisher.' I am well aware that a production of a book cover is a choreographed and negotiated dance between the writers, editors, publishing houses, and the designers, taking into consideration the readership, the market, and the socio-political climate in which a book comes out, among other things. I am also aware that each publishing house, given their size, budget, and their relationship with their authors operates differently in this process. Having said this, I choose to use the word 'the publisher' deliberately as the collective responsible for the end product that we see produced on the book cover. I do this because this paper does not have the scope, to seek out and address in detail the process involved in individual process that a book cover is produced. What I also would like to clarify is that I am aware that a lot of times the authors themselves have little input in the covers. Sometimes this lack of choice affects the intention of an author in the way the content of their book is represented. In this chapter, I am not concerned about this relationship. I only refer to the cover and examine how the work could be read solely based on the cover and not the intention of the author or the content.

Covering Women: Post-1979

The first narratives by Iranian writers in English emerged in the early days following the Islamic revolution of 1979 and at the beginnings of Iranian mass migration to other countries as the result of internal turmoil in Iran. Their appearance was within a historically and politically tainted framework which was consequently reflected on the kinds of covers chosen to represent them. As we know, the Middle East, generally and historically, has always fascinated the Western world as exotic and inaccessible, with veiled women, oppressed under the patriarchal rule. Iran, or Persia as it was known, has been no exception and has formed a significant part of this Orient that the Western world so craves to understand and unravel. As Lila Azam Zanganeh puts it, Iran has been present in the Western imagination since antiquity: '[W]hether as a haven of exotic sensuality or a stronghold of fanatic religiosity, Iran has, since ancient times, inflamed the popular imagination.' (2006, p. xi) The image of pre-revolutionary Iran that had flourished in the Western mind was one that frequently had its origin in dated explorer travelogues and tourist accounts, as well as exotic fictional narratives. Put another way, the representation of Iran throughout Western history fits Edward Said's definition of the Orient in *Orientalism*, as a land that 'had been since antiquity a place of romance, exotic beings, haunting memories and landscape, [and] remarkable experiences.' (1978, p. 1) However, despite these imaginative and wonderful representations of Persia and the Persians, they still reflect a sense of Western superiority. This is particularly evident in descriptions of the condition of Iranian women. In most representations, women, who occupied a separate territory, out of the Western male narrator's gaze, remained an enigma. Westerners, who were both 'fascinated and repelled by the veil' and by the situation of women, created the assumption and convention that 'veiled women were necessarily more oppressed, more passive, more ignorant than unveiled women,' which led to 'exaggerated statements about the imprisoned existence of women in "the Orient."' (Mabro 1991, p. 3) This Oriental understanding, particularly when it comes to an exotic representation of the country and women's situation, framed and still continues, to some degree, affect the context into which narratives about Iran and the Middle East are emerging.

However, the historical image of Persia as an exotic and wonderful land of adventure, and of its gracious people, began to dissipate in the wake of the 1979 revolution. While the onset of forced veiling of women in Iran reinforced some already-existing negative images, it was the ensuing American hostage crisis that led to the emergence of a strong anti-Iran attitude in the West. This incited many negative perceptions of Iran and Iranians, who were portrayed as 'non-rational,' 'hungry for martyrdom,' and 'unwilling to compromise.' (Mobasher, 2006, p. 110) Long forgotten were exotic utopian adventures into Persia and its harems. Instead, Iran became the demonic anti-American dystopia with escalating numbers of human rights violations. While the non-stop coverage of the hostage crisis in the Western media played an especially important role in the construction of this anti-Iranian attitude, this representation resonated far into the future, continuing to affect the way Iran and Iranians are seen and depicted in the West to this day. It was within this framework that the early narratives by Iranian writers in the West were received. And it was this Orientalist ideology, tainted by the hostility of the animosity between America and Iran as a Muslim country that was directly reflected on the covers of the few books that were emerging by Iranian writers in English at this time.

This is why the image of the veiled woman, *chador* clad, mysterious, and oppressed became the posterchild of Iranian (and generally Middle Eastern) experience in the West and began to make a repeated appearance on covers of books, some of which became best sellers. The first of these books, by Iranian writers, to reflect this were Sousan Azadi's *Out of Iran: One Woman's Escape from the Ayatollahs* (1987) and Cherry Mosteshar's *Unveiled: Life and Death Among the Ayatollahs* (1995), both of which recount the difficult lives of the narrators in Iran during the revolution, its aftermath and their eventual exile. Their covers reflect this too. Striking and bold, Mosteshar's is an all encompassing black, with only the eyes of a woman staring, not directly at the reader but into a distant horizon. This face interestingly is mocked with makeup. Bright blue eye shadow covers the eyelids and colorful brush strokes are drawn on the black to represent blush and a bright red lipstick where the lips are hidden under the blackness that represents the *chador*.

Azadi's cover, too, plays on a similar variation of the *chador*-clad woman. Here, unlike the made up face, an Iranian woman with very plain features almost totally covered, except for her nose, with a *chador*, carries a rifle in her hand. Behind her another *chador* covered figure, with her face showing but completely without emotion or expression, stares down, avoiding direct eye contact with the camera.

Such images reinforced the Western imagination of Iran. While Mosteshar's image seems to represent the West's imagination of the hidden desire of women to look beautiful and wear makeup in Iran, something that they assume is not possible, Azadi's seems to hint at the way the tyrannical regime (represented by the rifle the woman is holding) has taken away any kind of life or attraction in the women's all hidden and emotionless face. Both images, confirm for the Western reader what they already assume and know about life in Iran.

These images opened the floodgate of covers that were to represent Iran, and what they connoted fuelled the Western readers' imagination, as Iran continued to remain almost totally inaccessible to the rest of the world, as the result of the revolution and the eight-year war with Iraq. The representation of the *chador* covered woman specially reached its climax after the events of 9/11 when a large of wave books by Iranian writers, particularly women, flooded the Western markets, and the black covered face that covered these books became *the* symbol of the Iranian/Muslim experience and repression well into the late 2000s. Framed within America's 'War on Terror' and Iran's newly earned position within the 'axis of evil,' and given its still relatively inaccessible and seemingly hostile domestic landscape, after the events of 9/11, more than ever, there was now an interest in narratives about Iran, particularly those that promised entrance into the unknown world of its oppressed and mysterious women. This created what Jasmin Darznik says 'an insatiable curiosity for both the intimate details of ... lives [of Iranians] and descriptions of forbidden landscapes,' (2008, p. 57) and the books that appeared this time tapped right into this discourse, feeding that desire even before the reader opened the first page of the book. So prevalent became this visual representation that a quick glimpse at the body of work by Iranian writers between 2003 and 2009, reveals that nearly two-thirds of them use the *chador* clad or veiled woman in one way or another as their covers.

However, while the veil or *chador* was the staple symbol of these book covers, its meaning and symbolism shifted according to the kinds of narratives and stories as well as the context into which they are received. If we look at these covers closely, particularly in an American setting, they are telling of an Orientalism that uses these images as marketing strategies and affects directly how the books are marketed and consumed. Here, the presence of the veil, the shape of which changes accordingly, operates on several layers to invite curious readers to pick up these books accordingly. A glimpse at the different variations of the use of the veils is revealing of how its symbolism is used to frame the narratives and how they are read and received.

On the one hand, the picture of a *chador*-clad woman, an indistinguishable figure from any other in the shadows, such as on the covers of *My Prison, My Home* (2009) and *Persian Girls* (2006), appeal to the stereotypical Western imagination of Middle Eastern women. Women here are shadowy figures, hidden in the background, without any agency, just as the Western reader imagines them. This is the symbol of the passive and silenced woman, and her appearance on the cover is an invitation to the Western reader to unveil her.

On the other hand, others dare to break this silence and are stepping forward to seek recognition. The veiled women, with only their eyes peering out at the viewers, as on the covers of *Prisoner of Tehran* (2008) and *Journey from the Land of No* (2004), *Rage Against the Veil* (1999), *In the House of My Bibi* (2008) and *Watch Me* (2010), are inviting, yet challenging the viewer/reader to pick up the book to enter into their mysterious, hidden world. The eyes in these images, sharp in focus, distinguish each woman from the other under the veil, a humanizing strategy suggesting that the woman behind the veil 'can look back at the spectator mute but eloquent.' However, what is interesting to note is that despite this humanizing strategy, there is a sense of generalization, a kind of 'one woman's story is every woman's story' approach. If we look, for instance, at the covers of *Journey from the Land of No* and an edition of *Prisoner of Tehran*, it is the same eyes that are peering back at us, hinting at the similarity of these two narratives. All of these images, despite slight variation, tap 'into a [Western] fantasy of the illicit penetration of the hidden and gendered spaces of the "Islamic World."' (Whitlock, 2007, p. 59) They are 'invit[ing] and encourag[ing] the Western imperial gaze, offering Westerners a glimpse into the presumably forbidden world beneath the veil.' (Ibid.) This invitation is almost a call for acknowledgment by the Western reader, an appeal for recognition, by women who have so far been silenced in their own country. However, the fact that the Western reader is involved in this act of

FIGURE 9.1
A collage of cover images by Iranian women writers in English.

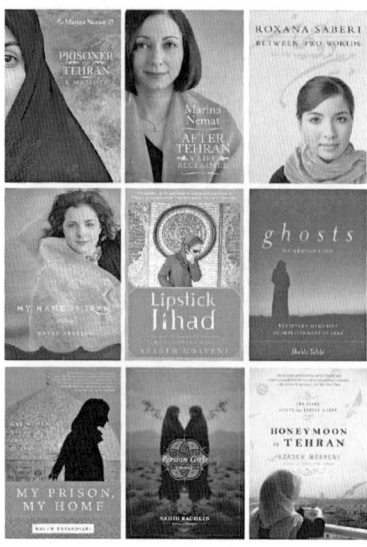

FIGURE 9.2

A collage of cover images of books by Iranian women writers in English.

unveiling and recognition operates on an acceptance of cultural dichotomy between the narrator and the reader, appealing, as Gillian Whitlock also reminds us, to the Western tradition of benevolence. It is only by the book being picked up by the Western reader that Iranian women can be recognized and thereby regain their sense of subjectivity. This recognition, however, operates on a presumption that Iranian women are oppressed, and imprisoned behind the veil, and need Western readers and values to liberate them from their social imprisonment.

The use of the images of young veiled girls—the kind of pictures usually used for passports, birth certificates, and school records in Iran—on such covers as *Living in Hell* (2004) and *The Last Living Slut* (2010), further highlights the dichotomy and the seemingly oppressive force bearing down on women's lives in Iran. On the cover of Omid's *Living in Hell* this message is emphasized further, as the girl's face is framed, bound, almost branded with the logo of the Islamic Republic, hinting at oppression under the regime.

The unveiled woman with the scarf around her neck, staring at the camera, invites readers into a different kind of story. These women, such as Ardalan and Saberi on the covers of *My Name is Iran* (2008) and *Between Two Worlds* (2010), are liberated. They have taken the chance to speak for themselves in line with Western traditions of freedom of speech. They are inviting the viewers to read about their passage from oppression to freedom, giving the impression that this is something that is offered to them thanks to the Western world. Here, their stories are not so much about the oppression, but about the process of liberation. These women appear to have demystified themselves by unveiling, and are offering curious readers a chance to glimpse into their lives, hailing the Western countries/readers for giving them the opportunity to 'unveil.'

It is not only the images that communicate the above-said messages to the readers. The titles and promotional blurbs also heighten these elements by feeding off the current socio-political interests of the times when the books are marketed. A survey reveals a set of key phrases in the titles of many of these memoirs, almost as conventional as the cover images. Titles such as *Unveiled: Life and Death Among the Ayatollahs*, *Out of Iran: One Woman's Escape from the Ayatollahs*, *In the House of My Bibi: Growing up in Revolutionary Iran*, *Honeymoon in Tehran: Two Years of Love and Danger in Iran* and *Rage Against the Veil: the Courageous Life and Death of an Islamic Dissident*, draw on the urgency of life, death, and revolution, and debated issues of veil and unveiling. They feed into American Orientalist perspectives, and are, as Gillian Whitlock argues, 'designed to grab the Western eye and with a glimpse of absolute difference, of the exotic.' At a time of America's declared 'war on terror,' and Iran's gained status in the 'axis of evil,' these titles were feeding into this discourse, and were 'a way of positioning them for metropolitan markets.' Other titles, such as Haleh Esfandiari's *My Prison, My Home: One Woman's Captivity in Iran* and Roxana Saberi's *Between Two Worlds: My Life and Captivity in Iran*, draw directly on the well-known American tradition of captivity, as they reframe the story of the American(-Iranian) woman caught this time in the web of extremist society. In both Esfandiari and Saberi's titles, for example, the word captivity, juxtaposed with the word Iran, reminiscent of the hostage crisis and looming hostility between Islam and the West, and Iran and America, transforms them immediately into a modern version of the captivity narrative.[1]

Covering Tehran: Post-2009

A shift began to gradually occur, however, in the late 2000s as the landscape of the kinds of narratives, and inevitably the covers of books emerging from Iran began to gradually change after the 2009 presidential elections, thanks to digital and social media. Although the Iranian government has a very strict censorship policy on Internet access, Iranians have been extremely active bloggers,

---

1   For further study of this refer to my detailed study of some of these book covers in the chapter on Iranian women's memoirs in *The Literature of the Iranian Diaspora: Meaning and Identity since the Islamic Revolution*, I.B. Tauris, 2015.

and ironically despite restrictions, Persian is one of the most frequent languages of blogosphere and it continued to be at the height of its reach in the early 2000s. However, as Niki Akhavan observes, after 2007 'the sheen of blogs and blogging was beginning to dull on the Iranian internet, and social networking sites were showing signs of becoming more popular among resident and Diaspora Iranians.' (2013, p. 9) This social networking played a significant part in the distribution and dissemination of information after the 2009 contested elections. As Rafizadeh and Alimardani argue 'the 2009 election was a watershed moment in illustrating the socio-political impact of new media,' (2013) as all parties involved began to rely heavily on social media to organize rallies and events, show support or discontent. In the meantime, social media also became a platform through which people in Iran began to immediately reach a global and digital audience as events unfolded when serious and deadly protests broke out after people accused the government of vote-rigging.

As Akhavan observes, 'protestors' much-touted uses of social media in the aftermath of the disputed election remain a hallmark example of how these platforms can successfully attract transnational attention and support.' (2013, p. 10) Social media, including Facebook pages and updates, YouTube clips and Tweets that were uploaded from mobile phones, played a significant role in bringing what was going on in Iran to the attention of the world, immediately and directly from those were affected by it. With the rapid circulation of clips from protests, a different Iran came into view. Here, women were no longer silent, passive and domestic. Rather, they could be seen and heard shouting and screaming slogans alongside men in opposition to the government. As the world witnessed through these new images and platforms, women such as Neda Agha Soltan, who was shot in the street and died on camera, suffered alongside men the violation of their rights as humans.

Out of the ashes of these protests, a new interest was born in Iran. The world was no longer interested in delayed stories by silenced and oppressed diasporic Iranian women. Rather, resting on the mere glimpses that social media was providing, people wanted to know what was going on in Iran right now and these images began to project a new kind of understanding of life in Iran, shifting the way Iran was seen previously by the world. Consequently, for the first time since the hostage crisis, the world began to distinguish between the Iranian people and its government. Here, not all Iranians were anti-Westerns it was previously believed after the events of the hostage crisis, and for the first time it was made clear how much the Iranian youth disagreed with the existing government and its policies. Furthermore, it brought into world attention some serious human rights issues and problems in Iran, the denial of which, before they were circulated on the Internet, would have been easy for the Iranian government. Now, there was an active interest in the stories of the generations of men and women who had lived silently under the Islamic regime for the last several decades and whose lives were affected by the 2009 elections and its aftermath.

Consequently, major publishers began to publish current and local stories that reflected this. Inevitably, there was also a shift in the kinds of images that the publishers used to represent these books. A glimpse into the cover of these books is revealing of the shifting interest in these narratives. Though still maintaining a sense of the exotic, mysterious, and not completely understood, they were no longer interested in the delayed narratives of oppressed women. Thus, the covers of the books suddenly became bolder, carrying a lot of visual stimulation that drew on the current situation. For example, Reza Kahlili's 2011 *A Time To Betray: The Astonishing Double Life of a CIA Agent Inside the Revolutionary Guards of Iran* is a great example of this shift.

Using Reza Kahlili as a pseudonym the narrator tells of his life as a CIA operative inside the Iranian Revolutionary Guards, Iran's notorious secret service responsible for the clampdowns on protestors. The bold cover, unlike anything before it, speaks directly to the urgent interests of the market then. Although it still hints at the exoticism of the location and Islamic fundamentalism, not through the veil but through a familiar gray motif of a mosque in the distant background, it adds another layer of meaning by stamping a large image of the then Iranian president Mahmoud Ahmadinejad in the foreground framed by the Iranian flag above and the United States flag below, and the words A TIME TO BETRAY stamped with large lettering on the Iranian flag. That an image of the most unpopular (in the eyes of both Iranians and the Western world) Iranian president since the Islamic revolution appears on the cover of a popular book, with a mosque, as a symbol of the feared Islamic system lurking in the background, is indicative of a major shift in the way these books are produced and marketed. To place Ahmadinejad's gazing face between the Iranian and American flags and the mosque in the background, positions him as the man who is leading the polarization of the relationship between the United States and Iran, still resting on the beliefs of fundamental Islamic thought. At the same time, given his unpopularity amongst Iranians following the post-election protests and horrific human rights violations, Ahmadinejad is not only presented as an enemy of the United States, but as also an enemy of his own people. As a representative of the Islamic government, symbolized by the mosque in the background, he is the one who is separating Iranian people from living with values, such as freedom of speech and respect for human life, that Western/American society upholds with pride. Thus, Kahlili's book, starting from its very cover, appears a challenge to the traditionally understood concept of us/them. As a result of the recent news from Iran, and people's opposition to the regime, a clear distinction has emerged between perceptions of the Iranian government and its people. Unlike at the time of the hostage crisis, when Iranians were collectively viewed as hostage takers, now Iranian people are no longer seen merely as anti-American fanatics. Considering the Iranian government's conflict with the American government, and Iranian people's recent opposition to the Iranian government, then the Iranian population can be seen in a favorable light by Americans, because they now appear to be fighting the same enemy. The blurb on the back of the book also hinges on this dichotomy, as it promises to take us on a man's mission to infiltrate the Iranian government and help overthrow it. On the dust jacket it reads:

> As Reza, a member of the elite Guards, my role was to look and act the part of a devout Muslim enforcing all the new rules laid down by the mullahs. A full black beard was a mandatory accessory to the Guards' uniform, and I sported one along with every other member of the Guards. Playing the part of a zealot did not come naturally to me, and there were times I had to do things I dreaded. [...] Back in Iran now, I knew that I would have to try and convince myself that doing these things allowed me to maintain my role—and maintaining my role allowed me to contribute to the downfall of the organisation to which I so fervently imitated allegiance.

The framing of Kahlili's book brings to our attention a new kind of captivity and freedom narrative. This is not the captivity of a single man or woman; rather the book appears to hint it is the imprisonment of a nation at the hands of a regime that must be overthrown in order for its people to gain freedom.

Another shifting interest in the types of narratives that were emerging was the emphasis on the city of Tehran, the imagination of which was feeding many through social media sites. That the city of Tehran should replace the image of the veiled woman is not a surprise since as Slaymaker believes foreign cities form a site for the representation and understanding of the Other. Here the city becomes a luring site of 'romantic and sexual attraction; and [the danger of] death,' (2007, p. 109) inviting and daring the outside other to enter it, to understand it and explore it. That is why Tehran, the bustling and busy city of nearly twelve million inhabitants, the relatively unknown capital of Iran until then, began to replace the veiled woman as the site of the Other on book covers. While prior to 2009, the readers were invited to unveil the Iranian woman, to get under their skin, now it was the city, its smog, its grim, its busyness and chaos, the dangers and romance, that allured them as a mysterious and exotic Other site to be understood.

Reflecting the lure and tension of the city, this can be seen in books such as Ramita Navai's *City of Lies: Love, Sex, Death and the Search for Truth in Tehran* (2014). A creative non-fiction, it takes the readers inside the less travelled streets of Tehran and gives us a glimpse into the lives of several groups of marginal people living across Tehran. Heightening its allure is the cover which is of a couple sitting on a bench on a lookout over a dense, smog covered landscape of this un-transparent city. Another edition of the book has the same layout, this time a couple looks over a similarly dense landscape at dusk. The bleak, inaccessible landscape of the city of Tehran, and the couple's shadowy figures, heightens the the mystery of what Tehran is like, appealing to the readers' interest to pick up the book to understand what is really going on under the skin of the city.

Some of the reviews of the book as cited on its Amazon page are reflective of how this book has drawn on the Otherness of the foreign city to intrigue readers: "A vivid, heartbreaking insight into survival under an oppressive regime. These are stories of characters we might see ourselves in, surviving in circumstances we can't imagine" writes, Shappi Khorsandi, author of *A Beginner's Guide to Acting English*; "Read this if you want to know about life, love and death in Tehran. Ramita Navai has written a fascinating, unforgettable book about the unbreakable human spirit in one of the world's great cities," recommends Jeremy Bowen, BBC Middle East Editor; and "One of the world's most exciting cities, as revealed by one of journalism's most exciting women. Navai slips effortlessly into the boots of earthy, urban writer to tour Tehran's ripped backsides in this intimate, grand guignol debut. She transports us through the Iranian capital's multiple personas with deft and knowing navigation: never short of love for even the lowliest of her fellow Tehranis. An intimate and devoted portrait, lifting a beautiful truth from a city masked in lies," tells us Anthony Loyd, author of *Another Bloody Love Letter and My War Gone by, I Miss it So.*

Other books, too, draw on this newly found interest of mysterious cityscape of Tehran. For example, the edited collection of stories by Akashic Press called *Tehran Noir* (2014), plays on the same theme. Published in the same series by the publisher as *Tel Aviv Noir, Brooklyn Noir, Belfast Noir*, this too, sets as its landscape a series of 'noir' stories from Tehran. A timely addition, published in 2014, when Tehran was now a common name in the news and social media with particular, yet mysterious appeal, the book uses as its cover the iconic image of Tehran's 'Freedom Square.' The square which was made famous by

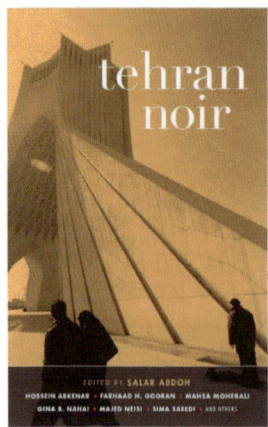 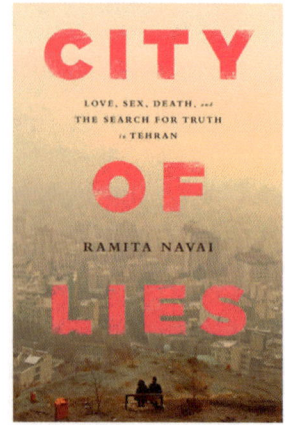 

FIGURE 9.3 *A collage of cover images of books by Iranian writers in English depicting Tehran as the city of desire. Images copyright to publishers.*

the Islamic revolution and once again re-surfaced in the Western vision during the 2009 uprisings, is by now, a well-known international landmark. Yet, in sepia and with a few shadowy figures looming at the bottom of the cover, the image adds to the intensity of the mystery, violence, and harshness that hides in the city, waiting to be unraveled.

Other titles too draw on Tehran as the entry point. Salar Abdoh's *Twilight at Tehran* (2014) for instance offers a similar promise. With a cover of a distant landscape of Tehran, this time not of the Freedom Tower but of the Milad Tower, Tehran's relatively new architectural addition, visible through the distant smog and pollution of the city, it promises entrance into this mysterious and conspicuous metropolis. The sense of violence and harshness that lies in the cityscape is heightened by the grading of red to orange that covers the landscape, and further emphasized by the quote on the cover by Dalia Sofer which reads: 'A remarkable meditation on violence, and on all the ways one bears witness to pain. Abdoh depicts a pulsating portrait of Tehran.'

Conclusion

The chapter has briefly demonstrated a sweeping analysis of the shifting nature of the kinds of covers used by Iranian writers and the publishers to frame these works. On the surface there appears to have been a definite shift in the covers of these books from the veiled women and their invitation to unveiling them, an appeal deeply rooted in the Western visual cultures, to the distant and impersonal landscape of the city of Tehran. However, what can be argued is that while the images of these covers might have appeared to change, their essential underlying meaning has not. What has happened is that now the Islamic woman as the site of the Other has been replaced by the city as the site of the Other. What this means is that while between 1979 and 2009, it was the women who were the subject of mystery, waiting to be unveiled and understood, now a similar theme of desire for unveiling continues. Now that which needs to be unveiled is the city of Tehran, the exotic, mysterious, inaccessible metropolis, and these books through their covers promise entry under her skin, into her hidden and intimate landscapes. Here, the woman waiting to be unveiled is now the city of Tehran. And yet, however we choose to see this shifting representation, it is one that will definitely change and continue to evolve, inevitably reflecting whatever new fantasy the Western reader might have of the East. What remains consistent though, despite the changing images, is the sense of mystery and allure offered by the Islamic Republic of Iran. While the In a digital world where access has become so immediate and all-encompassing one can never guess what the next alluring image might be to reflect the Iranian experience.

References

Abdoh, S. (2014). *Tehran at Twilight*. Brooklyn: Akashic Books.

Abdoh, S. (2014a). *Tehran Noir*. Brooklyn: Akashic Books.

Akhavan, N. (2013). *Electronic Iran*. New York: Rutgers.

Ardalan, D. (2008). *My Name is Iran*. New York: Holt Paperbacks.

Azadi, S. (1987). *Out of Iran: One Woman's Escape from the Ayatollahs*. London: Macdonald.

Darabi, P. (1999). *Rage Against the Veil: the Courageous Life and Death of an Islamic Dissident*. New York: Prometheus Books.

Darznik, J. (2008). The perils and seductions of home: return narratives of the Iranian diaspora. *MELUS*, 33(2), 55–71.

Esfandiari, H. (2009). *My Prison, My Home*. New York: Harper Collins.

Hakakian, R. (2004). *Journey from the Land of No*. Auckland: Bantam.

Kahlili, R. (2010). *A Time to Betray: the Astonishing Life of a CIA Double Agent inside Iran's Revolutionary Guard*. New York: Threshold Editions.

Kherad, N. (2008). *In the House of My Bibi: Growing Up in Revolutionary Iran*. Academic Chicago Publishers, IL.

Mabro, J. (1991). *Veiled Half-truths: Western Travelers' Perceptions of Middle Eastern Women*. New York: I.B. Tauris.

Mobasher, M. (2006). Cultural trauma and ethnic identity formation among Iranian immigrants in the United States. *American Behavioral Scientist*, 50(1),100–17.

Mosteshar, C. (1995). *Unveiled: Love and Death among the Ayatollahs*. London: Hodder and Stoughton.

Navai, R. (2014). *City of Lies: Love, Sex, Death, and the Search for Truth in Tehran*. New York: PublicAffairs.

Nemat, M. (2008). *Prisoner of Tehran*. New York: Free Press.

Omid, G. (2004). *Living in Hell*. Oklahama City, OK: Park Avenue Publishing.

Pazouki, R. (2010). *Watch Me*. Lulu.com.

Rachlin, N. (2006). *Persian Girls*. New York: Tarcher.

Rafizadeh, S. and Mahsa Alimardani. (2013, May 6). 'The Political Evolution of the Iranian Internet.' *Iran Media Program*. Retrieved from <http://www.iranmedia research.org/en/general/blog/227/13/05/06/1365>.

Saberi, R. (2010). *Between Two Worlds: My Life and Captivity in Iran*. New York: Harper Collins.

Said, E. (1978), *Orientalism*. New York: Penguin.

Shirazi, R. (2010). *The Last Living Slut: Born in Iran, Bred Backstage*. New York: Igniter.

Slaymaker, D. (2007). Yokomitsu Riichi's Others: Paris and Shanghai. In Rachael Hutchins & Mark Williams (Eds.), *Representing the Other in Modern Japanese Literature: A Critical Approach*, (pp. 109–124). New York: Routledge.

Whitlock, G. (2007). *Soft Weapons: Autobiography in Transit*. Chicago IL: University of Chicago Press.

Zanganeh, L. A. (2006). *My Sister, Guard your Veil; My Brother, Guard your Eyes: Uncensored Iranian Voices*. Boston MA: Beacon Press.

Index